TREKKING IN AUSTRIA'S STUBAI ALPS

HIKING AND MOUNTAINEERING ON THE STUBAI RUCKSACK ROUTE, GSCHNITZTALER RUNDTOUR AND STUBAI GLACIER TOUR

By Allan Hartley

JUNIPER HOUSE, MURLEY MOSS,
OXENHOLME ROAD, KENDAL, CUMBRIA LA9 7RL
www.cicerone.co.uk

© Allan Hartley 2024
Fourth edition 2024
Third edition 2018
Second edition 2003
First edition 1993
ISBN: 978 1 78631 065 1
eISBN: 978 1 78765 176 0

Printed in Czechia on behalf of Latitude Press Ltd on responsibly sourced paper.
A catalogue record for this book is available from the British Library.

Route mapping by Lovell Johns www.lovelljohns.com

Contains OpenStreetMap.org data © OpenStreetMap contributors, CC-BY-SA.
NASA relief data courtesy of ESRI.
All photographs are by the author unless otherwise stated.

To Marilyn

Acknowledgements

To the many members of the Austrian Alpine Club, Alpenverein Britannia, who have accompanied me over several decades of visiting the Stubai Alps, with particular thanks to my late wife Marilyn for her helpful support as I dealt with the trials and tribulations of being a guidebook writer.

Front cover: En route from Becher Haus to the Teplitzer Hut looking towards the Übeltalferner glacier and Botzer Stubai Glacier Tour South Tirol Extension

CONTENTS

Mountain safety 7
Route summary tables 10

INTRODUCTION 17
Villages of the Stubai and Stubaital 18
When to go 20
Getting there and back 21
Places to stay 24
Local services 26
Professional mountain guides (Bergführer) 27
Children 27
Austrian Alpine Club (ÖAV) 28
Huts 30
Hut meals and menus 34
Kit list 36
Route finding 38
Maps and guidebooks 39
Alpine walking skills 40
Glaciers and glacier travel 41
Health and safety 42
Electronic devices 45
Using this guide 46

TREK 1: STUBAI RUCKSACK ROUTE 50
Stage 1   Neder to Innsbrucker Hut 54
Excursion   Ascent of Habicht (3277m) 58
Excursion   Ascent of Kalkwand (2564m) 60
Stage 2   Innsbrucker Hut to Bremer Hut 61
Stage 3   Bremer Hut to Nürnberger Hut via Simmingjochl ... 67
Excursion   Ascent of Östlicher Feuerstein (3267m) from Simmingjochl ... 69
Excursion   Ascent of Aperer Feuerstein (2968m) 71
Stage 4   Nürnberger Hut to Sulzenau Hut via Niederl 72
Stage 4A   Nürnberger Hut to Sulzenau Hut via Mairspitze 74
Stage 4B   Nürnberger Hut to Sulzenau Hut via Wilder Freiger .. 77
Stage 5   Sulzenau Hut to Dresdner Hut via Peiljoch 81
Stage 5A   Sulzenau Hut to Dresdner Hut via Grosser Trögler . 84
Excursion   Ascent of Schaufelspitze (3333m) 86
Stage 6   Dresdner Hut to Neue Regensburger Hut via Grawagrubennieder . 88

Stage 7	Neue Regensburger Hut to Franz Senn Hut via Schrimmennieder	93
Excursion	To visit Rinnensee	96
Excursion	Ascent of Vordere Sommerwand (2677m)	97
Excursion	Ascent of Lisenser Fernerkogel (3299m)	98
Stage 8	Franz Senn Hut to Starkenburger Hut	101
Excursion	Ascent of Hoher Burgstall (2611m)	105
Stage 9	Starkenburger Hut to Neustift	106
Stage 9A	Starkenburger Hut to Fulpmes	110

TREK 2: STUBAI GLACIER TOUR 112

Stage 1	Mieders to Franz Senn Hut	116
Stage 2	Franz Senn Hut to Amberger Hut via Wildgratscharte	120
Stage 3	Amberger Hut to Hoch Stubai Hut via Wütenkarsattel	126
Stage 4	Hoch Stubai Hut to Hildesheimer Hut via Bildstöckljoch	129
Stage 5	Hildesheimer Hut to Müller Hut via Zuckerhütl	133
Stage 5A	Hildesheimer Hut to Siegerland Hut (alternative bad-weather route)	138
Stage 5B	Siegerland Hut to Müller Hut via Sonklarspitze	141
Stage 6	Müller Hut to Nürnberger Hut via Wilder Freiger	144
Stage 7	Nürnberger Hut to Ranalt	149

Trek 2A: South Tirol extension 151

Stage 6	Becherhaus or Müller Hut to Teplitzer Hut	152
Stage 7	Teplitzer Hut to Magdeburger Hut	155
Stages 8–10	See Gschnitztaler Rundtour Stages 5B–7	

TREK 3: GSCHNITZTALER RUNDTOUR 160

Stage 1	Trins to Blaser Hut	165
Stage 2	Blaser Hut to Padasterjochhaus	166
Stage 1A	Mieders to Maria Waldrast Monastery	170
Excursion	Ascent of Serles (2718m)	174
Excursion	Ascent of Lämpermahdspitze (2595m)	176
Stage 2A	Maria Waldrast Monastery to Padasterjochhaus	178
Excursion	Ascent of Kirchdachspitze (2840m)	180
Stage 3	Padasterjochhaus to Innsbrucker Hut via Trins and Gasthof Feuerstein	182
Stage 3A	Padasterjochhaus to Innsbrucker Hut via Hammerscharte	185
Stage 3B	Padasterjochhaus to Innsbrucker Hut via Padasterjoch, Silbersattel and Kirchdachspitze	189
Stage 4	Innsbrucker Hut to Bremer Hut	192

Stage 5	Bremer Hut to Austrian Tribulaunhaus	194
Stage 5A	Bremer Hut to Magdeburger Hut	198
Stage 5B	Magdeburger Hut to Italian Tribulaun Hut	201
Stage 5C	Italian Tribulaun Hut to Austrian Tribulaunhaus via Sandesjöchl	204
Stage 6	Austrian Tribulaunhaus to Truna Hut via Gstreinjöchl	206
Stage 7	Truna Hut to Trins or Steinach am Brenner	211

DAY WALKS AND EXCURSIONS 212

HUT DIRECTORY AND LOCATIONS 216
Amberger Hut (2135m) 217
Becherhaus (3195m) 218
Blaser Hut (2176m) 220
Bremer Hut (2413m) 221
Dresdner Hut (2308m) 222
Elfer Hut (2080m) 224
Franz Senn Hut (2147m) 225
Hildesheimer Hut (2900m) 227
Hoch Stubai Hut (3174m) 228
Hotel Klostergasthof Maria Waldrast Monastery (1638m) 230
Innsbrucker Hut (2369m) 232
Magdeburger Hut (2423m) 234
Müller Hut (3145m) 236
Neue Regensburger Hut (2286m) 238
Nürnberger Hut (2278m) 239
Padasterjochhaus (2232m) 240
Seducker Hochalm (2256m) 241
Siegerland Hut (2710m) 242
Starkenburger Hut (2237m) 243
Sulzenau Hut (2191m) 244
Teplitzer Hut (2586m) 245
Tribulaunhaus (Austrian) (2064m) 247
Tribulaun Hut (Italian) (2369m) 248
Truna Hut (1750m) 250

Appendix A	Useful contacts	252
Appendix B	German–English glossary	255
Appendix C	Further reading	258

Updates to this guide

While every effort is made by our authors to ensure the accuracy of guidebooks as they go to print, changes can occur during the lifetime of an edition. Any updates that we know of for this guide will be on the Cicerone website (www.cicerone.co.uk/1065/updates), so please check before planning your trip. We also advise that you check information about such things as transport, accommodation and shops locally. Even rights of way can be altered over time.

The route maps in this guide are derived from publicly available data, databases and crowd-sourced data. As such they have not been through the detailed checking procedures that would generally be applied to a published map from an official mapping agency, although naturally we have reviewed them closely in the light of local knowledge as part of the preparation of this guide.

We are always grateful for information about any discrepancies between a guidebook and the facts on the ground, sent by email to updates@cicerone.co.uk.

Register your book: To sign up to receive free updates, special offers and GPX files where available, create a Cicerone account and register your purchase via the 'My Account' tab at www.cicerone.co.uk.

At the Muttenjoch (Trek 3, Stage 6)

Tribulaun mountains

Mountain safety

Every mountain walk has its dangers, and those described in this guidebook are no exception. All who walk or climb in the mountains should recognise this and take responsibility for themselves and their companions along the way. The author and publisher have made every effort to ensure that the information contained in this guide was correct when it went to press, but, except for any liability that cannot be excluded by law, they cannot accept responsibility for any loss, injury or inconvenience sustained by any person using this book.

International distress signal *(emergency only)*
Six blasts on a whistle (and flashes with a torch after dark) spaced evenly for one minute, followed by a minute's pause. Repeat until an answer is received. The response is three signals per minute followed by a minute's pause.

Helicopter rescue
The following signals are used to communicate with a helicopter:

Help needed: raise both arms above head to form a 'Y'

Help not needed: raise one arm above head, extend other arm downward to form the diagonal of an N

Should you be involved with a helicopter rescue...
- Stay at least 50m+ from the helicopter.
- Do not approach the helicopter unless signalled by the winch man to do so.
- Do not approach the helicopter from behind.
- Ensure that all loose items of quipment are made secure.

Emergency telephone numbers
The following numbers can be dialled from a mobile phone even when the phone indicated that there is no reception from your service provider.
Fortunately, in Austria mobile phone reception is excellent.
- Mountain Rescue (Bergrettung) Austria 140
- Mountain Rescue (Buergrettung) Italy 118
- Red Cross (Rotes Kreutz) 144
- European emergency telephone number 112

Trekking in Austria's Stubai Alps

Relief in metres

Range	Range	Range
1200–1400	2600–2800	4000 and above
1000–1200	2400–2600	3800–4000
800–1000	2200–2400	3600–3800
600–800	2000–2200	3400–3600
400–600	1800–2000	3200–3400
200–400	1600–1800	3000–3200
0–200	1400–1600	2800–3000

At Sendersjochl (Stubai Rucksack Route, Stage 8)

At the Nürnberger Hut (Stubai Rucksack Route, Stage 3, Stubai Glacier Tour, Stage 6)

ROUTE SUMMARY TABLES

Trek 1: Stubai Rucksack Route

	Stage	Distance
1	Neder to Innsbrucker Hut	10.3km/8.3km
Excursion	*Ascent of Habicht*	*1.5km (+1.5km descent)*
Excursion	*Ascent of Kalkwand*	*1.0km (+1.0km descent)*
2	Innsbrucker Hut to Bremer Hut	10.4km
3	Bremer Hut to Nürnberger Hut	5.7km
Excursion	*Ascent of Östlicher Feuerstein*	*2.5km (+2.5km descent)*
Excursion	*Ascent of Aperer Feuerstein*	*1.25km (+1.25km descent)*
4	Nürnberger Hut to Sulzenau Hut via the Niederl	4.5km
4A	Nürnberger Hut to Sulzenau Hut via the Mairspitze	5.9km
4B	Nürnberger Hut to Sulzenau Hut via the Wilder Freiger	11.4km
5	Sulzenau Hut to Dresdner Hut via the Peiljoch	4.7km
5A	Sulzenau Hut to Dresdner Hut via the Grosser Trögler	5.6km
Excursion	*Ascent of Schaufelspitze*	*3.0km (+3.0km descent)*
6	Dresdner Hut to Neue Regensburger Hut	12.7km
7	Neue Regensburger Hut to Franz Senn Hut	9.1km
Excursion	*To visit Rinnensee*	*2.5km (+2.5km descent)*
Excursion	*Ascent of Vordere Sommerwand*	*1.5km (+1.5km descent)*
Excursion	*Ascent of Lisenser Fernerkogel*	*5.0km (+5.0km descent)*
8	Franz Senn Hut to Starkenburger Hut	15.8km
Excursion	*Ascent of Hoher Burgstall*	*1.0km (+1.0km descent)*
9	Starkenburger Hut to Neustift	5.6km
9A	Starkenburger Hut to Fulpmes	3.8km
Total (main route, no excursions)		**78.8km**

Route summary tables

Ascent	Descent	Time	Grade
1385m/810m	negligible/255m	5hr/5–6hr	
910m	*910m*	*4hr (+2½hr descent)*	*F*
200m	*200m*	*1hr (+¾hr descent)*	*F*
890m	850m	7–8hr	
465m	610m	3–4hr	
505m	*505m*	*2–2½hr (+2hr descent)*	*F*
280m	*280m*	*1hr (+1hr descent)*	*F*
395m	485m	3–4hr	
560m	645m	4hr+	F-
1180m	1265m	8–9hr	F+
505m	370m	4–5hr	
730m	595m	4–5hr	
1030m	*1030m*	*4hr (+3hr descent)*	*F*
880m	900m	6–8hr	
465m	605m	5–6hr	
515m	*515m*	*2½hr (+1hr return)*	*Walk*
530m	*530m*	*2hr (+1½hr descent)*	*Walk*
1120m	*1120m*	*4–6hr (+4hr descent)*	*PD*
805m	710m	6–7hr	
375m	*375m*	*1hr (+¾hr descent)*	*Walk*
negligible	1255m	2½hr	
175m	300m	3hr	
5790m	**5785m**	**9 days**	

Trek 2: Stubai Glacier Tour

	Stage	Distance
1	Mieders to Franz Senn Hut	14.5km from Neustift
Excursion	To visit Rinnensee	2.5km (+2.5km descent)
Excursion	Ascent of Vordere Sommerwand	1.5km (+1.5km descent)
Excursion	Ascent of Linsener Fernerkogel	5.0km 5.0km (+5.0km descent)
2	Franz Senn Hut to Amberger Hut	12.4km
3	Amberger Hut to Hoch Stubai Hut	8.3km
4	Hoch Stubai Hut to Hildesheimer Hut	5.9km
5	Hildesheimer Hut to Müller Hut via the Zuckerhütl	6.1km
5A	Hildesheimer Hut to Siegerland Hut (bad-weather route)	5.3km
5B	Siegerland Hut to Müller Hut via the Sonklarspitze	4.5km
6	Müller Hut to Nürnberger Hut	6.8km
7	Nürnberger Hut to Ranalt	5.9km
Total (main route, no excursions)		**59.9km**

South Tirol extension

	Stage	Distance
6	Becherhaus or Müller Hut to Teplitzer Hut	4.6km
7	Teplitzer Hut to Magdeburger Hut	7.0km
8	Magdeburger Hut to Italian Tribulaun Hut	5.7km
9	Italian Tribulaun Hut to Austrian Tribulaunhaus	4.5km
10	Austrian Tribulaunhaus to Truna Hut	10.1km
10A	Austrian Tribulaunhaus to Steinach am Brenner or Obernbergtal valley	13.8km/9.4km
11	Truna Hut to Trins or Steinach am Brenner	4.5km (Trins); 7.6km (Steinach)
Total (South Tirol extension only, main route)		**36.4km/39.5km**
Total (Stubai Glacier Tour + South Tirol extension, main route, no excursions)		**83.6km/86.7km**

Route summary tables

Ascent	Descent	Time	Grade
165m from Neustift	negligible	5hr	
515m	*515m*	*1½hr (+1hr return)*	*Walk*
530m	*530m*	*2hr (+1½hr descent)*	*Walk*
1120m	*1120m*	*4–6hr (+4hr descent)*	*PD*
1075m	1085m	6–8hr	
1110m	75m	5–6hr	
345m	615m	5–6hr	
850m	600m	5–6hr	PD
345m	530m	3hr	
775m	305m	5hr	F+
330m	1200m	4–5hr	F+
negligible	910m	2hr	
4875m	**4485m**	**7 days**	

Ascent	Descent	Time	Grade
60m	630m	4hr	F+
615m	775m	6–7hr	
610m	655m	4hr	
235m	550m	2½hr	
635m	980m	6hr	
890m/495m	790m/1170m	4hr	
35m (Trins); 60m (Steinach)	530m (Trins); 215m (Steinach)	4hr	
2190m/2215m	**4120m/3805m**	**6 days**	
6735m/6760m	**6495m/6180m**	**11 days**	

Trek 3: Gschnitztaler Rundtour

	Stage	Distance
1	Trins to Blaser Hut	4.4km
2	Blaser Hut to Padasterjochhaus	7.8km
1A	Mieders to Maria Waldrast Monastery	3.1km
Excursion	*Ascent of Serles*	*4.0km (+4.0km descent)*
Excursion	*Ascent of Lämpermahdspitze*	*1.0km (+1.0km descent)*
2A	Maria Waldrast Monastery to Padasterjochhaus	10.2km
Excursion	*Ascent of Kirchdachspitze*	*3km (+3km descent)*
3	Padasterjochhaus to Innsbrucker Hut via Trins and Feuerstein	19.2km
3A	Padasterjochhaus to Innsbrucker Hut via the Hammerscharte	13km
3B	Padasterjochhaus to the Innsbrucker Hut via Padasterjoch	10.7km
4	Innsbrucker to Bremer Hut	10.4km
5	Bremer Hut to Austrian Tribulaunhaus	10.1km
5A	Bremer Hut to Magdeburger Hut	5km
5B	Magdeburger Hut to Italian Tribulaun Hut	5.7km
5C	Italian Tribulaun Hut to Austrian Tribulaunhaus	4.5km
6	Austrian Tribulaunhaus to Truna Hut	10.3km
7	Truna Hut to Trins or Steinach am Brenner	4.5km (Trins); 7.6km (Steinach)
Total (main route, no excursions)		**66.7km/69.8km**

Route summary tables

Ascent	Descent	Time	Grade
1005m	45m	2½–3hr	
845m	785m	6hr/6–7hr	
160m	140m	1–2hr	
1075m	*1075m*	*3hr (+2½hr descent)*	*F*
210m	*210m*	*2hr (+1hr descent)*	
1245m	650m	6–7hr	
610m	*610m*	*2½–3hr (+2hr descent)*	*F*
1160m	1030m	6hr	
1290m	1160m	7–8hr	
1355m	1220m	7–8hr	
890m	850m	7–8hr	
680m	1030m	7–8hr	
565m	565m	5hr	
610m	655m	4hr	
235m	550m	2½hr	
635m	980m	6hr	
35m (Trins); 60m (Steinach)	530m (Trins); 215m (Steinach)	4hr	
5250m/5275m	**5250m/4945m**	**7 days**	

Negotiating the fixed cables, with the Tribulaun mountains providing the scenery (Trek 1, Excursion: Ascent of Habicht)

INTRODUCTION

Descending from the summit of the Wilder Freiger; easy ground looking towards the peaks of the Feuerstein (Trek 2, Stage 6)

The Stubai Alps are situated southwest of the old Austrian city of Innsbruck, in the province of Tirol. The area has no access difficulties and is easily reached by local bus service from Innsbruck in about 1hr.

Generally, the main peaks of the Stubai Alps follow the Wilder Freiger–Zuckerhütl mountain chain that straddles the border with Italy and embraces the area known as South Tirol (Südtirol), which refers to the Austrian territory that was annexed to Italy after World War 1.

The boundary of the Stubai Alps is generally recognised as being the Brenner Pass to the east and border with the Zillertal Alps range, the Sölden valley in the Ötztal Alps to the west, the mountains of the Italian South Tirol to the south and the Inn valley and Karwendel Mountains to the north. The highest mountain in the Stubai valley is the Zuckerhütl at 3505m, with a further 130 peaks over 3000m, many of which have glaciers and permanent snow cover.

This guidebook concentrates on two tours within the main Stubaital valley: the Stubai Rucksack Route, known in German as the Stubaier Höhenweg or Stubaier Runde Tour, and the Stubai Glacier Tour or Stubaier Gletscher Tour.

Each tour comprises a multi-day hut-to-hut walk with a comprehensive route description for each day, along with information about the huts and recommended climbs and excursions that may be undertaken en route.

As with my other books, this guide has been written to provide as much flexibility as possible to give participants various options that arise when hut-to-hut touring. The familiar Rucksack Route by definition means you will require no more than the ubiquitous rucksack and a pair of boots, while the very essence of the Glacier Tour requires you to carry mountaineering paraphernalia to cross the glaciers. Both are great options and can be undertaken within the span of a two-week holiday.

In this edition a third tour has been added to embrace the growing popularity of the Gschnitztaler Rundtour.

Whatever your aspirations, the Stubai is a splendid area for all mountain enthusiasts to explore. It is rightly recognised as ideal for first-time visitors to the Alps, particularly family groups with adventurous children and, perhaps more so, for aspiring alpinists, who should not judge the Stubai to be a tame area in comparison to the higher mountains of the Western Alps, as these mountains can challenge even the most experienced.

Whether you seek high-altitude walking through stunning scenery or relish greater challenges, you will not be disappointed.

Gruss Gott und sehr gut Stubaier Bergtouren.

VILLAGES OF THE STUBAI AND STUBAITAL

From the entrance to the valley at Schönberg to its head at Mutterbergalm, the Stubaital valley, or Stubaital in German, is everything Tirolean, with pretty chalet-style houses and organised charm. As you travel up the length of the some 27km valley, you first reach the trio of villages of Telfes, Mieders and Fulpmes and, lastly, Neustift, the Stubaital's main village and administrative centre.

Telfes, the first of the trio of Stubaital villages, prides itself on being a centre for adventure sports, principally mountain biking and paragliding, and boasts of being the sunniest place in the Stubai valley. While **Mieders**, at a tad short of 1000m, is more of a hillside village, located off the valley floor on the northern slopes of the Serleskamm ridge and the mountain known locally as King Serles.

If the weather is poor and you are looking for something to do, take the Serles cable car to the top lift and visit Maria Waldrast Monastery, then ride down the hill on the summer toboggan run. It's guaranteed to get your blood racing!

Fulpmes, the third of the trio of villages, established itself in the 16th century as a community for smelting iron ore brought in from Eastern Austria, gradually developing into a village of blacksmiths and manufacturers of iron products and eventually becoming famous as the home

of Stubai climbing equipment. Less known is the narrow-gauge railway built in 1904, which serves the village from Innsbruck. It was built to support the emerging steel industry until it became more profitable for the railway to transport passengers and tourists than carry iron ore. Equally less known is the fact that the village is a centre for hand-painted children's toys, principally Tiorlean dolls.

Neustift is the largest of the Stubaital villages and includes the outlying hamlets of Neder, Ranalt and Mutterberg. After Sölden in the Ötztal valley, it is the second-largest village in the Tirol.

Neustift's real claim to fame is that it was home to Franz Senn, who was the village priest in Neustift from 1881 until his untimely death from pneumonia, aged 52, on 31 January 1884. It was during his time in the village that he worked with his close friends Johann Stüdl and Karl Hofmann on establishing the German and Austrian Alpine Club. While Franz Senn is synonymous with the Stubai valley, the latter two are better known for their pioneering work around the Grossglockner.

The Franz Senn Hut, which features several times throughout the guidebook, is named in his honour. Those with time on their hands may wish to visit Saint George's Church cemetery, where he is buried. On the main street in Neustift there is a fitting memorial in his honour; see www.stubai.at.

Franz Senn

WHEN TO GO

The summer season usually starts in mid June and ends in late September.

June is early season and not the best time to visit as it is not unusual to find large amounts of old snow lying on the north-facing slopes, such as on the Simmingjochl, Grawagrubennieder and Schrimmennieder.

In July, the weather will be warmer and the winter snow will have receded further, although there will be more people in the mountains and at the huts.

August is seen as the peak season, when most Europeans take their holidays and the huts are at their busiest. The weather is at its most settled, although it is not unusual to see cloud build up late morning, with thunderstorms appearing in the evening. As an aside, August is when most of the villages in the Stubaital hold their summer church festivals, known as *Kirchentage*; they are worth a visit, good fun and enjoyed by all.

September announces the arrival of autumn, and the weather will be cooler and the huts quieter as the end of the season approaches.

The author's personal choice for a two-week holiday is either the middle of July or the first two weeks in September.

Glacier Tour

Sadly, with the erosion and decline of many of the Stubai glaciers, some of it exacerbated for the needs of skiers, the Glacier Tour is now best undertaken early in the season when the huts have just reopened and when plenty of snow cover remains on the glaciers, such as should exist in late June and early July. Once into August the route starts to become more problematic.

GETTING THERE AND BACK

Getting to Austria is relatively straightforward no matter how you decide to travel. For the purpose of these treks, you will probably arrive in Austria in the medieval city of Innsbruck, the provincial capital of the Tirol. Thereafter, all starting points for the Stubai tours are individually described from Innsbruck within each section.

By air

Even if you travel by air, which is without doubt the quickest way to get to Austria, you do not always have sufficient time to leave the UK in the early morning, catch a train from Innsbruck and then make your way to one of the huts before nightfall. At best you should plan to stay overnight in Innsbruck or Neustift and then continue your journey the day after. However, if you have no hold-ups, it is just about possible to get to Neustift by early evening and perhaps overnight at the Elfer Hut, chasing the last lift at 16:30.

Both British Airways and Lufthansa operate several flights a day from London, Manchester and Birmingham. Other carriers offer services from Luton, Stanstead and Gatwick. See Appendix A for airline websites.

Of course, travelling by air gets you to mainland Europe quickly, but you may lose precious time transferring to the *Hauptbahnhof* (railway station), and may experience frustrating delays and hold-ups just finding your way about.

At Munich, the airport connects directly with the regional railway network, where there are frequent trains every 20min or so. From the arrivals hall, follow the train signs 'DB' and 'S'. This is a similar set-up to the London Underground, which means you need a prepaid ticket before getting on the train. You can buy your ticket to Innsbruck, *hin und zuruck* (round-trip ticket), at the Deutsche

TREKKING IN AUSTRIA'S STUBAI ALPS

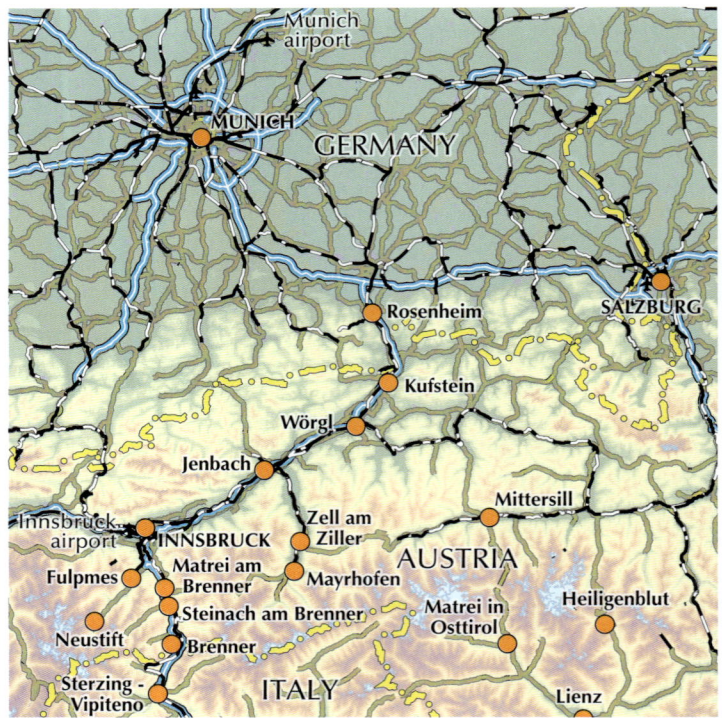

Bundesbahn (DB) railway booking office in the arrivals hall, adjacent to the concession counters for car hire and hotel reservations. Express trains run every 2hr or so.

Once on your journey you will need to leave the regional train at München Ost (Munich East); listen to the announcements and change platforms to get on one of the *Schnellzug* (intercity trains). Look out for the matrix signboards at the station, and on the sides of the trains, and board the first one displaying Innsbruck, Brennero, Venezia or Venedig; any destination heading into Italy or Switzerland will do, as they all have to go via Innsbruck.

There is also a DB ticket office at Munich East station, located on the lower level alongside shops and fast-food outlets. With express trains it is also possible to pay on the train, sometimes at a premium.

Train tickets can also be purchased in advance and online, including seat reservations, by visiting www.bahn.de. Click on the drop-down menu to access the website in English.

At Salzburg, take the 'Line 2' bus service from the airport to the railway station, where a rail ticket can be purchased to Innsbruck. The journey time is around 2hr, travelling west along the Inn valley.

At Innsbruck airport there is a regular shuttle-bus service plus taxis to get you to Innsbruck railway station. The onward journey is by bus for the Stubaital or by train for Steinach am Brenner and the Gschnitztaler Rundtour.

Airport transfers

A further alternative is to make a reservation with Four Seasons Travel (tel 0043 512 58 41 57 www.tirol-taxi.at), who specialise in coach or minibus transfers to and from Munich or Salzburg airports to Innsbruck. If you are a group of say eight, this can be more cost- and time-effective, as you will be collected at the airport and driven directly to your destination in Innsbruck. Otherwise, if you are a two or a three, make a reservation to travel on one of its luxury coaches. The overall journey time is about 2hr, depending on connections.

At Innsbruck airport, there is a bus service plus taxis to get you to Innsbruck city centre and the main railway station, followed by the regional bus service for the Stubaital.

By rail

Consult with Trainline and Eurostar, but the two most commonly used routes are as follows. Each route will get you to Innsbruck within 18hr of leaving London.

- London–Dover–Calais–Paris–Zurich–Innsbruck
- London–Dover–Ostend–Brussels–Munich–Innsbruck

See these websites for further details:

- German Railways – Deutsche Bundesbahn (DB): www.bahn.de
- Austrian Railways – Österreichische Bundesbahnen (ÖBB): www.oebb.at and fahrplan.oebb.at
- Postbus: www.postbus.at

By road

For the most direct route, take the Dover–Ostend channel crossing, then use the motorway system to travel to Munich and into Austria at Kufstein, then make the short drive up the Inn valley to Innsbruck.

Whatever your chosen route, consult with your motoring organisation before setting out. If there is more than one driver, it is possible to get to Innsbruck in around 15hr from Calais or Ostend.

It is also important when parking your car to consider the return journey and getting back to your vehicle, which is not always easy when you drop down into another valley. It is best to leave your car at one of the major towns with good railway connections to Innsbruck.

Approaching the Starkenburger Hut (Trek 1, Stage 8)

The return journey

This note is mainly for people travelling by air rather than those travelling by road and rail. The last day of your vacation needs to be devoted to making the journey home. See individual sections for descriptions.

The journey time from Innsbruck to Munich airport is around 2½hr, from Salzburg 2hr.

From Neustift the Postbus times to Innsbruck are 09:33 / 10:33 / 11:33.

From Innsbruck the trains to Munich are currently at 08:38 / 10:38 / 12:37 / 14:37 / 16:37 / 18:37 / 20:37.

From Innsbruck the trains to Salzburg are roughly every 2hr: 09:30 / 11:30 / 13:30.

Remember to change trains at Munich East and get on the regional shuttle-service train S8 marked '*Flughafen*' (airport).

See Appendix B for a glossary of some useful German–English words and phrases to use when travelling.

PLACES TO STAY

There is no shortage of good places to stay throughout Austria, as the whole country is geared to tourism and catering for visitors.

Hotels

Obviously, hotels in Innsbruck will be more expensive than hotels and guest houses in the surrounding local villages. If you are not bothered about nightlife, you will find good bargains in the villages of Neustift, Telfes, Fulpmes and Mieders.

In Innsbruck, hotels can be booked from the tourist information centre at the entrance to the Old Town Square, the Altstadt, or in advance via the internet. See Appendix A for a handful of recommendations.

In Steinach am Brenner, starting point for the Gschnitztaler Rundtour, the Aktivhotel zur Rose (tel 0043 5272 6221 info@hotelrose.at) is the hotel of choice, located within a 10min walk from the village railway station. The hotel is managed by Herr Franz and the Holzmann family, who provide good, inexpensive hotel accommodation. You can also leave surplus bags there to pick up on your return.

In Neustift, the main centre of the Stubaital, hotels tend to cater to the tourist trade, but there is an abundance of guest houses and small hotels where climbers and walkers will feel more at home, and if you are booking huts via the internet, many huts have family connections with guest houses and hotels in the valley and will be happy to make recommendations. In terms of recommendations, the Hotel Berghof (www.berghof-tirol.com info@berghof-tirol.com), located adjacent to the Elfer cable-car station, is a very good place to stay. In Neustift, the tourist information office is located in the village square; see www.stubai.at.

If you have to stay overnight in Salzburg, the family-run Das Grüne Hotel zur Post (tel 0043 662 8323390 info@hotelzurpost.info) is located 5min from the airport and a 15min walk from the centre of this fine old city.

Youth hostels (Verein Volkshaus)

Innsbruck has three youth-hostel-type hotels reasonably close to the railway

---

VISITING INNSBRUCK

Capital city of the province of Tirol, and named after the river on which it stands, Innsbruck is overlooked by the Karwendel group of mountains and became famous as a centre for Winter Olympics sports. The city is well worth a visit in its own right, with the right mix of city life and the cultural history of the Old Town, Altstadt, as well as the ÖAV Alpenverein-Museum. Located within the Hofburg Imperial Palace in the Old Town, it has many fine exhibits from the golden age of alpinism, perhaps the most notable being memorabilia of Hermann Buhl's ascent of Nanga Parbat in the Karakoram mountains of Northern Pakistan.

The museum is open Monday to Saturday during normal business hours.

station and the tourist part of the city. To check their availability, visit www.jungehotels.at; see Appendix A for further details.

Campsites
For those travelling by road who wish to camp, good campsites can be found throughout the region; see Appendix A for details.

Groups intending to camp should enquire from the campsite warden about reduced fees while they are away; this is referred to as *leeres Zelt*.

LOCAL SERVICES

Tourist offices
In Innsbruck, the main tourist office is located at the entrance to the Old Town Square, Altstadt, on Museum Strasse, at the road junction of Burg Graben and Maria Therasien Strasse. This is the only bureau in Innsbruck with a money-exchange facility that is open on a Sunday. Other satellite offices are located throughout the city.

In Neustift, the tourist office is located in the village square, adjacent to the town hall; see www.neustift-stubaital.gv.at and www.stubai.at.

In Steinach am Brenner, tourist information can be found at Tourismusverband Wipptal, located on the main road in Steinach, on the ground floor of the town's *Rathaus* (town hall).

See also www.austriatourism.com.

Post offices and mail
Post offices are open Monday to Friday from 08:00 to 12:00 then 14:00 to 18:00. They have a fax facility and a money-exchange service.

In Innsbruck, post offices are located on Mark Stainer Strasse, near the entrance to the Altstadt, and on Maximilian Strasse, near the Triumphal Arch. In Neustift, it is located on the main street, Scheibe Dorf, near the church.

Post to Austria usually takes about five days from the UK. At the huts, postcards can be purchased and mailed from the hut's post box. The mail is then taken down the valley, usually once a week, and deposited at the main post office. Not surprisingly, post to the UK will take 10 to 20 days.

Places to leave luggage
There are left-luggage facilities at all railway stations. However, for security reasons there may be restrictions on using the luggage lockers for longer than 48hr. It is advised that you leave a note with your belongings stating who you are, where you are going and when you will be back, along with your passport number and mobile telephone number.

Alternatively, should you be staying at one of the hotels, most hoteliers are quite happy to store luggage until you return.

PROFESSIONAL MOUNTAIN GUIDES (BERGFÜHRER)

Should you require the services of a professional mountain guide, these can be hired; see Appendix A for more information.

CHILDREN

I have been asked many times about the suitability of hut-to-hut touring for children. Most children I know, or have met, love visiting the various huts and the sense of freedom it bestows on them. The Austrian Alpine Club also actively encourages children to participate in mountain activities.

The author's own daughter has traversed the entire length of the Rucksack Route and undertook the rigours of the Glacier Tour, climbing several peaks along the way, when she was 14 years old.

If children are capable of ascending Ben Nevis, Snowdon or the round of Helvellyn, they will surely enjoy some of these tours.

But only parents can decide, as some of the days are quite long, particularly the Innsbrucker Hut to Bremer Hut and the Dresdner Hut to Neue Regensburger Hut connections. Children need to be fit, happy to be in the mountains for long periods of time

Youngsters of Alpenverein Britannia having some fun at the Franz Senn Hut

and easily entertained, i.e., enjoy reading books, playing scrabble or simply chit-chatting. However, the best solution is that they have a friend(s) with them for company and are allowed to have adequate rest days.

AUSTRIAN ALPINE CLUB (ÖAV)

(Österreichischer Alpenverein founded 1862)

Huts throughout the Stubai are administered by the Austrian and German Alpine Clubs, the ÖAV and DAV, respectively, except those in South Tirol, which are owned and administered by the Italian Alpine Club (CAI) or its regional equivalent, the Alpenverein Südtirol (AVS).

The Österreichischer Alpenverein (ÖAV), which translates as the Austrian Alpine Association, was founded in 1862 to foster and encourage the sport of mountaineering. Its founding is largely credited to Franz Senn, who was the village priest in Neustift (Stubai valley) until his untimely death from pneumonia aged 52, and his associates Johann Stüdl, a wealthy Prague business man, and Karl Hofmann, a young lawyer from Munich, who was sadly killed in action a few years later, fighting on the streets of Sedan in the Franco-Prussian War. Both men, Stüdl and Hofmann, are more closely associated with the development of mountaineering in the Venediger and Glockner groups of mountains. Hofmann himself was a very talented mountaineer.

Celebrating its 160th anniversary in 2022, the Alpenverein was the first Alpine Club to be established in mainland Europe. Presently, the Club has just over 650,000 members in 197 *Sektions* (sections) that embrace all facets of mountaineering. Membership is open to anyone, without exception, who has a love of the mountains, regardless of age or ability.

The Club's principal activities include developing mountain huts, marking and maintaining footpaths, producing maps, organising mountaineering courses and tackling environmental issues, particularly those deemed to be spoiling the aesthetic appeal of the mountains, such as littering or inappropriate signage and graffiti.

The establishment of the UK section, Alpenverein Britannia, is largely credited to Major Walter Ingham and Henry Crowther, who both had strong links with Austria. Walter, while a UK citizen, spent many years in Vienna, including several years with the Control Commission just after World War 2.

Henry, born Heinrich Kraus, came from the eastern city of Graz. He was an electrical engineer but work in Austria in the 1930s was dire, so he accepted a posting as manager of the Austrian Tourist Office in London. As National Socialism took hold of Austria, he was ordered by Hitler to return to Austria, which he refused to do. As war approached, Heinrich was

Austrian Alpine Club (ÖAV)

Clockwise from top L: edelweiss, Austria's elusive national flower; globe flower or butterball; alpine aster; mountain houseleek

interned on the Isle of Man. During this time, he became a naturalised British citizen and changed his name to the more English-sounding Henry. After the war both men got together to re-establish their growing interest in the travel and tourism business, one of their plans being to establish an English Sektion of the Austrian Alpine Club.

In 1948, just after World War 2, the UK Sektion of the ÖAV was formed to foster Anglo-Austrian relationships between like-minded people in the spirit of mountaineering and to make it easier for British mountaineers in the immediate post-war years to visit the Eastern Alps.

Presently, Alpenverein Britannia is one of the largest UK mountaineering clubs, with over 13,000 members, ranking 12th in the Alpenverein as a whole. The Club organises its own activities and has a regular programme of indoor and outdoor meets. It also has its own website (www.alpenverein.at/britannia) and produces a quarterly newsletter. The Club runs training courses for its members, both in the UK and in Austria, through the Alpenverein-Akademie mountaineering school. The Austrian Alpine Club (UK) enjoys full reciprocal rights agreements with all other Alpine Clubs: in France (CAF), Switzerland (CAS), Italy (CAI) and Germany (DAV). This means that should you cross from the Stubai into South Tirol to stay at the Becherhaus Hut, for instance, you will pay the same fees as those enjoyed by members of the Italian Alpine Club and vice versa.

Anyone intending to undertake a hut-to-hut tour anywhere in Austria is strongly recommended to join Alpenverein Britannia. Apart from the real benefit of enjoying preferential treatment and reduced costs at the huts, perhaps the main advantage of being a member is that of belonging; this feeling of friendliness, referred to as *Gemütlichkeit* (homely), is greatly cherished and fostered by everyone and will be experienced many times when visiting various huts, particularly over a number of years.

Membership of the Austrian Alpine Club is, as previously noted, open to all regardless of age or ability and is recommended for everyone wishing to avail themselves of the benefits of reduced hut rates and the provision of mountain rescue insurance. There are different categories for adults, seniors, juniors, juveniles, children and family groups. Membership is renewed annually.

On acceptance of membership, the Club provides an internet link packed full of useful information: www.alpenverein.at/britannia/membership/member-benefits.php. See Appendix A for full contact details.

HUTS

The word 'hut' is a misnomer as all the huts in the Stubai Alps, as described here, are more akin to mountain inns or guest houses and

At the Hildesheimer Hut, looking towards the Pfaffenferner glacier and the Pfaffenschneide (Trek 2, Stage 4)

provide simple overnight accommodation and some form of restaurant service. This means that the mountain traveller does not have to return to the valley every few days to stock up on provisions.

Collectively, there are well over 1000 huts in Austria, half of which are owned by the Austrian and German Alpine Clubs. In the Stubai Alps there are a total of 30 ÖAV and DAV huts, most of which are open from the end of June to mid September. All of the huts in the Stubai have a *Hüttenwirt* (hut guardian), traditionally a *Bergführer* (mountain guide) and his family. Each hut has simple sleeping accommodation in the form of a *Matratzenlager* (mixed dormitory) with blankets and pillows and a small number of *Bettzimmer* (bedrooms) with duvets and sheets.

In addition to sleeping accommodation, each hut will have some form of restaurant service offering a number of traditional dishes (see Appendix B). The menu generally comprises *Bergsteigeressen* (mountaineers' food): soup, a choice of main meals, cold meats, cheese and sometimes cakes and sweets. All huts serve tea, coffee, beer, wine and so forth, and most huts will have a small shop where visitors can buy postcards, chocolate and biscuits.

On arrival at the hut, you should first remove your boots and store them in the boot rack, which will be close to the front door. You should also hang your ice axe, crampons, rope and other clobber on the racks provided because such paraphernalia is not permitted in the dormitories and bedrooms. If you are wet on arrival,

On the Übeltalferner glacier, approaching the Müller Hut (Trek 2, Stage 5B)

your waterproofs should be shaken as dry as possible outside and hung up to dry with your ice tackle. If you are in a group, do not mill around the doorway, and make sure your group leaves its surplus water and as much dirt off boots outside as possible. Many of the huts are spotlessly clean and, for the benefit of all guests, like to remain that way.

You should then establish contact with the Hüttenwirt to obtain your overnight accommodation. (A maximum of three nights is the Club rule but, generally, this is not rigidly enforced.) You will usually find this most important person in the *Küche* (kitchen), *Gastestube* (dining room) or *Bureau* (office).

Having found the Hüttenwirt it is important to greet him or her by saying *Gruss Gott* (good day) and introduce yourself. Mention if you and your group are members of Alpenverein Britannia of the Austrian Alpine Club (or another Alpine Club) and tell them that you would like some accommodation. (Note it is advisable to book ahead to ensure there is a room available.) The Hüttenwirt is then likely to ask for your membership card(s), which may be retained overnight or until your departure, when you will be asked to pay.

If you do not speak German and feel uncomfortable attempting to ask for rooms in German, write down the following phrase: *Ich/wir hatte(n) gern ein Zimmer oder Matratzenlager, bitte* (I/we would like a room or dormitory, please). Be polite and always use *bitte* (please) and *danke* (thank you). As obvious as this may seem, these polite gestures are extremely important and will go a long way to ensuring a pleasant stay.

Should the hut be full, you may have to take up residence in the *Winterraum* (winter room), which is usually the reserve of ski mountaineers and those visiting when the hut is closed. The winter room is generally an annexe to the hut and may double as a storeroom or shelter for animals, as is the case at the Starkenburger Hut. While the winter room can be quite cosy, remember to keep your gear off the floor, as it is usually the home of the hut's more permanent four-pawed furry residents.

Should the hut be beyond full, you will be provided with a mattress for *Notlager*, which roughly translates as 'sleeping with the furniture', be it on the floor, in the corridors, on tables, on benches or simply anywhere you can lie down.

Only on very rare occasions will you be asked to move on by the Hüttenwirt and only when bed space has been secured at an adjacent hut and only when there is sufficient daylight for you to reach your destination. In the Stubai Alps this is a rare scenario, however, which means your only option would be the cosy but somewhat noisy situation of 'sleeping with the furniture'.

At the hut you will also require a *Schlafsack* (sheet sleeping bag) for use with the blankets and bedding provided by the hut; this is to minimise the amount of washing required and, thereby, reduce water pollution downstream of the hut. Note that this is a compulsory requirement. If you do not have one, the Hüttenwirt will hire you one.

You will also require a pair of hut shoes for wandering around the hut, as many ÖAV huts do not provide them. Wearing boots upstairs is strictly *Verboten* (forbidden).

Each hut will have some form of male and female washrooms and toilets, ranging from excellent at the Franz Senn, Sulzenau and Amberger Huts to more modest at say the Bremer Hut to basic but adequate facilities at the Müller and Hoch Stubai Huts, simply due to the fact that they have a limited water supply.

However, it does seem likely that the provision of hot water at some huts will gradually diminish as the Club moves towards more simple and basic necessities in an effort to minimise the use of fuel and water.

Elsewhere in the hut, usually near the front door, you will find the *Trockenraum* (drying room), where wet clothes can be dried.

Thereafter, the heart and soul of the hut is the dining room. Here you will find all manner of activities going on: groups planning their next day, people celebrating a climb or a birthday or people just chatting. The atmosphere is best described as Gemütlichkeit, a homely ambience that is fostered and cherished throughout the whole of Austria.

At the end of your stay, remember to make your bed, fold your blankets and check you haven't forgotten anything. Search out the Hüttenwirt and thank him/her and the staff for a pleasant stay. Remember to collect your membership card if it has not already been given back to you. Finally, fill in the hut book to record your stay and indicate where you are going next.

Hut reservations
Even if you are travelling solo, it is recommended that you contact the hut, either by phone or email, prior to your arrival, more so if you are travelling as a group, as all the huts on the Stubai Rucksack Route get very busy, particularly at weekends and during the peak holiday season in August.

If you are travelling as a group, it is also recommended that you book your accommodation early, making enquiries up to six months before your intended visit. Don't leave it too late or you will find the smaller huts will be fully booked.

Most of the huts in the Stubai Alps now have websites and email addresses, which makes it easier than ever to get in touch directly and make a reservation online. There is also an attempt by the ÖAV, DAV and AVS to rationalise various online hut reservation practices into one amalgamated platform, which will allow individuals and groups to make hut reservations and payments at a one-stop shop via the internet: see www.alpenverein.at/huetten and www.alpsonline.org/guest/login. See 'Hut directory' also for details.

Having made your reservation, remember to reconfirm your booking directly with the hut just before you travel and again by phone the day before your visit, to let them know you're on your way and will turn up.

Reservation cancellations
Because of the ease with which huts can now be booked over the internet and by phone, abuse of this facility is beginning to become an issue, particularly when reservations are made and folk do not turn up; this results in not only a loss of business for the huts but also in a significant waste of food. Some huts are now asking for deposits to offset some of this risk. Note that in Austrian law, if you make a reservation and do not cancel in adequate time, you are still liable for the full costs, or part of, incurred by the hut. Most huts are businesses, and it is only polite that should you have to cancel your reservation you make every effort to do so – if not, don't be surprised if you receive a bill!

HUT MEALS AND MENUS

All huts have some sort of restaurant service to cover the three daily meals: *Frühstück* (breakfast), *Mittagessen* (lunch) and *Abendessen* (dinner). Tea, coffee, hot chocolate, lemonade, cola, beer, wine and schnapps are all available at the huts. Drinks are served in *Viertel* (quarter) or *Halbe* (half) litres or in *gross* (large) or *klein* (small) and may be *heiss* (hot) or *kalt* (cold).

Breakfast is served from approximately 06:00 to 07:30 and usually comprises two or three slices of bread, a portion of butter, jam and cheese, and a choice of tea or coffee. If you do not finish it, take it with you as you pay for it all! Thereafter, no meals are available until lunchtime because the hut staff are busy with general housekeeping. Breakfast is seen as the worst value for money, but unless you are carrying your own provisions you will have little choice other than to accept it.

Lunch and dinner are the main meals of the day and are served with a selection of vegetables or salad, and there will be vegetarian (*Vegetarische*) options. Lunchtime is usually from 12:00 to 14:00 but varies from hut to hut. However, it is possible to purchase simple meals, such as *Suppe* (soup), *Käsebrot* (cheese bread) and *Apfelstrudl* (apple strudel), at most of the huts throughout the afternoon.

Dinner is generally served from 18:00 to 19:30. Apart from the dishes listed on the menu, Bergsteigeressen will also be available; literally translated, it means 'mountaineers' food' and in reality, that is what it is – even if it is potluck what you get. However, it is a low-priced meal and must contain a minimum of 500 calories. The meal generally comprises spaghetti or other pasta, potatoes, some meat or sausage, sometimes a fried egg or maybe a dumpling. There is no hard and fast rule other than it is relatively inexpensive and there is usually a lot of it.

Siegerland Hut interior

Appendix B lists many of the items found on a typical hut *Speisekarte* (menu), as well as some useful words and phrases when ordering food and drink.

Generally, before ordering meals, you must first organise a table. There is no formality, but sometimes groups of tables may be marked *privat* (private) or *Reservierung* (reservation) when mountaineering training courses are being run. Once you have sat down, one of the *Kellnerinnen* (waitresses) will take your order. Alternatively, you may have to go to the counter or *Küche* (kitchen) to order, or there may be a sign marked *Selbstbedienung*, which means self-service.

The general rule for paying for food and drink is by way of an accumulative bill. Therefore, visitors are advised to note their consumption to aid checking at the time of paying. Take note, these bills/lists can be considerable when staying at a hut for more than a couple of nights.

Because of the excellent service the huts provide, there is little need to carry your own food. However, many people bring their own dry rations: tea, coffee, bread, cheese, etc. This allows you to make your own snacks, and by borrowing cups and purchasing *ein Liter Teewasser* (a litre of water for tea), you can brew up at a small cost.

The only option not provided for is self-catering, and it does seem a little pointless when all the meals are reasonably priced.

As a guideline for working out a budget, typical meal costs can be equated to similar prices for a decent bar meal plus drinks in most British pubs. The half-board cost is currently €55–65, depending on the category of hut.

KIT LIST

In terms of how much kit to take, the following is a good rule of thumb: one on, one off and the odd spare.

When travelling as a group, try to share items to minimise each person's load. For example, you will only need one comprehensive first-aid kit, one repair kit, one set of maps, one guidebook, one phrase book, one pair of binoculars and one set of spare batteries if all the headlamps are the same.

- Rucksack (50L)
- Boots (suitable for all seasons)
- Trekking poles (optional)
- Socks x 2 pairs
- Trousers
- Shorts (optional)
- Underwear x 3
- Shirts x 2
- Light fleece pullover
- Light windproof jacket
- Waterproofs: jacket and trousers
- Hat and gloves
- Gaiters (optional)
- Headlamp-cum-torch
- Toiletries plus pack towel
- Water bottle or thermos flask

- First-aid kit with sun cream and lip salve
- Sunglasses plus spare pair
- Repair kit: needle and thread, super glue, candle, binding wire
- Pocket knife
- Selection of polythene bags
- Maps and compass
- Whistle
- Notepad and pencil
- Stubai Alps guidebook – that is, this one!
- Emergency gear, bivvy bag, food rations
- Personal optional items, such as German phrase book, camera, binoculars
- Hut wear: a lightweight change of clothes, hut shoes or socks, trousers, shirt, sheet sleeping bag and inflatable pillow

Also recommended for walkers: a set of microspikes and a 2.4m-long x 10mm-wide Dyneema tape sling with a large jumbo-sized screwgate karabiner.

Should you intend to climb some of the peaks, you will need to add the following to the above list – and know how to use them:

- Ice axe
- Crampons
- 2 x large slings with screwgate karabiners
- 3 x Prusik loops
- Harness
- Ice screw
- 2 x spare karabiners
- A length of rope, such as 50m x 9mm, for each group of three people

All kitted out for glacier travel at the Wütenkarsattel pass, with the Hoch Stubai Hut in the centre (Trek 2, Stage 3)

- A few odds and ends, such as a small selection of slings with nuts, a pulley, a universal rock piton

For crevasse rescue you will generally need five karabiners at your disposal.

The following items are also useful within a group: altimeter, ice hammer, deadman, or other snow anchor belay device, and Prusiking devices, such as a Petzl Tibloc or Wild Country Ropeman.

ROUTE FINDING

Paths, tracks and waymarks

Paths throughout the Stubai are waymarked roughly every hundred metres or so with a daub of red paint.

At intersections, paths frequently have a signpost or, alternatively, a red-and-white paint marker with a designated path number; this in turn is cross-referenced to maps and guidebooks, including this one.

Paths throughout, such as on the Stubai Rucksack Route, vary from traditional mountain paths to tracks across boulder fields and rough ground. Participants will also encounter steep ground, late summer snow and fixed cables here and there, which have been installed to aid your stability.

Paths for hut-to-hut routes are frequently marked with a signpost just outside the hut; these give the standard time in hours for the distance between huts without stops and display a colour-code difficulty grade of blue, red or black.

Routes onto and across glaciers are by definition Black Mountain Trails and for the experienced only, as tracks onto and across glaciers are not normally marked because the route may vary from year to year. Also, if venturing onto glaciers, you are expected to have the necessary know-how and route-finding skills, plus the required equipment. However, sometimes the local guides will place marker poles on the glacier to aid route finding, such as those on the heavily crevassed Sulzenauferner glacier.

Difficult ground at the Hoachwand–Stubenscharte corridor (Trek 2A, Stage 8)

Where the route description refers to the left or right bank of a river, stream or glacier, this is when viewed in the direction of flow, which means that in ascent the left bank will be on the right. To avoid confusion, efforts have been made throughout the text to add a compass bearing to ensure participants go in the right direction.

Given the above, no great demand will be made on the individual's route-finding skills, except on routes noted in the text as having the odd navigational difficulty.

Map-makers have also endeavoured to enable better route interpretation by providing different types of path markings: solid red lines for easy trails, dashed red lines for footpaths and dotted red lines for narrow, steep paths; supporting symbols have been added to show fixed cables and ladders.

However, as with all mountains, the Stubai Alps included, route finding is made much more difficult in mist, rain and snow.

While the information provided is as accurate as possible, this may change from year to year due to landslips, avalanches and erosion.

MAPS AND GUIDEBOOKS

The following two maps are required for the Stubai Rucksack Route and Stubai Glacier Tour. The maps are published by the Austrian Alpine Club and are available from the UK Section of the Austrian Alpine Club.

Alpenvereinskarte (1:25,000)
- Sheet 31/1 Stubaier Alpen: Hochstubai
- Sheet 31/2 Stubaier Alpen: Sellrain

Other useful Alpenvereinskarte maps (1:25,000)
- 31/3 Brennerberge
- 31/5 Innsbruck

Also recommended, since the maps cover the complete region at a glance and are available from major map retailers:
- **Freytag & Berndt Wanderkarte:** Sheet 24, 1:100,000 Stubaieralpen
- **Kompass Wanderkarte:** Sheet 83, 1:50,000 Stubaieralpen: Serleskamm
- **Verlag W. Mayr:** Sheet 18, 1:35,000 Stubaital

Books

For guidebooks, websites and other reading, see Appendix C.

Alpenvereinaktiv app

The Alpenverein has also developed mapping software, Alpenvereinaktiv, for use on mobile phones and digital tablets, which can be accessed via Alpenvereinaktiv.com. The Alpenverein is keen to promote the use of Alpenvereinaktiv, first as a tour-planning tool and as a physical tool while undertaking a tour.

The Alpenvereinaktiv app offers three levels of access: the basic app is free and includes tour planning, height profiles, commentary and photos; this is followed by the Pro and Pro+ versions, which can be purchased as a monthly or annual subscription and include GPS tracking, 3D video and satellite photos.

Mountain terminology

Appendix B provides a glossary of German–English words that may be useful when route finding and navigating in the Stubai.

ALPINE WALKING SKILLS

So, how do these skills differ in the Stubai from walking elsewhere?

Put simply, and as mentioned in the route-grading segment, it's the variance in the terrain that makes Alpine walking different. On a single walk you may encounter easy paths, stone-covered tracks, large rocky boulder fields, paths with fixed cables, and the odd patch of hard-packed snow. Sometimes, just the strength-sapping distances involved when carrying a touring rucksack can make Alpine walking far more of a challenge.

Boots: It is essential that you have a relatively stiff boot with good ankle support and a stout Vibram-type rubber sole. Many of the walks involve sustained hard walking over rocky slopes and glacial debris, plus encounters with patches of old, hard snow. It is important to think of your boots as tools that can be used to kick steps and jam into rocky cracks without causing damage to your feet. While flexible boots may be a tad lighter and more comfortable, they are no match for a good pair of four-season mountaineering boots when it comes to dealing with difficult ground.

A protected gangway path en route to the Peiljoch (Trek 1, Stage 5)

Microspikes: While crampons are normally associated with climbers, a pair of these little tools often comes in handy when the weather decides to dump some unseasonable snow in July or August, and they may help provide you with a little extra security when you get up close to some old, hard-packed snow.

Improvised harness: Many of the routes are equipped with fixed cables to provide some support over stretches of difficult terrain. While these may be relatively easy to cross, it is the consequences of a fall that should be borne in mind. Also, not everyone has a head for heights, and the use of an improvised harness will help to give you confidence and security of passage. Constructed from a 2.4m-long by 10mm-wide Dyneema sling, three or four overhand knots and a large jumbo-sized screwgate karabiner, the sling will allow you to clip into those fixed cables whenever the need arises and arrest a fall when you least expect it.

These slings can also be daisy-chained together to provide a useful short rope should the need arise, provided everyone carries one.

Trekking poles: Almost standard accessories for most folk these days but in the Alps trekking poles come into their own, especially when crossing glacial streams and traversing steep patches of old snow.

GLACIERS AND GLACIER TRAVEL

While relatively small compared with the glaciers of the Ötztal and Venediger, the glaciers of the Stubai are in the heartland of the Tirol and the Eastern Alps, with the glaciers of the Zuckerhütl and the Wilder Freiger covering the greatest area, while the Sulzenauferner glacier, adjacent to the Zuckerhütl and Wilder Pfaff, remains the longest in the range. Quite a few of the mountaineering routes described in this guide involve crossing or negotiating glaciers that can be heavily crevassed depending on the time of year, the conditions changing from season to season, and can take several hours to cross.

It goes without saying that before committing to climbing these peaks, you should have the requisite skills and equipment to navigate such glacial terrain safely. Should this be your first foray into glacier territory, you are strongly advised to undertake some formal training beforehand.

The UK Section of the Austrian Alpine Club organises basic training in glacier crossing and crevasse rescue through the ÖAV Alpenverein subsidiary WELTbewegend, the commercial arm of Alpenverein Edelweiss in Vienna; see www.alpenverein.at/britannia/activities/training.php or contact the AAC (UK) office for details www.alpenverein.at/britannia.

TREKKING IN AUSTRIA'S STUBAI ALPS

Plas y Brenin National Outdoor Centre in North Wales and Glenmore Lodge in Scotland also run similar introductory alpine skills courses, where you can practise crevasse-rescue techniques on the safe, dry land of local crags and climbing walls; contact www.pyb.co.uk and www.glenmorelodge.org.uk.

A further alternative is to hire a professional mountain guide for a day via British Mountain Guides www.bmg.org.uk.

A very informative DVD, *Alpine Essentials*, is also available from the British Mountaineering Council (BMC).

The motto is to practise before you go.

HEALTH AND SAFETY

Fitness
While you do not have to be super fit to undertake these tours, it is essential that participants are used to walking for 6hr continuously while carrying a touring-sized rucksack weighing in the region of 12–15kg (significantly less without mountaineering equipment).

Altitude
The average altitude experienced on the tour is in the region of 2500–3000m (8000–10,000ft). It is, therefore, uncommon for people visiting the Stubai to suffer badly from altitude sickness.

HEALTH AND SAFETY

However, that's not to say you won't feel the effects of altitude, such as feeling out of puff, experiencing a mild headache or walking at a slowed pace, particularly on the higher peaks, the Zuckerhütl and Wilder Freiger.

The best defence against the effects of altitude is to be as fit as possible, eat and drink normally and ensure you get adequate rest and sleep. However, should you experience symptoms that persist or worsen, it would be prudent to descend to a lower altitude.

Mountain rescue and personal insurance

All the routes described involve sustained activity in a high mountain environment. Inevitably, this increases the risk of an accident taking place, such as a severe fall, breaking a limb or some other serious mishap, resulting in the mountain rescue team being called out.

As noted elsewhere, one of the benefits of membership of the ÖAV is mountain rescue insurance in case of accidents. This can be supplemented by a specialist insurance company, details of which are available from the Austrian Alpine Club (UK) or by simply scanning the advertisement sections in one of the many climbing magazines. Similarly, the BMC has an excellent insurance policy, which can be obtained separately to membership.

View from the summit of Wilder Freiger, looking across the Übeltalferner glacier towards Becherhaus and the Italian South Tirol (Trek 1, Stage 4B)

The value of insurance should not be underestimated; the cost of a mountain rescue can be considerable when helicopters, police and professional mountain guides are involved, unlike in the UK, where mountain rescue services are generally provided free of charge by the local authority's public services department and groups of enthusiastic volunteers. In the Alpine regions, most countries will charge the hapless victim. Be warned!

Mountain rescue is as much about prevention as it is about cure so before you go, please check all your gear and practise constructing your improvised, rudimentary harness as well as the time-consuming tasks of putting on crampons/harnesses and roping up. Most importantly, practise your crevasse-rescue techniques.

Global Health Insurance Card (GHIC)

This card, previously known as the EHIC (European Health Insurance Card) and E111, is available free from any post office or online. To qualify for the card, you must be living legally in the UK; see www.nhs.uk for details of eligibility. Simply fill out the form and you will receive a credit-card-sized GHIC identity card, which entitles you to free medical care in any EU member state, in this case Austria. Should you be unfortunate to need medical attention while on holiday, this card will help you to pay your way.

However, the GHIC entitles you only to those services provided free in the member state; it does not cover any aspect of medical repatriation. In Neustift and neighbouring villages, the nearest hospital-clinic where the GHIC card is valid is the General Hospital in Innsbruck.

It is important that you take out good personal travel insurance to supplement that provided by the GHIC.

Doctors

Should you need to visit a doctor or pharmacist, look out for the green cross sign usually displayed outside a general practitioner's clinic. In Neustift there is a doctor's practice and *Apotheke* (pharmacy) on the main road opposite the church.

Coronavirus pandemic

As a result of the Coronavirus pandemic in 2020, restrictions were put in place; many of these affected air, train and bus travel, but they also affected how hut accommodation operated. Post-Covid-19, some restrictions at huts may continue for the foreseeable, such as the requirement for a sheet sleeping bag. Hopefully, all restrictions will ease over time, but until such time, check the latest guidelines before you go.

Emergency telephone numbers

The following numbers can be dialled from a mobile phone, even when the phone indicates there is no reception from your service provider. Fortunately, mobile phone reception is excellent in Austria.

On the Wildgratscharte (Trek 2, Stage 2)

It is worthwhile popping these numbers into your mobile phone, then you don't have to look them up should the need arise:
- *Bergrettung* (mountain rescue), Austria 140
- Mountain rescue, Italy 118
- *Rotes Kreutz* (Red Cross) 144
- European emergency phone number 112

Helicopter rescue
In the event of a helicopter rescue:
- Remain at least 50m from the helicopter
- Do not approach the helicopter unless the winch man signals you to do so
- Do not approach the helicopter from behind
- Ensure that all loose items of equipment are made secure

ELECTRONIC DEVICES
Folk who are wedded to and rely heavily on their mobile phone or tablet should note that the electrical infrastructure in most huts is, at best, extremely modest, with few if any places to recharge your phone, tablet or camera battery. Some huts have started to provide a common multi-gang USB charging unit in dining rooms, but these tend to fill up quickly with devices when the hut is busy. It is recommended that you take (perhaps as part of a group kit) a portable USB battery pack and a twin or triple USB charging socket, which will allow you to extend any USB provision provided by the hut. For cameras, the best option is to carry enough spare batteries to last the length of the tour.

At the Seescharte, so named because you can see lots of Alpine Sees (Trek 1, Stage 4B)

USING THIS GUIDE

Route descriptions and maps
As previously mentioned, the routes described follow recognised paths and tracks corresponding to those indicated on maps and signposts.

However, to aid route finding across unfamiliar ground, each daily tour itinerary is fully described and illustrated with a map indicating the main topographical features that will be observed en route.

Route grading
The routes described are for people who are already involved in some sort of mountain activity on a regular basis. The tours range from moderate to quite strenuous, and you will need to be able to carry a full rucksack for an average of 6–7hr each day. In terms of alpine grading, the majority of the routes fall into the mountaineering grade of 'easy to moderate', comprising sustained mountain walking and requiring the ability to negotiate steep ground, scramble over rocks, cross late summer snow and make use of fixed cables, as well as having a good head for heights.

To help participants determine what they can expect to encounter on the popular routes between huts, the Alpenverein (ÖAV and DAV) has devised a colour-coded system for marking fingerposts, similar to the skiing grades of blue, red and black, with blue being the easiest and black the hardest. The trekking grades are as follows:

- **Blue** – routes on wide tracks within permanently settled regions in the forest. No prior mountain experience or specialist equipment is required.

Mountain trails: Routes mostly above the treeline. Basic alpine experience and knowledge are required. Mountain trails are divided into red and black trails, according to their level of difficulty.

- **Red mountain trails** – narrow routes of intermediate difficulty with steep sections, secured footpaths (fixed cables) or short climbing sections (scrambling). Alpine experience, good physical shape, surefootedness and mountaineering equipment are required; see 'Kit list' for guidance.
- **Black mountain trails** – very difficult, narrow paths with many steep sections and precipices, secured footpaths (fixed cables) and longer climbing sections (scrambling). Alpine experience, excellent stamina, surefootedness, a good head for heights and specialist hiking equipment are absolutely essential; see 'Kit list' for guidance.

Most of the trekking/hiking described in this guidebook follows red and black routes and blue approach routes.

The ascents of the peaks are all graded mountaineering routes ranging from easy, as in the Alpine grade of Facile (F), which has no significant difficulties, to peaks that are moderately difficult to climb and have an Alpine grade of Peu Difficile (PD), requiring good mountaineering skills.

Standard times

At the beginning of each route description, a standard time in hours is given as an estimate of the time required to walk from hut to hut. This time is generally on the generous side compared with those given by the Alpenverein, the huts themselves and the times specified on the route direction signs. The time stated is the number of hours spent on the move and does not include lunch stops and other breaks. Most British parties find it difficult to attain the Alpenverein times. Be advised that this is of no consequence, as a good number of the quoted times are unattainable and seem to have been set by very fit athletes. With this in mind, the route descriptions in this book quote the actual time required when carrying a heavy touring rucksack.

If in doubt, you can always work out an approximate time yourself by calculating the sum of 20min per km and 1hr per 300m of ascent.

Participants undertaking the tour with children are advised to add at least 1hr to the standard time to allow for frequent picnic stops. Similarly, aspiring alpinists should make due allowance to the standard time while they learn the rudiments of glacier travel and the time-consuming activity of roping up and adding and removing crampons.

Spellings

You may well encounter discrepancies in the spelling of place names between those used in this book and those found on signposts, in the huts and on maps. This is an issue across German-speaking countries which use the *Eszett*, ß, and umlauts on the 'ä', the 'ö' and the 'ü'. In practice, this shouldn't cause confusion as long as travellers are aware of it. In this guidebook the *Eszett* is presented as a double 's', as in *weiss*.

GPX tracks

GPX tracks for the routes in this guidebook are available to download free at www.cicerone.co.uk/1065/GPX. If you have not bought the book through the Cicerone website, or have bought the book without opening an account, please register your purchase in your Cicerone library to access GPX and update information.

A GPS device is an excellent aid to navigation, but you should also carry a map and compass and know-how to use them. GPX files are provided in good faith, but in view of the profusion of formats and devices, neither the author nor the publisher accepts responsibility for their use. We provide files in a single standard GPX format that works on most devices and systems, but you may need to convert files to your preferred format using a GPX converter, such as gpsvisualizer.com or one of the many other apps and online converters available.

ESSENTIAL FOREIGN TERMS

Bergschrund gap between the mountain and the ice of the glacier
Gemütlichkeit homely/cosy
Gesprutt route is closed/barred
Hüttenwirt hut guardian
Klettersteig aided climbing trail
Matratzenlager dormitory-style accommodation
Seilbahn material goods hoist

At the Kreuzjoch, looking towards Schlicker Seespitze (Trek 1, Stage 9A)

STUBAI RUCKSACK ROUTE

At Grünausee, looking towards the Wilder Freiger (Trek 1, Stage 4A)

TREK 1
Stubai Rucksack Route

Start	Neder
Finish	Neustift or Fulpmes
Standard time	9 days (excluding excursions)
Distance	78.8km
Ascent	5790m
Descent	5785m

The central Stubai Alps are served by a total of 14 huts, providing an unlimited combination of hut-to-hut walks and tours. Specifically, it is possible to link eight huts together to form the Stubai Rucksack Route, known in German as the Stubaier Runde Tour and more recently as the Stubaier Höhenweg, the complete traverse of which is possible without having to cross glaciers or difficult passes. This makes the route ideal for mountain walkers, families and others with limited alpine experience. However, that's not to say you won't encounter snow, steep ground or the

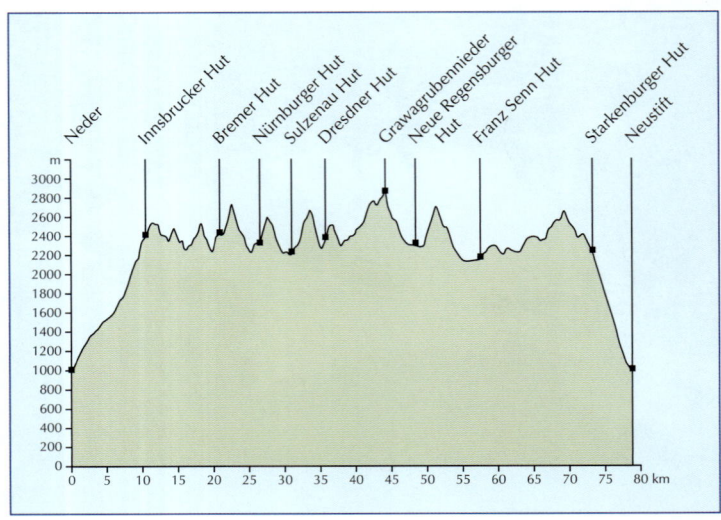

STUBAI RUCKSACK ROUTE

odd scramble here and there. Also recommended is the ascent of several mountains along the route, which are attainable for those with sufficient experience.

The route starts at Neder, a small village a few miles before Neustift and goes first to the Innsbrucker Hut then to each of the following huts in turn, Bremer, Nürnberger, Sulzenau, Dresdner, Neue Regensburger, Franz Senn, Starkenburger, ending back at Neustift or Fulpmes.

Apart from the Bremer Hut, each hut connects directly with the main Stubaital valley, making it possible to connect or finish the route according to your preference.

The length of the tour is about 80km and involves around 6000m of ascent and descent.

The route can be done in either direction, although the clockwise route, as described here, is seen as being marginally easier.

Additionally, since the second edition we have recommended that participants consider starting the tour by following either Stage 1 or 2 of the Gschnitztaler Rundtour, especially starting from the wonderful monastery inn of Hotel Klostergasthof Maria Waldrast, to include the peaks and passes of the Serleskamm ridge. This option provides participants with the opportunity to climb Serles (2718m), also known as King Serles, perhaps the most important mountain of the Serleskamm ridge, followed by the Kesselspitze (2728m) and the Kirchdachspitze (2840m), the mountain with the 'church roof' and 'spire'.

Extending the tour by a few days makes better use of your time for a two-week holiday, as well as giving you the opportunity to visit a little-known and much-neglected eastern part of the Stubai Alps.

Route summary
- Stage 1 Neder to Innsbrucker Hut
- Excursions from Innsbrucker Hut
  - Ascent of Habicht
  - Ascent of Kalkwand
- Stage 2 Innsbrucker Hut to Bremer Hut

Single file only (Trek 1, Stage 9A)

- Stage 3 Bremer Hut to Nürnberger Hut
- Excursions from Simmingjochl
  - Ascent of Östlicher Feuerstein
  - Ascent of Aperer Feuerstein
- Stage 4 Nürnberger Hut to Sulzenau Hut via Niederl
- Stage 4A Nürnberger Hut to Sulzenau Hut via Mairspitze
- Stage 4B Nürnberger Hut to Sulzenau Hut via Wilder Freiger
- Stage 5 Sulzenau Hut to Dresdner Hut via Peiljoch
- Stage 5A Sulzenau Hut to Dresdner Hut via Grosser Trögler
- Excursions from Dresdner Hut
  - Ascent of Schaufelspitze
- Stage 6 Dresdner Hut to Neue Regensburger Hut
- Stage 7 Neue Regensburger Hut to Franz Senn Hut
- Excursions from Franz Senn Hut
  - To visit Rinnensee
  - Ascent of Sommerwand
  - Ascent of Lisenser Fernerkogel
- Stage 8 Franz Senn Hut to Starkenburger Hut
- Excursions from Starkenburger Hut
  - Ascent of Hoher Burgstall
- Stage 9 Starkenburger Hut to Neustift
- Stage 9A Starkenburger Hut to Fulpmes

Getting to the start

From Innsbruck a regular bus service runs up the Stubaital valley from the bus station that adjoins the main railway station. At *Steig* (stage) B, signs clearly indicate 'Stubaital Mutterbergalm', at the bus stop and on the bus itself.

The journey to Neder, a pleasant ride of about 1hr, crosses the Europa Bridge en route to the Italian border on the Brenner Pass, where the whole of the Stubaital valley stretches out before you. As you approach Neder, familiarise yourself with the style of the village road signs; on the approach, the sign states the name of the village. As you leave the village, a similar sign is displayed with a red stripe across it, which tells you that you have now left the village.

INNSBRUCK TO NEUSTIFT

The following bus timetable has remained unchanged for the past ten years: 09:05 / 09:35 / 10:05 / 10:35 / 11:05 then every hour up to 17:00; see www.ivb.at.

STAGE 1
Neder to Innsbrucker Hut

Start	Neder (964m)
Standard time	5hr, although 6hr more likely
Distance	10.3km/8.3km via Elfer cable car
Ascent	1385m/810m via Elfer cable car
Descent	Negligible/255m via Elfer cable car

This is a fine walk and an appropriate introduction to the Stubai Rucksack Route. The scenery is particularly good, but perhaps more akin to the Dolomites than the snow-covered peaks of the Stubai Alps. The towering spires of the Serleskamm and Tribulaun cannot fail to impress.

CAUTIONARY NOTES

The route presents no difficulty, other than it is quite a long day with a lot of uphill for the first day. Walkers need to be mindful of this and be on their way early.

TO THE KARALM BY VEHICLE

If you are early, enjoy the walk and get into the feel of things. However, if you are late, a minibus-cum-taxi service runs up to the Pinnisalm and Karalm, the alm with boulders, which will halve the journey time. The minibus pick-up point in Neder (signposted) is in the car park, just behind the bus shelter, and there is another one at the Herzebenalm.

Alternatively, take the main Postbus service into the centre of Neustift, where you can hire a similar minibus service from outside the *Tourismusverband* (tourist information office). If you are travelling as a group, it is easier and more cost effective to arrange your own taxi service as follows:

Pinnis Shuttle Neustifter Funktaxi tel 0043 664 2877 000
Neustift tourist office 09:00
Neder 09:05
See 'Innsbrucker Hut' in 'Hut directory'.

STAGE 1 – NEDER TO INNSBRUCKER HUT

From the bus stop and bridge at Neder, a hut signpost is located just across the road, pointing the way up the Pinnistal valley. This single-track road goes as far as Karalm (7.5km).

For those intending to walk, after about 3km from Neder the Pinnistal valley opens up after passing through some narrows known as the **split stone**, a gigantic boulder that is almost, but not quite, split in half, to reveal the towering rock spires of the Serleskamm, which provides some interesting, dramatic scenery, particularly for aspiring rock climbers, with the impressive rock walls of the Kirchdachspitze ahead.

As you approach the **Pinnisalm**, the north-easterly slopes of the Habicht (3277m) dominate your view right up to the Pinnisjoch on which, just out of sight, sits the Innsbrucker Hut.

Whatever you do, don't stay too long at the popular tourist spot at the Pinnisalm. **2hr** It is better to take your refreshments at the Innsbrucker Hut, which has unrivalled views of the Tribulaun mountains. Beyond the Pinnisalm, the path quickly steepens, first gradually to the Karalm, then more abruptly, with 600m gained over 5km, the last 200m of which zigzags up to the Pinnisjoch and the **Innsbrucker Hut**. **3hr**

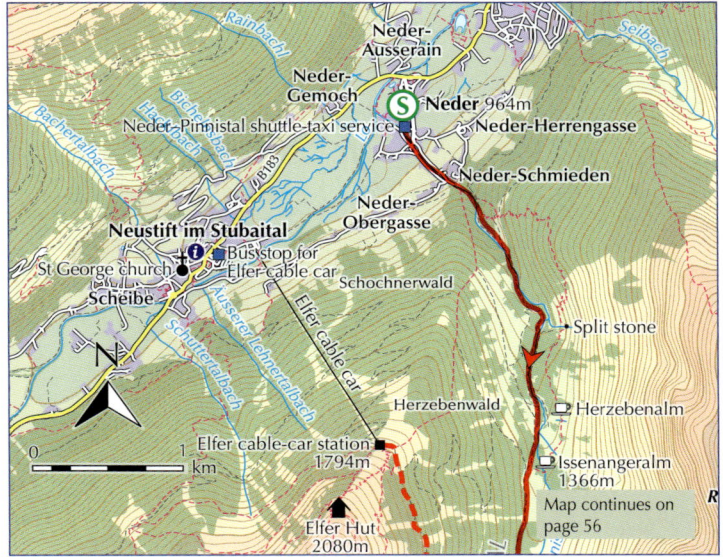

TREKKING IN AUSTRIA'S STUBAI ALPS

Via the Elfer cable car

As a further alternative, you can take the Elfer cable car to avoid the meander through the streets of Neder and the road traffic up to the split rock. You could then overnight at the Elfer Hut or simply pick up the broad trail just beyond the cable-car station for the 1hr pleasant walk past the tourist attraction and viewpoint of the Elfer Sundial before continuing through the forest to the Pinnisalm and eventually the Innsbrucker Hut.

At the Pinnisalm, the Innsbrucker Hut is located on col to the right

EXCURSION
Ascent of Habicht (3277m)

Start	Innsbrucker Hut (2369m)
Standard time	4hr (+2½hr for descent)
Distance	1.5km (+1.5km for descent)
Ascent	910m
Descent	910m
Grade	F
Note	For map, see Stage 1

Known as Hawk Mountain – *Habicht* meaning 'hawk' in German, probably so-called on account that it stands tall and surveys all around – Habicht, like its close neighbour Serles, is evident on the approach into Innsbruck railway station, standing proud and dominating the head of the Pinnistal valley.

First climbed in 1836, this superb mountain is the highest in the eastern Stubai Alps. The mountain is best viewed from the Bremer, Tribulaun and Starkenburger huts, the latter having a good view of the north face and what remains of the Mischbachferner glacier, which in its day was the hardest route on the mountain and once one of the premier ice climbs in the Tirol. Sadly, the route has ceased to exist, succumbing to the ever-growing list of glaciers lost to global warming.

The ordinary route via the eastern flank is a popular outing from the Innsbrucker Hut; therefore, not surprisingly, in summer the route up the mountain is a well-beaten trail.

Living up to its name as Hawk Mountain, Habicht offers excellent panoramic views in all directions from its summit, particularly of the main peaks of the central Stubai Alps, the Tribulaun and Serleskamm groups, plus the distant peaks of the Dolomites, Zillertal and Ötztal. Sharp eyes will be able to locate the Starkenburger Hut across the void to the north.

From the hut turn immediately left with the Habicht signposts indicating the start of the route. Head west at first, then south-west over rocky slopes of blocks on blocks to the foot of the south-east ridge, marked by several **memorial cairns. A short 1hr**

EXCURSION – ASCENT OF HABICHT (3277M)

CAUTIONARY NOTES

The time on the signpost just outside the hut states 3hr to the summit of Habicht. This is rarely achieved and 4hr is much more realistic.

While the route is not technically difficult, it does call for reasonable scrambling skills and a good head for heights while negotiating the steep rock sections and fixed cables.

Because the route is well frequented, some rocks are now quite polished, which can be problematic in descent when the rocks are wet as the rock strata leads and slopes in the wrong direction.

In good weather, route finding is not a problem, but in mist be careful, particularly in descent. Make sure to descend what remains of the Habicht glacier due east, retracing as far as is practicable one's own steps. Do not go north-east as the snow slope of the glacier ends in a sudden drop.

Cross over a short level section of boulders to where the ridge ramps up significantly. Climb this, following splashes of red paint that mark the way. This section involves good scrambling over broken slabs, aided by fixed cables on the steeper exposed sections – make use of your improvised harness. The ridge finally emerges on a broad col at the edge of what remains of the Habicht glacier. **2hr**

Cross the snow slope of the glacier west and scramble up shattered rocks, moving slightly south-west to gain the summit ridge, using more fixed cables. Continue over easier ground to the large ornate cross on the summit of **Habicht**. **1hr+**

In descent return by the same route, allowing around 2½hr.

At the memorial cairn; note the Kirchdachspitze in the distance (the mountain with the 'church roof' and 'spire')

EXCURSION
Ascent of Kalkwand (2564m)

Start	Innsbrucker Hut (2369m)
Standard time	1hr (+¾hr for descent)
Distance	1.0km (+1.0km for descent)
Ascent	200m
Descent	200m
Grade	F
Note	For map, see Stage 1

Note this is a walk not a climb; it's just something to do should you have a bit of free time.

This short excursion from the Innsbrucker Hut takes you to the highest peak at the southern end of the Serleskamm ridge. From the Pinnisjoch (signpost), a small track leads north-east to the summit. **About 1 hr**

At the Innsbrucker Hut looking towards the Kalkwand and Pinnisjoch

STAGE 2
Innsbrucker Hut to Bremer Hut

Start	Innsbrucker Hut (2369m)
Standard time	7–8hr
Distance	10.4km
Ascent	890m
Descent	850m

Characterised by lots of up and down, with plenty of challenge and some of the best scenery on the Stubai Rucksack Route, this wonderful walk has benefitted from the replacement of the majority of its fixed cables and staples, making the route much safer.

As you leave the hut, the unrivalled views of the Tribulaun peaks continue to dominate the horizon until you reach the first col on the Alfairkamm, from where there is a particularly fine retrospective view of the Innsbrucker Hut and the rock pinnacles of the Serleskamm group.

By the time the route reaches the Pramarnspitze, the magic of the Tribulaun peaks will have given way to the snow-capped peaks of the Feuerstein and Pflerscher Hochjoch and a fabulous view of the Gschnitztal valley. The day is superbly rounded off with a finish at the magnificently sited Bremer Hut.

CAUTIONARY NOTES

While the standard time for the route is given as 7hr, this is rarely achieved, and most parties will take around 8hr, particularly when carrying a touring rucksack. You are advised to be on your way by 07:00 and no later than 08:00.

Note that the path descending from the Pramarnspitze is on the scrappy side due to a combination of poor ground and lack of maintenance.

Because the route crosses a number of ridges and spurs, patches of old snow tend to linger on the north-facing slopes and in the gullies, in particular, north of the Alfairkamm, opposite the Innsbrucker Hut, and on the northern side of the col when crossing the Äussere Wetterspitze. Neither is insurmountable, but they can be problematic. While the route is adequately waymarked, it is best avoided in bad weather.

TREKKING IN AUSTRIA'S STUBAI ALPS

> ### ESCAPE ROUTES
>
> Should you be unfortunate to have bad weather while at the Innsbrucker Hut but still wish to make the journey to the Bremer Hut, the most straightforward way is to follow Route 60 down the steep track of the Alfairalm into the Gschnitztal valley to Feuerstein. **2hr** You can also arrange for rucksacks to be transported between the two huts, making use of the *Seilbahn* (materials goods hoist). From Gasthof Feuerstein, follow Route 102 on the Central Alpine Way to the hut. **3hr**
>
> Alternatively, abandon this stage and proceed to the Nürnberger Hut by returning down the Pinnistal valley, making use of the minibus-cum-taxi service then the Stubaital bus service from Neder to the bus stop for the Nürnberger Hut, and on to the hut.

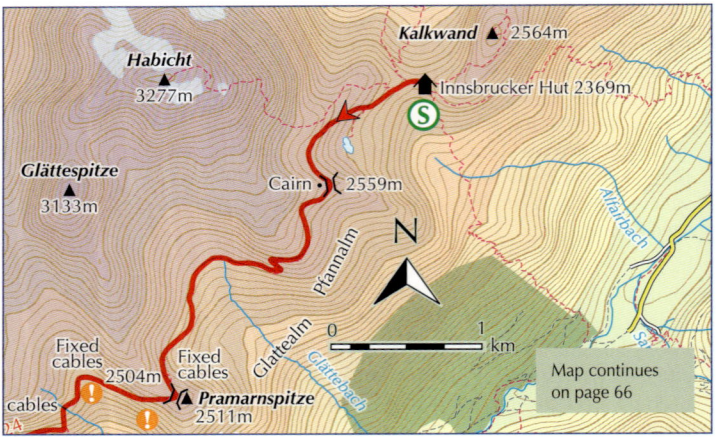

Pick up the trail from behind the hut (signpost) and follow Route 124 south-west, contouring across the hillside over rocky broken ground to an obvious col at 2559m with a **large stone cairn** on a spur off the Alfairkamm, above a tiny lake. **A short 1hr**

The col is clearly visible from the hut and the approach is frequently snow covered early in the season. There are excellent views hereabouts of the Serleskamm and Kirchdachspitze.

Crossing one of the many streams

From the col, the route continues to traverse the hillside south-west above Pfannalm and Glattealm, roughly on or around the 2500m contour, to a **saddle (2504m)** at the foot of the Glattespitze's south-east ridge, west of the rock outcrop of Pramarnspitze. **2½–3hr**

The path descends steeply west, with fixed cables in places to aid stability, into a broad couloir of Beilgrube above Traulalm. Continue around the open rocky combe and ascend the rocky slopes south to round the Ochsenkogl's east ridge, traversing west along the 2200m contour into the boulder-strewn slopes above Traulalm to a stream at Plattental, 2400m.

Here ascend south along broken, rocky ground, crossing a number of small spurs, to an obvious **col (2590m)** on the east ridge of the Äussere Wetterspitze. **1½hr** The slope just before the col is often snow covered late into the season and will require a little extra care to climb. From the top of the col, the Bremer Hut is clearly visible across the Simmingalm void, complete with its little sea!

From the col, descend steep rocks, protected by fixed cables, zigzagging south-east to round the foot of the ridge, then traverse south on the northern slopes of the Simmingalm. Cross the Simmingalm basin south-west, where after

Peaks of the Tribulaun

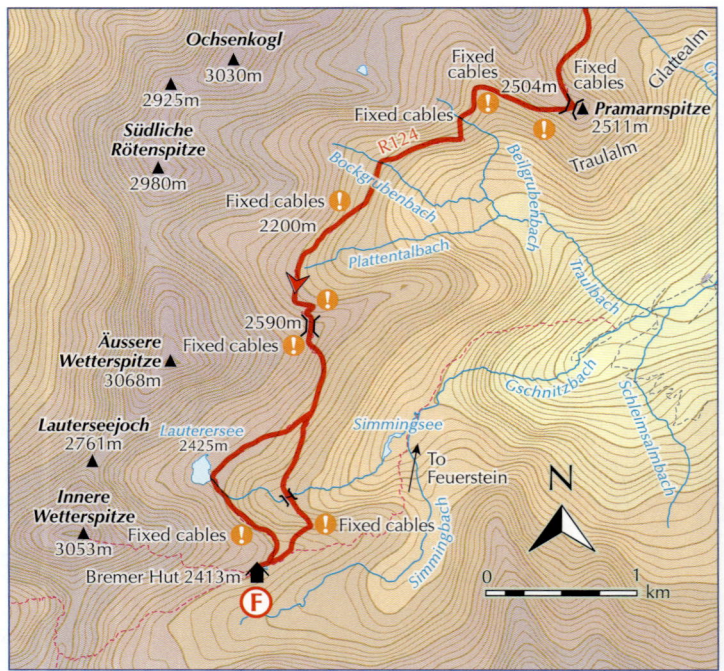

a short distance you will reach a junction of paths that lead to the hut (signpost). **1hr** If the weather is good, continue to the **Lauterersee (2425m)**, thereafter following the track to the foot of the Innere Wetterspitze east ridge. Ascend steep, broken rocks, with good scrambling aided by fixed cables, to emerge on the broad plateau just below the **Bremer Hut**. **1½hr**

Alternatively, if the weather is poor, or if you're feeling all but done in, continue to follow the slightly longer but easier regular way on Route 124, over rock-strewn boulder slopes around the head of the Simmingalm couloir. Climb through the steep rock face, making use of the fixed cables, metal staples and a ladder, eventually emerging some distance below the hut. Join up with the main track coming up from the Gschnitztal valley head at Feuerstein and continue on to the **Bremer Hut**. **1½hr**

This track variation came into being several years ago when the Jubiläumssteig was established, along with the Gschnitztaler Rundtour.

STAGE 3
Bremer Hut to Nürnberger Hut via Simmingjochl

Start	Bremer Hut (2413m)
Standard time	3–4hr
Distance	5.7km
Ascent	465m
Descent	610m

This splendid day out is full of scenic interest, in particular, the north faces of the Pflerscher Hochjoch and Feuerstein. The view of the Wilder Freiger from the Simmingjochl is particularly good, where it is not unusual for those with sharp eyes to see the dawn patrol of climbers crossing the upper snow slopes of the Wilder Freiger Ferner glacier on their way up the mountain.

CAUTIONARY NOTES

The fixed-cable sections and the couloir on the north side of the Simmingjochl can prove difficult to negotiate when snow covered, as is frequently the case early in the season.

Participants should also note that in recent years the rocks on both sides of the Simmingjochl, more so on the western side, appear to be prone to landslips. This may cause the route to change, particularly those areas around the fixed-cable sections. In such circumstances, members of the party are advised to stay close to each other for support and to avoid knocking rocks down on each other.

From the hut, proceed west along the obvious path on **Route 102**. The path rises steadily across grass and rocky slopes amid fine scenery until just below the Simmingjochl (2764m), when it rises steeply, aided by fixed cables, to the col and the tiny **police hut** still used by the border police. **1hr+** From here there are excellent views of the Feuerstein and across the void to the Wilder Freiger.

From the col, descend north across steep, rocky slopes, aided by fixed cables, to the head of a couloir, which is frequently snow covered, then continue to a point below the Innere Wetterspitze.

Proceed west down scree slopes, along a reasonably marked path into the upper basin of the Grübl cirque at 2420m. The area is characterised by its glacial debris, with large boulders strewn all over the place, and the many streams and **ponds** that congregate there. **1hr** From here, take time to recce the route to the Sulzenau Hut, since the Nürnberger Hut, Niederl, Mairspitze and Wilder Freiger are all clearly visible to the west.

Continue to follow the obvious path descending first south-west, then north-west, then south-west again over broken ground and some very steep rock sections with fixed cables that lead to the raging torrents of the Langentalbach coming off the Grüblferner glacier. Cross the wooden planks that form the rickety **bridge** and proceed in a north-westerly direction, scrambling up and over slabs, following a line of fixed cables, to the substantial four-storey **Nürnberger Hut**. **1hr**

Crossing the Langentalbach river

EXCURSION
Ascent of Östlicher Feuerstein (3267m) from Simmingjochl

Start	Police hut
Standard time	About 2–2½hr, depending on conditions (+2hr for descent)
Distance	2.5km (+2.5km for descent)
Ascent	505m
Descent	505m
Grade	F
Note	For map, see Stage 3

On this fine route up a particularly neglected mountain, you are most likely to discover that you have the mountain to yourself.

From the summit, the mountain affords some fine panoramic views, particularly towards the Habicht and then along the Frontier Ridge into South Tirol. From the summit, those with sharp eyes will be able to locate the Becherhaus on its rocky knoll to the left of the Wilder Freiger. It is stunning indeed!

CAUTIONARY NOTES

While crevasses are not normally a problem, the mountain is in a state of flux, particularly the Bergschrund running parallel with the north-west ridge. This is likely to disappear in the not-too-distant future, leaving the underlying rocks unstable. In such circumstances, you may wish to try gaining access by point 3166m on the south-west ridge from the Pflerscher Hochjoch then traversing the exposed rocky ridge to the summit.

From the summit, the route across to the west summit and beyond may look tempting to aspiring alpinists; however, the route is not recommended due to the increased difficulty and corresponding increase in exposure. The descent route beyond the Westlicher Feuerstein via the Weites Tuerl, Hohe Wand and Grüblferner glacier has long been abandoned due to the unstable nature of the rock.

Trekking in Austria's Stubai Alps

From the police hut, where parties may leave their rucksacks, head south along the ridge to gain the Aperer Feuerstein glacier a little above point 2749m. Continue heading in a southerly direction towards the **Nürnberger Scharte** (2914m). At an appropriate point, move off left, heading towards point 2958m on the west side of the ridge and continue south-east up the glacier to below **point 3026m**. Tackle up and contour across the glacier in a south-easterly arc, to below the Feuerstein's north-west ridge, which has some crevasse danger at the edges, then climb steepening snow slopes to gain the north-west ridge. Continue up the rocky ridge, scrambling over loose rocks and scree, to the large metal cross on the summit of **Östlicher Feuerstein**. **2–2½hr**

In descent, return by the same route or alternatively proceed north-east towards the Pflerscher Hochjoch, descending steep, rocky slopes to gain the glacier's upper apron, then cross through the heart of the glacier, back towards the **Nürnberger Scharte** and eventually the police hut. **Allow 2hr**

Bremer Hut to the Nurnberger Hut. Ascent of Ost Feuerstein

EXCURSION
Ascent of Aperer Feuerstein (2968m)

Start	Police hut
Standard time	About 1hr (+ 1hr for descent)
Distance	1.25km (+1.25km for descent)
Ascent	280m
Descent	280m
Grade	F, easy walk with some scrambling
Note	For map, see Stage 3

For those who feel the Östlicher Feuerstein is too difficult an undertaking, particularly if you don't have the necessary equipment, the Aperer Feuerstein is a worthwhile alternative excursion, providing first-class views of the Feuerstein and Wilder Freiger mountains.

From the police hut, head south along the ridge to gain the Aperer Feuerstein glacier at 2749m. Proceed south up the snow slope to the **Nürnberger Scharte (2914m)**. Scramble north-west up the obvious rock ridge to the summit of **Alperer Feuerstein**. **About 1hr**

From the summit, retrace your tracks in descent to the Nürnberger Scharte and back to the police hut. **About 1hr**

Alternatively, continue south to point 2852m, then descend steeply west, down rocks of dubious quality, to gain the remnants of the Grüblferner glacier. Continue along the rocky boulder trail over difficult ground until the path joins the normal route to cross the Langentalbach river at the rickety footbridge. **1½hr to footbridge plus ½hr to hut**

STAGE 4
Nürnberger Hut to Sulzenau Hut via Niederl

Start	Nürnberger Hut (2278m)
Standard time	3–4hr
Distance	4.5km
Ascent	395m
Descent	485m

There is a choice of three routes to the Sulzenau Hut and these are described in order of difficulty.

CAUTIONARY NOTES

The only caution needed is in descending the very steep rock faces, more so on the west side of the Niederl. Anyone who is not entirely vertigo-free should descend the rocks with a partner for a little moral support, making good use of their improvised harness for added security.

From the hut, proceed west for a few minutes, following Route 102, along the Central Alpine Way, to a signpost pointing the way to the Niederl Mairspitze.

Continue west, up and over rocky slabs in a series of zigzag-type staircases, gradual at first then steeper at the top and aided by fixed cables, to the **Niederl (2627m)**, an obvious col with a large wooden cross on the ridge connecting the Urfallspitze with the Mairspitze. **1hr** Stunning views stretch in all directions, particularly of the Wilder Freiger and Feuerstein mountains.

From the Niederl, descend a very steep rock face, traversing to and fro along a series of ledges protected by fixed cables, to a **tiny lake** that makes a good picnic stop. Continue west along a good path to its junction with the path coming from the Mairspitze. **1hr**

Thereafter, proceed south-west to the **Grünausee lake**, which provides a spectacular view of the Wilder Freiger and its glacier system. Follow the track north-west on the right bank of the Grünaubach stream to a couple of **footbridges**. Cross these and head west-north-west over easy ground to the very modern **Sulzenau Hut**. **1hr**

STAGE 4 – NÜRNBERGER HUT TO SULZENAU HUT VIA NIEDERL

STAGE 4A
Nürnberger Hut to Sulzenau Hut via Mairspitze

Start	Nürnberger Hut (2278m)
Standard time	4hr+
Distance	5.9km
Ascent	560m
Descent	645m
Grade	F-
Note	For map, see Stage 4

Stages 4 and 4A are famed for their panoramic views of the Wilder Freiger. Likewise, each location provides a good vantage point for reviewing the previous day's activity or for reccying the forthcoming route across the Peiljoch or Grosser Trögler to the Dresdner Hut.

Throughout the initial part of the day, the scenery is dominated by good views of the Wilder Freiger and the peaks of the Feuerstein, as well as the backdrop across the void of the Simmingjochl with its tiny police hut.

Thereafter, the tiny lakes above Grünausee provide ideal sites for picnics, particularly if you remembered to purchase extra tasty provisions such as Apfelstrudl and filled your water bottle with beer or wine. Here you can sit back and enjoy the view of the Wilder Freiger mirrored on the surface of the lakes – just super!

Overall, it's an excellent day with some truly memorable scenery, although a little short on duration. Enjoy!

CAUTIONARY NOTES

The only caution needed is in descending the very steep rock faces, more so on the west side of the Niederl. Anyone who is not entirely vertigo-free should descend the rocks with a partner for a little moral support, making good use of their improvised harness for added security.

From the hut, proceed west on **Route 102** for a short distance to a signpost where the routes to the Niederl and Mairspitze split.

Now ascend the gradually steepening rocky path, first traversing north-west then north in the direction of an obvious ridge. Scramble over rocks with fixed cables to gain the ridge at point 2553m. Enjoy good retrospective views back to the Nürnberger Hut and across the void to the peaks of the Feuerstein and the police hut on the Simmingjochl. Continue west, scrambling along the ridge, aided by fixed cables on the steeper sections, to a double col on the Mairspitze south ridge. **1½hr** The views are superb hereabouts.

Looking towards the Wilder Freiger and Grünausee

Cross the col into a dip to the main col at **2742m**, then proceed north along the obvious ridge via point 2775m, rising steeply for a short distance before continuing more gradually to the craggy top with its park bench seat and large **summit cross**. ¾hr

Trekking in Austria's Stubai Alps

From the summit, return to the col by the same route (signpost), and with the Sulzenau Hut in clear view, descend the steep rocks, heading south-west and making use of fixed cables, to a **small lake** at 2552m on the old glacier basin of the Schafgrübl – another good picnic stop. Continue on the obvious path to rejoin the path from the Niederl, Route 102, a little further on (signpost). **1hr** The views of the Wilder Freiger are stunning.

The route from here on is as described in Stage 4, via the Niederl. **1hr**

On the Mairspitze

STAGE 4B
Nürnberger Hut to Sulzenau Hut via Wilder Freiger

Start	Nürnberger Hut (2278m)
Standard time	8–9hr (about 4–5hr to summit of Wilder Freiger)
Distance	11.4km
Ascent	1180m
Descent	1265m
Grade	F+
Note	For map, see Stage 4

This is an extremely popular route up a beautiful, snow-capped mountain, perhaps the most scenic of all the mountains in the Stubai Alps, so early birds should be on their way by 06:00 to avoid the rush. An early start will allow you to enjoy the cool pre-dawn air for most of the way to the Seescharte, by which time the sun will have illuminated the snow slopes of the twin peaks of the Feuerstein to spectacular effect.

The Seescharte, an ideal place for a second breakfast stop, enjoys a fair amount of sunshine, with many flowers growing in its vicinity, including the vivid blue spring gentian and pink moss campion. From here the route opens up to provide some spectacular glacier scenery, particularly along the rocky ridge south of the Gamsspitzl.

However, it's the panorama from the summit of Wilder Freiger that is perhaps the most extensive in the region, for the summit is placed among the Stubai's biggest mountains and its largest glaciers. The view into Italy, across the snowy peaks of South Tirol and beyond to the Dolomites, is immense, with the lonely Becherhaus and Müller Hut standing isolated in the near distance.

From the hut (signpost) head south, over rocks, on a well-defined track for 15min to a signpost, where the track splits.

The track heading off south-east will be familiar as it is Route 102, which leads to the Simmingjochl and the Bremer Hut.

Our route continues south along the well-defined rocky path, then turns southwest, following a series of zigzags below the Urfallspitze. The route continues south-west along the Urfallspitze's east flank and rises steadily up and over boulders before finally giving way to a gap in the ridge at the **Seescharte** (2762m). **2hr**

> **CAUTIONARY NOTES**
>
> While not a serious undertaking, the Wilder Freiger is a big mountain set among the Stubai's largest glaciers, and warm air from the Italian south quickly condenses to form thick cloud, making route finding across the summit snows very hazardous. By mid-morning, the mountain frequently starts to cloud up.
>
> In cloudy conditions it is essential to retrace your steps to the Signalgipfel and the large stone cairn before the Gamsspitzl. Do not descend directly from the summit across the Grüblferner glacier to point 3324m, as climbers are frequently led over easy ground into a series of big crevasses on the 3300m contour. While crevasses are not normally a problem on the upper slopes, they do exist and have become more prevalent in recent years due to minimal winters and warmer summers.

Apart from the excellent view, the Seescharte provides an opportunity for you to deposit and stash some of the contents of your rucksack, allowing you to make a lighter ascent of the mountain.

From the Seescharte, continue south-west over rocks and boulders, passing below points 2954m and 2934m, to a permanent large patch of snow south of the **Gamsspitzl** (3051m). Get onto the snow by descending west for a few metres. Cross the snow in a southerly direction to the foot of an obvious rocky ridge around point 3065m. Scramble along the rocky ridge, over boulders and blocks, in a south-westerly direction and amid spectacular glacial scenery, until its end at the junction of the old track coming from the col below the Gamsspitzl (3065m), marked by a large stone cairn at 3127m. Proceed south along the rocky ridge, very exposed in places, until it joins the Wilder Freiger Ferner and Grüblferner glacier systems proper at around 3220m.

Tackle up and proceed south up the broad snow ridge, avoiding obvious crevasses, to point 3324m. Now head south-west over the snowfield to the **Signalgipfel** (3392m), where the ruins of the abandoned border police hut remind us of a bygone era, when the border was patrolled by police and alpine troops.

From this overlook of the Übeltalferner glacier and peaks of South Tirol, continue north-west up the snowfield, handrailing the edge of a rocky ridge, making good use of the fixed cables, to the summit of **Wilder Freiger** with its large wooden cross. **2–3hr**

STAGE 4B – NÜRNBERGER HUT TO SULZENAU HUT VIA WILDER FREIGER

Excellent **views** abound in all directions, particularly of the Übeltalferner glacier and the remarkable Becherhaus and Müller Hut, both standing in splendid isolation. Those with knowledge of the Dolomites will be able to locate the three towering spires of Drei Zinnen (or Tre Cime di Lavaredo, if you prefer the more poetic Italian name) and the snowy white mantel of the Marmolada, the Queen of the Dolomites. Closer at hand across the glacial void stand Botzer and the Sonklarspitze.

The Müller Hut can just be seen from the Signalgipfel, while to the west and on the northern horizon lie all of the Stubai's main peaks, from the Zuckerhütl around to the Schrankogel and Ruderhofspitze and across the Stubaital valley, in a wide panoramic arc, to the Habicht. On the far horizon stand the peaks of the Ötztal in the west, with the Zillertal and Venediger to the east. The Dolomites lie to the south, the Karwendel Mountains and the German Alps to the north.

To descend retrace your steps back to the **Seescharte**. About 2hr

Cross the Seescharte onto the west flank of the Urfallspitze and descend the steep snow slope that forms the remnants of the Kleiner Grünauferner glacier. Descend the snow slope, what was the glacier's right bank, keeping close to the rocks, heading north-west, until it gives way to glacial debris and easier ground at its foot. Here the route is waymarked by the usual daubs of red paint. The Sulzenau Hut and the small alpine tarn of Grünausee are clearly visible from here on.

Approaching the summit

The path continues north-west and descends rapidly towards the **Grünausee**, where it joins routes coming from the Nürnberger Hut via the Niederl and Mairspitze. **1hr**

There are good views from here of the ice fall off the Wilder Freiger Ferner glacier. Also, keep an eye open for the Grawagrubennieder, the highest pass on the Stubai Rucksack Route, which is clearly visible across the void below the Seespitze to the north-west. From Grünausee, continue north-west on the obvious path of Route 102 to the modern **Sulzenau Hut**. **1hr**

Ascent of Wilder Freiger

STAGE 5
Sulzenau Hut to Dresdner Hut via Peiljoch

Start	Sulzenau Hut (2191m)
Standard time	4–5hr
Distance	4.7km
Ascent	505m
Descent	370m

Leaving the conviviality of the Sulzenau Hut behind, you have a choice of two routes to the Dresdner Hut. This pleasant trek is a little short on duration, although it is ideal as a semi-rest day, to keep the party moving.

While this route may not have the scenic interest of the Grosser Trögler, it provides a suitable poor-weather alternative, plus an opportunity to have a closer inspection of the Sulzenauferner glacier system and what remains of the ice fall.

The Peiljoch is characterised by so many stone cairns – built by enthusiastic, if somewhat amateur, stonemasons – that it is more reminiscent of sacred ground in the mighty Himalayas than the Austrian Tirol.

Once across the Peiljoch, there are some excellent views of the neighbouring peaks, particularly the Schaufelspitze, Stubaier Wildspitze and across to the Daunkogel and Ruderhofspitze.

CAUTIONARY NOTES

In poor weather, particularly cloud, some additional care needs to be exercised on the fixed cables and on making sure you keep to the correct track immediately below the Peiljoch, at point 2580m. Here a path of sorts continues south-west onto the Sulzenauferner glacier, and it is not uncommon for the right-hand turn up to the Peiljoch to be missed. Remember to bear right at the signpost for the Zuckerhütl-Peiljoch.

From the hut, follow **Route 102** on the Central Alpine Way, heading south-west for a short distance, until you reach the branch track to the Grosser Trögler (signpost). The Peiljoch is also known as the Beiljoch, so don't be confused as one and both are the same. Proceed west, passing the branch track for the Lübecker Weg and Route 136 on the left and the crags used by the ÖAV Alpenverein-Akademie on the right.

Carry on for another short distance to a second signpost for the Peiljoch that indicates a scenic route following the river to the left and the regular route to the right. Continue right, following the regular route west over rocky ground, then south-west along the left-hand moraine of the Sulzenauferner glacier. There are fixed cables in places and a metal plank gangway leading across the edge of an exposed rock buttress.

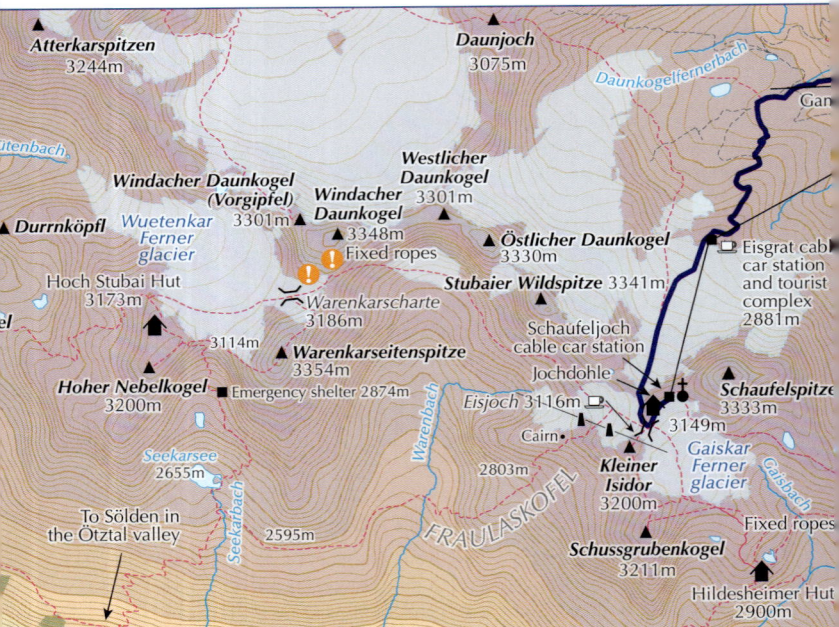

Continue south-east across the flank of the Grosser Trögler until immediately below the Peiljoch and what remains of the snout of the Sulzenauferner glacier at **point 2580m**. At the signpost for the Zuckerhütl, now redundant, bear right and proceed north-west up a steep path to the **Peiljoch** (2676m), characterised by its many stone cairns. About **1½ –2hr** The views are stunning towards the Sulzenauferner glacier and the Wilder Pfaff.

From the col, descend rocks north-west across a broad couloir, then continue more steeply down a ridge along a staircase of rocks and boulders, exposed

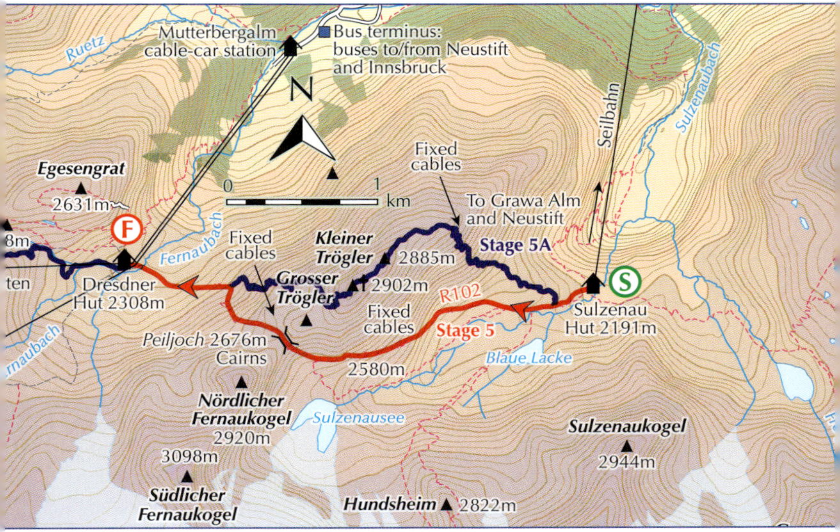

STAGE 5 – SULZENAU HUT TO DRESDNER HUT VIA PEILJOCH

in places but aided by fixed cables on the difficult bits, until the path joins with the route coming from the Grosser Trögler from the east (signpost). **About 1hr**

The Dresdner Hut is now clearly visible a little above the Stubaitalbahn cable-car station. There are also good views towards the Schaufelspitze and the peaks of the Daunkogel, but sadly the view is cluttered with all the ski-tow pylons and other modern-day mechanisations.

Continue as before, descending the obvious path west, then northwest, over rocks and grassy slopes, on past the cable-car station to the very commercial **Dresdner Hut**. **1½hr**

At the Peiljoch, looking towards the Zuckerhütl

STAGE 5A
Sulzenau Hut to Dresdner Hut via Grosser Trögler

Start	Sulzenau Hut (2191m)
Standard time	4–5hr
Distance	5.6km
Ascent	730m
Descent	595m
Note	For map, see Stage 5

This is a justifiably popular route with a truly magnificent view of the Zuckerhütl (3505m), the Stubai's highest mountain, and its attendant Sulzenauferner glacier. It is from the summit of the Grosser Trögler that the meaning of the name of the Zuckerhütl, German for sugarloaf, becomes apparent. Equally, the summit is a good place to recce the route across the void to the north, to the Neue Regensburger Hut, which can be seen from as far as the high pass of the Grawagrubennieder.

CAUTIONARY NOTES

On a few short sections new fixed cables have been fitted on both sides of the mountain, making it easier, but a little brute force will be required to climb a number of rock steps.

From the hut follow **Route 102** south for a short distance until you reach the branch track and signpost. Route 102 continues to the Dresdner Hut via the Peiljoch. From the signpost the route to the Grosser Trögler turns north-west, heading over grassy slopes and the broken, rocky ground of the Hohe Salze. At point 2500m, the path steepens and climbs in a series of zigzags through a rock barrier, with fixed cables on the steeper sections, to a broad ridge north of the Kleiner Trögler.

> The scenery is excellent in all directions from here on, plus this small plateau is famed for its profusion of **alpine flowers**, particularly the vivid blue spring gentian and the ever-elusive edelweiss.

STAGE 5A – SULZENAU HUT TO DRESDNER HUT VIA GROSSER TRÖGLER

Proceed south-west along the ridge on a good track, encountering rock scrambles here and there, to the summit of **Grosser Trögler**. **2½hr** Here you will find a large wooden cross inscribed in the memory of Peter Hofer, a professional guide who was hut warden at the Dresdner Hut from 1936 to 1966. Peter Hofer's family continues the tradition of managing the hut, where they have now been custodians for over 100 years.

From the summit, descend steeply over rocky slabs, first south-west then turning west-north-west, through a narrow couloir in a series of steep zigzags to the junction of the track from the Peiljoch. Pick up the track for **Route 102** and head west, then north-west, over grass and rocks to the **Dresdner Hut**. **1½hr**

Summit view of the Wilder Pfaff and Zuckerhütl

EXCURSION
Ascent of Schaufelspitze (3333m)

Start	Dresdner Hut (2308m)
Standard time	4hr (+3hr for descent)
Distance	3.0km
Ascent	1030m
Descent	1030m
Grade	F
Note	For map, see Stage 5

Dominating the head of the valley above the Dresdner Hut, this pleasant, popular mountain is nicknamed the 'shovel peak' because of its broad summit.

Sadly, the main viewpoints are overshadowed by the ski-tow pylons and other man-made structures that now boast of having the highest restaurant facility in the Tirol, all constructed to satisfy the appetites of skiers and day trippers from Innsbruck. Despite my quip of disdain, if you have children with you, the Eisgrat recreation area is a good place to take them for a little respite from the rigours of hut-to-hut touring.

There are, however, a number of places that remain relatively untouched, providing uncluttered vistas. The first of these is found when crossing the Daunkogel glacier, around the 3000m contour, looking west along the glacier to the Stubaier Wildspitze. Another is from the glacier plateau of the Eisjoch, looking towards the Ötztal and, finally, from the summit, looking west to the Zuckerhütl.

CAUTIONARY NOTES

There are crevasses along the upper section of the route, but these are easily bypassed. The only other risk comes from any mechanisations or activities taking place on the glacier. The best advice is to keep well out of the way.

From the hut, head west, following Route 135 for a short distance until you reach a stream complete with footbridge and signpost for Eisee. From here, Route 135 continues to the Neue Regensburger Hut. Cross the stream and continue west through the rocky area of the **Gamsgarten**, ascending steadily to a large open area

Excursion – Ascent of Schaufelspitze (3333m)

at the foot of the Daunkogel glacier, complete with cable-car station and small lake for generating snow.

Here the track forks (signpost). The right-hand track goes to the Daunjoch and across to the Hoch Stubai or Amberger huts. Follow the left-hand path south-west on Route 102, over glacial debris, heading for the obvious **Eisgrat cable-car station** at the foot of the Schaufelferner glacier.

Continue south up the rocks above the Schaufelferner glacier's right bank to the Eisgrat cable-car station at 2881m. You now have two options, if you count taking the cable car to the Schaufeljoch on the Isidornieder.

The first option is to get onto the glacier and cross it south, following the line of the ski-tow pylons to the obvious col, the Eisjoch (3116m). **3hr** There are some crevasses on the 3000m contour, but these are not normally a problem, as they are continually filled in by the snow plough for the benefit of skiers.

Head south across the Bildstöckljoch and onto the upper snows of the Windacher Ferner glacier to the **Eisjoch** (3116m), which offers a full-blown restaurant and Imbiss refreshments kiosk. The summit is clearly visible from here, and there are excellent views towards the Ötztal and an unusual view of the Zuckerhütl.

From the Eisjoch, turn north-east and cross the upper snow slopes of the Gaisskarferner glacier to another small col, the Isidornieder (3158m), named after the patron Saint Isidor, which shares the space with the Schaufeljoch cable-car station, famed for its aerial walkway that boasts of being the Top of Tirol. Continue east and proceed over rocks and boulders, following a path of sorts, on past a little chapel and eventually arriving at the summit of **Schaufelspitze** with its large wooden cross. **1hr**

Via the cable car

Your second option is to make use of the cable car to or from the Dresdner Hut to the Eisgrat recreation area, then take the cable car to the top station at Isidornieder-Schaufeljoch and walk onto the summit of Schaufelspitze. About a 3hr walk from the hut or a ½hr walk from the Schaufeljoch cable-car station.

Participants may wish to consider this mode of ascent as an afternoon excursion after crossing the Peiljoch or Grosser Trögler in the morning.

At Schaufeljoch Chapel

STAGE 6
Dresdner Hut to Neue Regensburger Hut via Grawagrubennieder

Start	Dresdner Hut (2308m)
Standard time	6hr; this is rarely achieved and 8hr should be allowed
Distance	12.7km
Ascent	880m
Descent	900m

The second longest trek of the Stubai Rucksack Route, this fine outing is quite demanding and involves a lot of up and down, including a crossing of the Grawagrubennieder (2881m), the highest pass on the route.

The first highlight of the day is the tiny lake of Mutterbergersee, where a fine view of the Schaufelspitze is mirrored on its surface. Thereafter, negotiating the high-level path midway between the rocky spurs below the Schafspitze and Gamsspitze provides some great scenery across the Stubaital valley to the main snow-capped peaks along the Austrian–Italian border.

Once across the Grawagrubennieder, with all the difficult ground over, the walk along the cotton-grass-fringed Falbesonertal valley to the very popular Neue Regensburger Hut is one of the most scenically pleasant of the Stubai Rucksack Route, with an excellent view of the Ruderhofspitze before the Habicht returns into view.

CAUTIONARY NOTES

While the route has a liberal number of sections with fixed cables, the only real danger is in crossing the Grawagrubennieder. In descent, the route is a grotty affair, being a mix of snow, ice, rocks, scree and other loose rubble – and this is no place to be caught in bad weather!

At its lower edge, where the rocks reach the debris left behind from the retreating Hochmoosferner glacier, route finding is not always obvious. Care also needs to be exercised in getting onto the remains of the glacier, which these days is likely to be a mix of old snow and ice. Look for marker poles and the usual daubs of red paint.

Stage 6 – Dresdner Hut to Neue Regensburger Hut via Grawagrubennieder

From the hut, follow Route 135 west on a broad ski piste to a signposted junction with the path leading to the Schaufelspitze. Take the right-hand fork and head north-west over rocks to a **col (2506m)** and signpost on the west ridge of the Egesengrat, overlooking the Wilde Grube. **About 1hr**

The col is home to a family of **Murmeltiere (marmots)**. If you proceed quietly, you may be lucky enough to catch sight of this somewhat illusive furry mountain dweller.

The area overlooking the Wilde Grube was at one time a very wild place indeed, where many streams congregated. The dramatic German name of the 'wild ditch' was as direct and to the point as the place itself.

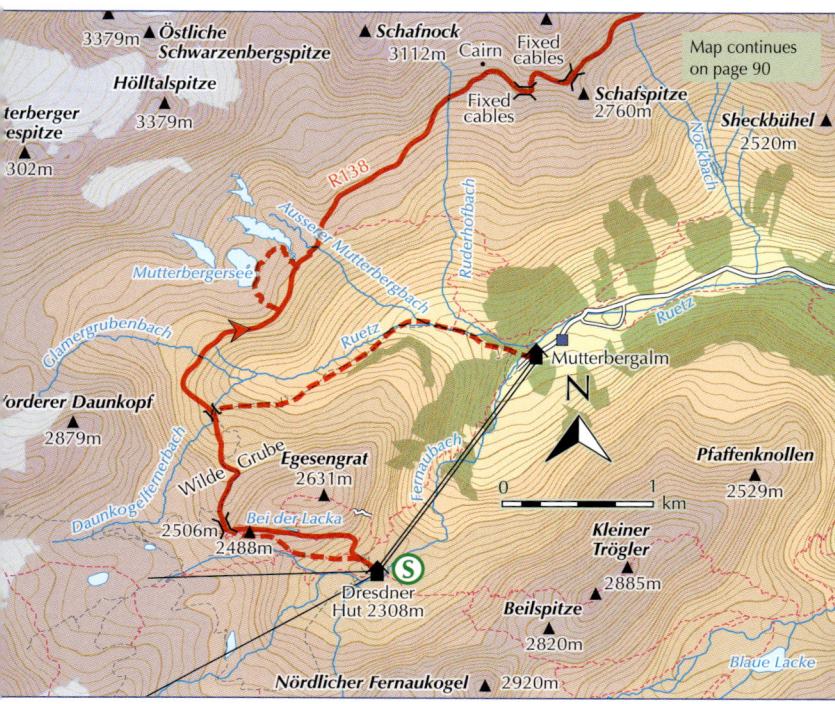

TREKKING IN AUSTRIA'S STUBAI ALPS

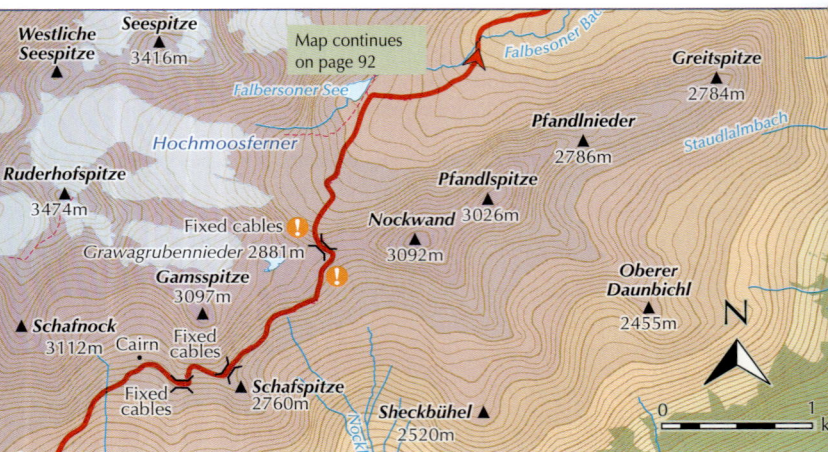

Via the high-level path

Alternatively, just outside the hut pick up the various signposts for the *Klettersteig* (protected climbing route) and the Rundwanderweg circular tour. Here take the more scenic high-level path to Bei der Lacka, initially climbing steadily on past the rock buttress with the Klettersteig climbing routes, then levelling out to pass the small alpine tarn before dropping down and following a rocky path to the **col (2506m)** and signpost. **A short 1hr** Views from the col are excellent.

Main route

From the col, either descend north on the original route, negotiating a steep path of boulders to join the obvious haulage road constructed by the Stubai Glacier Company, or proceed along the newly constructed track around the head of the couloir to pick up the graded road, then follow it down into the Wilde Grube, trudging around various tight bends until you reach a **footbridge** (a signpost boldly declares 'NRH 5hr'). **1hr**

> ### EXIT ROUTE
>
> If the weather is deteriorating at this stage, you are advised to duck out and follow the service road to Mutterbergalm, then take the bus to Falbeson, followed by the 3hr walk to the hut.

STAGE 6 – DRESDNER HUT TO NEUE REGENSBURGER HUT VIA GRAWAGRUBENNIEDER

At the Dresdner Hut, looking towards the Grosser Trögler (left) and the V-shaped gap of the Peiljoch pass

To continue, cross the streams. The track then contours around the open couloir of the Glamergrube, climbing steadily on a good path across the steep hillside of alpine pasture to reach the southern end of the **Mutterbergersee** (2485m) (signpost). **About 1hr**

If the weather is good, you are advised to make the 1hr detour to the small **Mutterbergersee** alpine lake to enjoy the best panoramic view there is of the Schaufelspitze, mirrored on its surface. Enjoy a short break, and a second breakfast, before descending to rejoin the route proper once more (signpost).

Continue on the good path for a short distance to another signpost that declares the hut is a mere 3hr away. In reality, it will take you about 2½hr to reach this point without the detour to the lake, and getting to the Grawagrubennieder will take a further 2hr before descending to the hut.

Continue north-east on the path, now on **Route 138**, ascending steadily across the southern flank of the Ruderhofspitze, in the direction of a col with a very large stone cairn. Climb the rocks, making use of the fixed cables to reach the col and signpost. This **cairn** marks the approximate halfway point in the day's promenade and provides an excellent panoramic view across the main Stubaital valley to the snow-covered peaks of the Wilder Freiger, Wilder Pfaff and Zuckerhütl. The Dresdner Hut is just about visible from here.

From the col, descend the very steep rock flank, fixed cables in place, and continue east, contouring across a rocky couloir to another col on the **Schafspitze** (2760m). Scramble down steep rocks, making use of the fixed cables. Continue north-east across the rocky southern flank of the Gamsspitze in a series of rock steps and zigzags to the **Grawagrubennieder** (2881m), a col on the east ridge of the Ruderhofspitze (signpost). **2–3hr** The route is partly waymarked with marker poles for a short distance before the col.

From the col, with its fine views of the Ruderhofspitze and Hochmoosferner (the 'high moss glacier') ahead, descend north on steep ground of loose rocks and other dubious terrain in a series of zigzags, fixed cables in place, to reach the foot of what remains of the once-mighty Hochmoosferner glacier. This is marked by a permanently fixed aluminium ladder; it's not for our use but more so for summer skiers going in the other direction. It is, however, a very good indicator that you are on the correct route.

Get onto the glacier, likely just a patch of old snow these days, and look for route markers and cairns. Cross the glacier snow, heading north over difficult, broken ground strewn with large boulders. Be careful at the lower edges, as the rocks and rubble overlie bare ice, concealing a number of hidden crevasses. Allow 1hr for this descent. Once on easier ground continue north-east through boulders and other glacial debris of moraines to reach the **Falbesoner See** alpine tarn (signpost).

With the hut now in sight, the route proceeds to descend more easily on a good path, heading north-east, to enter the picturesque, flat, marshy valley along the Falbesonertal to reach the very pleasant **Neue Regensburger Hut**. **2hr**

STAGE 7
Neue Regensburger Hut to Franz Senn Hut via Schrimmennieder

Start	Neue Regensburger Hut (2286m)
Standard time	5–6hr
Distance	9.1km
Ascent	465m
Descent	605m

After the very long walk from the Dresdner Hut to the Neue Regensburger Hut, Stage 7 can be considered a semi-rest day of sorts.

Sadly, the route is a little hemmed in and doesn't have the magnificent views of the previous day's outing. However, the view from the Schrimmennieder, down the valley to Ranalt and the Habicht, is quite spectacular. Likewise, the views of the snow-capped peaks of the Alpeiner, on the approach to the Franz Senn Hut, are quite impressive, particularly if the alpenrose bushes are still in flower.

CAUTIONARY NOTES

Once the most straightforward trek on the Stubai Rucksack Route, this route is now challenging, particularly on the Franz Senn side of the Schrimmennieder, due to a huge avalanche that occurred off the Platzenturm.

The descent from the Schrimmennieder to point 2496m is straightforward; however, the section from the small footbridge at 2445m, followed by 200m through the boulder slopes and streams, is ankle-twisting, leg-snapping terrain and demands great care.

Needless to say, this is not a place to be in very poor weather, particularly if the rocks are snow covered.

From the pleasant Neue Regensburger Hut, follow Route 133, north-east, along the level path of the **Windtratten** to the foot of the ridge coming down from the Summerwantl (signpost). **¾hr** Turn left, north-west, and ascend steep slopes, over slabby rocks, boulders and scree, traversing the couloir in a series of long looping zigzags, up to the broad col of the **Schrimmennieder** (2706m). **About 2hr** Great

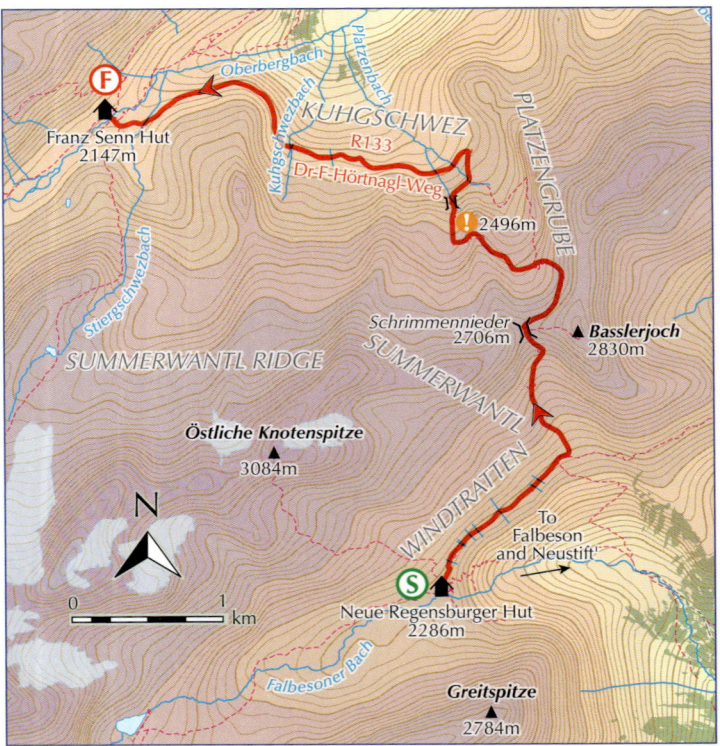

views stretch down the valley towards Ranalt and across the void to the Habicht. (Signpost at the col states 2½hr to the hut.)

For those with sufficient energy, a short 1hr detour can made to the Basslerjoch (2830m).

Descend north-east from the col, over broken, rocky ground, partly paved with a fine rock staircase, on the Dr-F-Hörtnagl-Weg. Continue down through the **Platzengrube** couloir in a wide arc where after a series of steep zigzags it levels out and turns left, west (signpost).

At this point the original route continued to gradually descend the couloir until an avalanche changed the route irrevocably.

STAGE 7 – NEUE REGENSBURGER HUT TO FRANZ SENN HUT VIA SCHRIMMENNIEDER

Continue to follow the bouldery but easy-to-follow track west, across the flank of the Kuhgschwez to point 2496m. Descend north on the steep, difficult, broken ground to a small **footbridge** at 2445m, thereafter descending via a series of zigzags over rocks, boulders and streams until the ground finally eases (signpost and junction of the original route). **1½hr**

Continue west to follow the well-laid-out rocky trail, sometimes paved, across the **Kuhgschwez** couloir, just north of the Uelasgrat and Gschwezgrat spurs coming down from the Östliche Knotenspitze, before finally rounding the foot of the Gschwezgrat ridge to reveal the very impressive **Franz Senn Hut**. **1½hr**

At the Franz Senn Hut

TREKKING IN AUSTRIA'S STUBAI ALPS

EXCURSION
To visit Rinnensee

Start	Franz Senn Hut (2147m)
Standard time	About 2½hr (+1hr return)
Distance	2.5km (+2.5km return)
Ascent	515m
Descent	515m

This lovely walk takes in the delightful alpine lake of Rinnensee, with its magnificent views of the Ruderhofspitze and Seespitze, and is an ideal picnic spot with many photographic opportunities.

Follow the route description for the Lisenser Fernerkogel. Return by the same route.

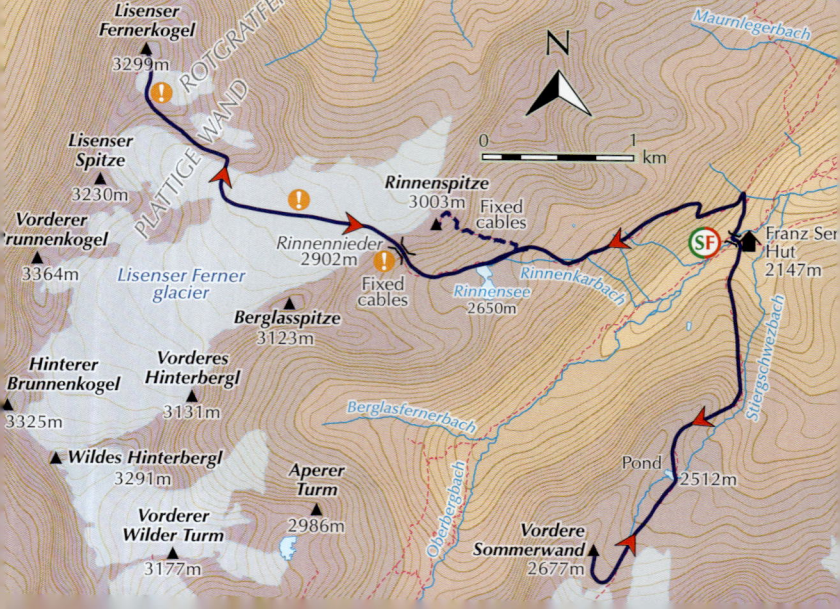

EXCURSION
Ascent of Vordere Sommerwand (2677m)

Start	Franz Senn Hut (2147m)
Standard time	About 2hr (+1½hr for descent)
Distance	1.5km (+1.5km for descent)
Ascent	530m
Descent	530m
Note	For map, see 'Excursion: To visit Rinnensee'

This pleasant walk to the lower summit provides a good view of the Seespitze and Kräulspitze. But more specifically, the Sommerwand is famed for its profusion of alpine flowers, including the shy edelweiss, which grows on its south-facing slopes.

From the hut, follow the well-marked path south (signpost), over rock and grassy slopes around the foot of the Vordere Sommerwand's long ridge, then head south-west to a signpost. The path ahead continues south-west, over what remains of the Sommerwand glacier, to the Kräulscharte. From the signpost, turn right, north, up a series of zigzags along a rock path to the rocky terrace of **Vordere Sommerwand**. **About 2hr**

Return by the same route.

EXCURSION
Ascent of Lisenser Fernerkogel (3299m)

Start	Franz Senn Hut (2147m)
Standard time	4hr; this is rarely achieved and 6hr is more realistic (+4hr minimum for descent)
Distance	5.0km (+5.0km for descent)
Ascent	1120m
Descent	1120m
Grade	PD
Note	For map, see 'Excursion: To visit Rinnensee'

This highly recommended excursion embraces many scenic attractions, notably the view up the Alpeiner valley with its glaciers and snow-capped peaks. The Rinnensee, with the peaks of the Ruderhofspitze, Seespitze and Kräulspitze mirrored on its surface, usually provides aspiring photographers with a variety of photogenic opportunities and is a lovely place for a picnic or a short day excursion.

Beyond the Rinnensee, the Rinnennieder provides a good mountaineering situation. Being isolated and a little exposed on both sides of the ridge, it affords a degree of excitement, plus the first real opportunity to see the Lisenser Fernerkogel mountain and its attendant glaciers.

Crossing the glaciers and scrambling up the rocks is good wholesome mountaineering and thoroughly enjoyable. And once you've attained the summit, the view is one of the most extensive in the entire Alps and, without doubt, the best in the Eastern Alps.

It is the Stubai peaks that dominate the scenery, especially the Schrankogel and beyond to the Zuckerhütl, Wilder Freiger and Habicht. Beyond the Stubai, on the far horizon, are the Ötztal, Zillertal, South Tirol, Dolomites, Kalkkögel and Karwendel, while those with sharp eyes will be able to locate the Westfalenhaus nestling in the Langtal valley over 1000m below.

If you are blessed with clear blue skies, spend as much time as possible absorbing the panoramic view, for it is magnificent.

EXCURSION – ASCENT OF LISENSER FERNERKOGEL (3299M)

CAUTIONARY NOTES

Due to global warming and the recession of the Lisenser Ferner glacier in recent years, getting onto the glacier below the Rinnennieder and off the glacier to access the Plattige Wand terrace can be problematic. Bergschrunds exist at both sides; although usually small and easily crossed, they do exist, varying from season to season. Similarly, the crevasses on the Rotgratferner glacier, which run parallel and diagonally to it, will involve some route-finding skills.

Thereafter, the ascent of the summit rocks along the south ridge requires a degree of care, as the midsection is loose, difficult ground, and the exposure on the west side of the ridge is very airy with a spectacular drop. Participants who are not totally vertigo-free are advised to keep to the bulk of the mountain.

From the hut, cross the Alpeinerbach stream and follow Route 132 for about 15min up the grassy path leading to the Lisens valley and the Starkenburger Hut until it branches off left (signpost). Turn left, and head south-west on a good path, over grass and rock-strewn slopes, ascending steadily over boulders with zigzags in places, to the **Rinnensee alpine lake** (2650m). **About 1½hr** The beautiful reflections of the Seespitze and Ruderhofspitze on the surface of the Rinnensee make this a great place for a picnic or breakfast stop. En route you will pass a park bench commemorating Harry Parkes. Harry was a very active member of what was then the ÖAV Sektion Britannia, having a great love of the Tirol and the Stubai in particular.

Continue west for a short distance, then head north-west up steep, rocky slopes with fixed cables to the **Rinnennieder (2902m)**, a broad col overlooking the Lisenser Ferner glacier. The col provides stunning scenery and is an excellent vantage point from which to recce the route up the mountain, which can be seen immediately opposite, to the north-west. **2hr**

Descend the rocks on the west side of the col to the edge of the **Lisenser Ferner glacier** (Bergschrund). Get onto the glacier and cross it north-west – crevasses midway – to the base of the rock barrier, the **Plattige Wand**. Look out for a large painted red circle that indicates the way.

Scramble up the rocks around the 3000m contour and traverse north-east along a rock terrace for a short distance to gain the **Rotgratferner glacier** at point 3045m. Get onto the glacier and ascend north-west up the steep slope, right bank, parallel to the Rotgratspitze's south-east ridge, until it is possible to cross the glacier north-west above a series of crevasses to the opposite bank, below the summit. Gain the rocks and scramble over boulders and slabs, which are loose in places, up the short but very exposed south ridge to the summit of **Lisenser Fernerkogel** with its slender metal cross. **About 2–2½hr**

From the summit, reverse the route in its entirety. Allow a minimum of 4hr, depending on the state of the glacier.

On the Plattige Wand terrace

STAGE 8
Franz Senn Hut to Starkenburger Hut

Start	Franz Senn Hut (2147m)
Standard time	6–7hr
Distance	15.8km
Ascent	805m
Descent	710m

This walk, the longest day of the Stubai Rucksack Route, is full of scenic interest and is a fitting way to end the tour.

Early in the day the scenery is dominated by views back to the Franz Senn Hut, including a memorable view of the snow-capped peaks of the Alpeiner, particularly Ruderhofspitze and Schrankogel.

Once you arrive at the tiny shepherd's hut at Seducker Hochalm, whose carved motto reads 'my kingdom is a flock of white sheep and my little hut is my castle', the peaks of the Alpeiner will have eased back and merged with the whole of the Stubai. For anyone looking for a super-duper mountain experience, the Seducker Hochalm has just eight beds, but what a place to stay, a reminder of a time when all alpine huts were like this.

Thereafter, the jagged limestone peaks of the Kalkkögel, which are more akin to the Dolomites than the Stubai, and known colloquially as the Dolomites of the North, become evident and announce the end of the tour.

Once at the Starkenburger Hut, the immediate scenery is dominated by a fine view of the Habicht. Perhaps, however, the most spectacular of panoramic views is seen when the sun goes down; then the sunset and night skies viewed from the Starkenburger Hut are truly memorable.

CAUTIONARY NOTES

This is a long day out so be on your way early, by 08:00.

Leaving behind the most impressive Franz Senn Hut, cross over the bridge and head north-east on **Route 132**, along a steep grassy path, bypassing the track leading to the Lisenser Fernerkogel, to its junction with Route 117, where a prominent

TREKKING IN AUSTRIA'S STUBAI ALPS

stream is crossed. Route 132, the left branch, continues over the Grosse Horntal into the Lisens valley.

Continue north-east along the Franz-Senn-Weg on **Route 117**, following a good path over grass and rocky slopes, crossing a number of rocky spurs on the southern flank of the Schaldersspitze and on to a small hut at **Seducker Hochalm** (2256m), also known as Sedugg Hochalm. **2–2½hr** As you look back, there is an excellent view of the Ruderhofspitze.

This tiny **alm** was once a shepherd's hut but was also used by chamois hunters. The hut is located a little before the halfway stage, and if the family who now manage the hut are in residence, this is an ideal opportunity for refreshments. However, do not linger too long as there is still a long way to go; the sign by the hut indicates that the Starkenburger Hut is 4½hr away.

Panorama above the Obernbergtal valley, looking back towards the Franz Senn Hut

Trekking in Austria's Stubai Alps

The hut is located at the junction of Route 118, which leads over the Wildkopfscharte to the Potsdamer Hut. Continue north-east along Route 117, on a good path contouring across the hillside high above the Obergtal valley on the 2300m contour, past the Schwarzhorn, until it climbs steadily to the col at **Sendersjöchl** (2477m). **1½hr** This overlooks the Senders and Fotscher valleys to the north, while in reverse there are excellent panoramic views across the whole of the Stubai.

Continue north-east, along the broad ridge to the Steinkogel (2589m), with its excellent view of the jagged peaks of the Kalkkögel. Descend slightly, contouring north-east over scree slopes to the **Seejöchl** (2518m) overlooking the tiny lake, signpost and junction with routes from the Adolf Pichler Hut. **1½hr**

From here on, follow Route 116 south-east, traversing the scree slopes below the Schlicker Seespitze, Riepenwand and Hoher Burgstall, on a good but slightly exposed path, to the very picturesque **Starkenburger Hut**. **1½hr**

Looking towards the Kalkkögel, with the Seejöchl far left and the Schlicker Scharte gap in the centre

EXCURSION
Ascent of Hoher Burgstall (2611m)

Start	Starkenburger Hut (2237m)
Standard time	1hr (+¾hr for descent)
Distance	1.0km
Ascent	375m
Descent	375m
Note	For map, see Stage 9

Note that this is a walk not a climb. This short excursion from the hut and takes about 1hr.

From the hut, head north on Route 115 (signpost), through the metal avalanche barriers, up scree slopes on an obvious path to a large cross on the summit of **Hoher Burgstall**. **1hr**

Return by the same route or continue to traverse the mountain, descending to the Sennjoch Hut, ideal for a break before departing for the **Kreuzjoch cable-car station** and, eventually, Fulpmes. Excellent views stretch in all directions.

Starkenburger Hut to the village of Fulpmes. Passing the avalanche barriers

STAGE 9
Starkenburger Hut to Neustift

Start	Starkenburger Hut (2237m)
Standard time	2½hr
Distance	5.6km
Ascent	Negligible
Descent	1255m

From the hut follow the service road, descending south-east, bypassing the gravel track road to **Schönegg**. **About ¼hr** Continue south-east on Route 115, through trees and alpine meadows, along a steep, well-marked path to the outskirts of **Neustift**. The scenery here is excellent.

Proceed south-east along the road into the village square, past the church and on to the main road and bus stop marked with a letter 'H', for the bus ride back to Innsbruck. **About 2hr**

Bus Service: Neustift to Innsbruck at 09:33 / 10:33 / 11:33

STAGE 9 – STARKENBURGER HUT TO NEUSTIFT

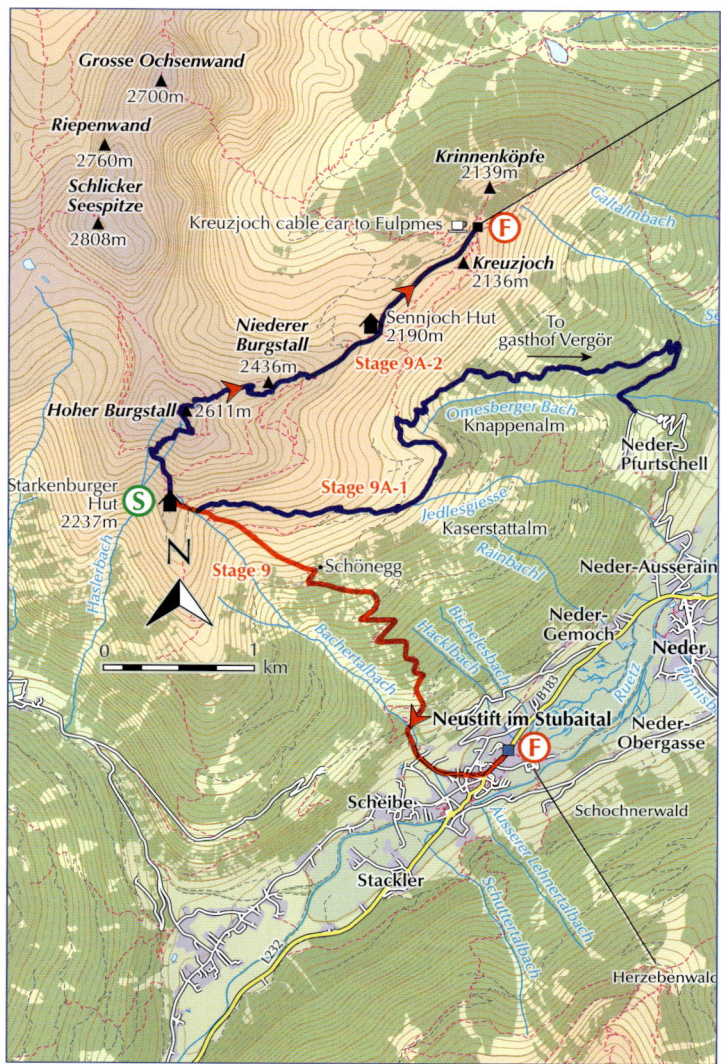

At Kreuzjoch recreation area, looking towards the peaks of the Kalkkögel and Schlicker Seespitze (Trek 1, Stage 9A)

STAGE 9A
Starkenburger Hut to Fulpmes

Start	Starkenburger Hut (2237m)
Standard time	3hr
Distance	3.8km (not including cable car)
Ascent	175m (not including cable car)
Descent	300m (not including cable car)
Note	For map, see Stage 9

From the hut follow the hut service road east on Route 116 for several km to **Kaserstattalm (1830m)** and Knappenalm. Continue along the service road for 1km, then turn south-east and descend through the forest to Gasthof Vergör (1266m). Thereafter, if your intention is to descend direct to Fulpmes, continue to follow the service road north-east until it comes to a natural conclusion in **Fulpmes**. **About 3hr**

Bus service: Fulpmes to Innsbruck at 09:48 / 10:48 / 11:48

Via the Kreuzjoch cable car
If your intention is to make use of the cable car at Kreuzjoch, from the hut, proceed north for a short distance to a signpost and pick up the well-marked trail, heading north-east through the avalanche barriers, for 1km to another signpost. Continue, contouring under the **Niederer Burgstall** to the Sennjoch Hut farm complex and **Sennjoch** at 2190m. This is a good place for a break. Thereafter, follow the well-marked trail, mingling with other tourists, to the **Kreuzjoch cable-car station** and tourist complex. **2½hr** Enjoy the excellent views of the limestone peaks of Kalkkögel and the many satellite peaks that make up the Schlicker Seespitze.

If you have time at the Kreuzjoch, take the 10min stroll to the Panoramaweg StubaiBlick viewpoint, complete with information boards that point out the mountains near and far and all the associated folklore legends.

STUBAI GLACIER TOUR

On the Schwarzenbergferner glacier, looking towards the Schrankogel (Stage 2)

TREK 2
Stubai Glacier Tour

Start	Mieders
Finish	Ranalt
Standard time	7 days (excluding excursions)
Distance	59.9km
Ascent	4875m
Descent	4485m

By way of introduction, it's important to first make a clarification about the name of the route, as the original route name has become confused over the years with the better-known Stubai Rucksack Route.

The Stubai Rucksack Route, which is its original English name, or the Stubaier Runde Tour in German, has now become known by default as the Stubaier Höhenweg. However, the Stubai Glacier Tour was originally known as the Stubaier Höhenweg. Over the years, the Stubai Rucksack Route (Runde Tour) gained popularity while that of the Glacier Tour declined as a result of border tensions along South Tirol in the late 1960s and early 1970s, exacerbated by the difficulty of crossing into Italy and the occupation of the Müller Hut and Becherhaus by the Italian Alpine Troops Command, the Alpini. Over the past 50 years, this swing in popularity has resulted in the route names becoming reversed.

Today if you say you are undertaking the Stubai Höhenweg, you will be understood to be doing the Stubai Rucksack Route or Runde Tour. If you say you are undertaking the Stubaier Gletscher Tour, you will be understood to be doing just that.

The route, as the name implies, involves much glacier work, which makes it a prerequisite that participants have the necessary skills to deal with the great variety of terrain that will be crossed.

Although the route is intended for the more experienced, it is also ideal for first-time visitors and those wishing to climb in the Alps for the first time. However, before doing so, each person should be able to use an ice axe and crampons, be able to belay on rock and ice, be familiar with rope management for glacier travel and be practised in Prusiking and crevasse-rescue techniques.

While the tour is undoubtedly tough, it is not unremittingly demanding. It will, therefore, suit aspiring alpinists wanting to develop their alpine experience without feeling over-committed and out of their depth, as is often the case in the

TREK 2 – STUBAI GLACIER TOUR

higher mountains of the Western Alps. As a word of encouragement, the route has been successfully undertaken by several young teenagers in the English section of the Austrian Alpine Club, Alpenverein Britannia, although it must be stressed that each had received formal winter training or had attended basic rock-and-ice training courses.

As with the Stubai Rucksack Route, the Glacier Tour is a hut-to-hut tour and while the Rucksack Route skirts around the mountains to avoid the glaciers, the very essence of the Glacier Tour is to traverse them. The reward for this effort is the infinite variety of glacier scenery from the many peaks and passes that the route crosses.

The tour starts at the fabulous Franz Senn Hut, then moves to the Amberger Hut via the challenging Wildgratscharte, opposite the Schrankogel's north face. From the

TREKKING IN AUSTRIA'S STUBAI ALPS

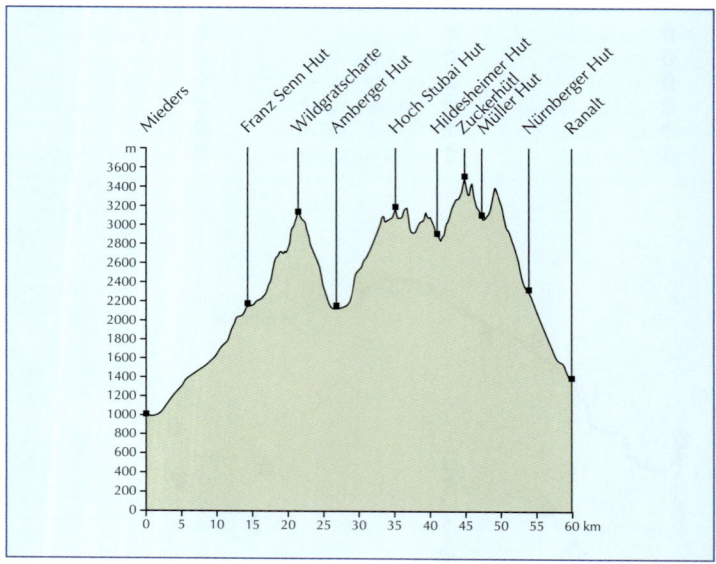

Amberger Hut, the route continues to the highest hut in the Stubai Alps, the Hoch Stubai Hut, via the spectacular Sulztalferner glacier. Thereafter, a long, descending traverse of the Warenkarferner and Windacher Ferner glaciers leads to the popular Hildesheimer Hut. From this premier hut, the route goes into Italy via the Frontier Ridge, across the Stubai's highest peak, the Zuckerhütl, and its close neighbour, the Wilder Pfaff, to the once-derelict Müller Hut on the Austria–Italy border with South Tirol.

The final part of the Glacier Tour crosses the Übeltalferner glacier and the impressive Wilder Freiger to end at the splendid Nürnberger Hut. All in all, it is six days of superb mountaineering.

For those with additional time, the Glacier Tour can be extended with the South Tirol extension, for several more days of exploring the peaks of South Tirol. The extension visits the Teplitzer Hut, Magdeburger Hut and the Italian Tribulaun Hut before crossing the border back into Austria to the Tribulaunhaus, bringing the tour to an end at the road head at Feuerstein. Or you can choose to continue to the Truna Hut and end the tour at Trins, in the Gschnitztal valley, or at Steinach am Brenner, in the Wipptal valley of the Brenner Pass.

Trek 2 – Stubai Glacier Tour

Route summary
- Stage 1 Mieders to Franz Senn Hut
- For excursions from the Franz Senn Hut, see the Stubai Rucksack Route
  - To visit Rinnensee
  - Ascent of Sommerwand
  - Ascent of Lisenser Fernerkogel
- Stage 2 Franz Senn Hut to Amberger Hut via Wildgratscharte
- Stage 3 Amberger Hut to Hoch Stubai Hut via Wütenkarsattel
- Stage 4 Hoch Stubai Hut to Hildesheimer Hut via Bildstöckljoch
- Stage 5 Hildesheimer Hut to Müller Hut via Zuckerhütl
- Stage 5A Hildesheimer Hut to Siegerland Hut (alternative bad-weather route)
- Stage 5B Siegerland Hut to Müller Hut via Sonklarspitze
- Stage 6 Müller Hut to Nürnberger Hut via Wilder Freiger
- Stage 7 Nürnberger Hut to Ranalt

South Tirol extension
- Stage 6 Becherhaus or Müller Hut to Teplitzer Hut
- Stage 7 Teplitzer Hut to Magdeburger Hut
- Stage 8 Magdeburger Hut to Italian Tribulaun Hut or Austrian Tribulaunhaus
- Stage 8A Italian Tribulaun Hut to Austrian Tribulaunhaus via Sandesjöchl
- Stage 9 Austrian Tribulaunhaus to Truna Hut via Gstreinjöchl
- Stage 10 Truna Hut to Steinach am Brenner or Obernbergtal valley

Getting to the start

A regular bus service operates from Innsbruck; see Stubai Rucksack Route description for the bus timetable and journey to Neustift. Take the bus as far as Neustift Ortsmitte. Neustift is the main village in the Stubaital, a little to the north-east of the junction with the Obernbergtal valley.

From Neustift, you have the following options:

1. Walk down the main road for 2.5km, turning right at the signpost into a cluster of chalet-type houses that is Milders.
2. Get off the bus at the fourth stop after Neustift, at Milders Ortsmitte, thereafter walking the few remaining metres to the centre of Milders.
3. If there are a few of you, get off the bus in Neustift and go to the tourist office and hire a taxi to take you all the way to the Oberiss Hut. This may seem a bit expensive, but it is good value and will save precious time getting to the hut, which would be better spent having an afternoon stroll on the Sommerwand.

STAGE 1
Mieders to Franz Senn Hut

Start	Mieders (952m)
Standard time	5hr
Distance	14.5km from Neustift
Ascent	1165m from Neustift
Descent	Negligible

Overall, this walk is a disappointing trudge. As the Obernbergtal is a steep-sided valley, the views are restricted until beyond Seduck, when parts of the Kalkkögel (Starkenburger Hut) and Schwarzhorn (Franz Senn Way) become more visible. This confinement, coupled with the disadvantage of following a road, laden with a heavy rucksack, is not the best of mountaineering experiences. It is better to make use of the transport available and then enjoy one of the short excursions from the hut, to the Rinnensee or up the Sommerwand. (See Stubai Rucksack Route itinerary for both route descriptions.)

TO THE OBERISSALM BY VEHICLE

A regular minibus service operates from the village square in Milders up the Obernbergtal valley to the Oberissalm (1742m). If you have difficulty in locating the minibus-cum-jeep-service bus stop, make enquiries at the Hotel Almhof Danler in the village square.

The jeep service generally runs at 09:00, 10:00 and 15:00.

A taxi service is also available from the hotel for those who wish to get to the hut quickly: tel 05226 2626 or 05226 3333.

Alternatively, telephone Neustifter Funktaxi: 05226 2877 or 0664 287 7000.

For those wishing to enjoy the walk and get into the feel of things, follow the road from Neustift for 1.5km to a signpost for Route 131. Follow this west to bypass **Milders** until it regains the road. The route now follows the road on and off, but always runs adjacent to it, first to **Bärenbad** (1248m), then to **Seduck** (1472m),

STAGE 1 – MIEDERS TO FRANZ SENN HUT

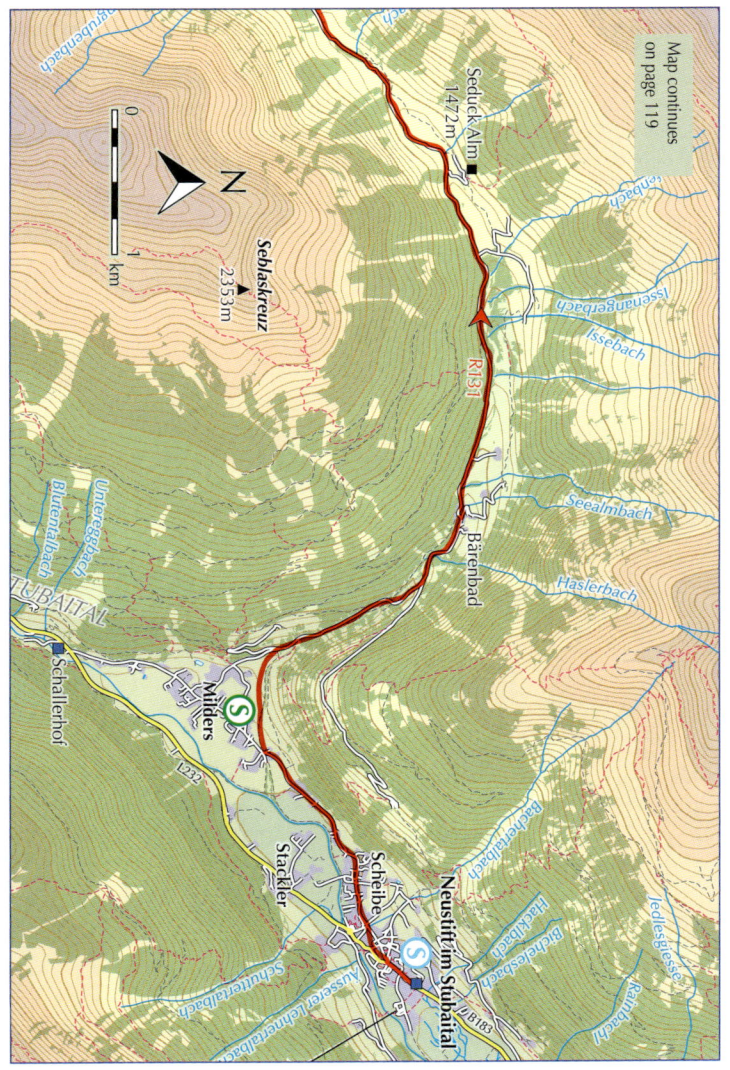

Stöcklenalm (1598m) and finally the **Oberissalm** (1742m). **3½hr and 8km from Milders**

From the popular Oberissalm (restaurant) there is a Seilbahn for the Franz Senn Hut. For a small charge, rucksacks can be hoisted the final 400m to the hut.

After the Oberissalm, the path steepens in a series of zigzags, rising 300m in a short distance, finally levelling out just before the **Franz Senn Hut**. **1½hr**

Approaching the Franz Senn Hut

STAGE 1 – MIEDERS TO FRANZ SENN HUT

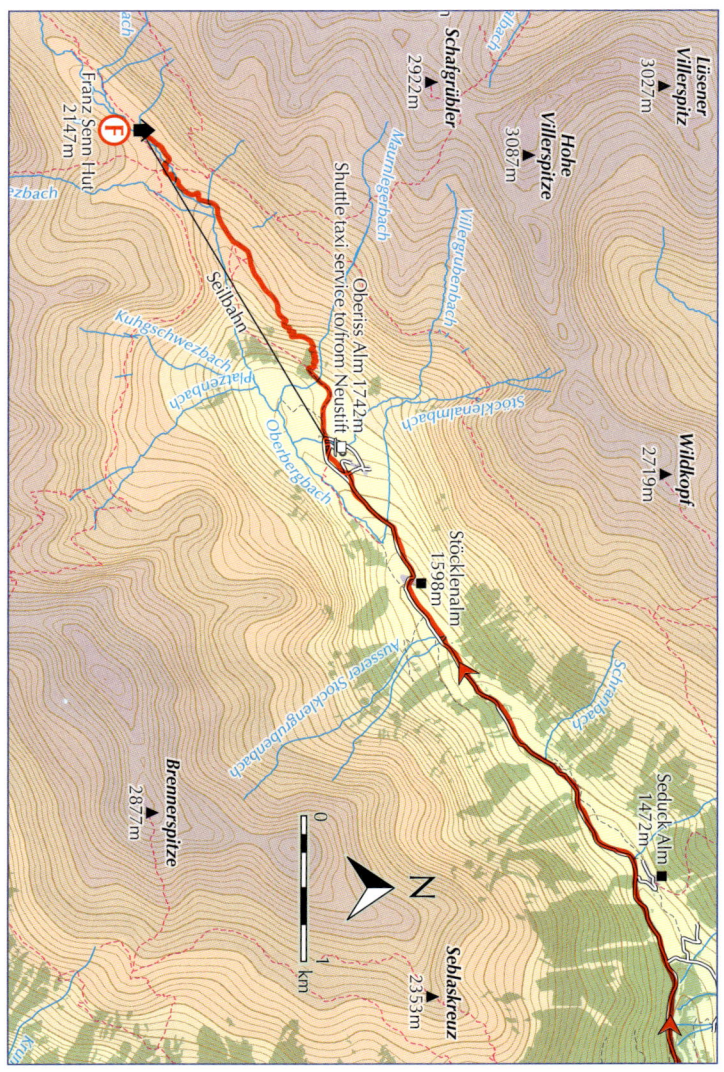

STAGE 2
Franz Senn Hut to Amberger Hut via Wildgratscharte

Start	Franz Senn Hut (2147m)
Standard time	6–8hr
Distance	12.4km
Ascent	1075m
Descent	1085m

This excellent day out is full of scenic variety, interest and challenge. The main event of the day is the crossing of the Wildgratscharte, from which the views are superb; the col itself is just big enough to accommodate two people standing. On one side you have the expanse of glaciers across to the Ruderhofspitze and on the other the dominant wedge of the north-east face of the Schrankogel, first climbed in 1923, which used to provide one of the best snow climbs in the region. The 50-degree slope has also been skied down (1935) but unfortunately both are now only possible during the depths of winter.

Approaching the Wildgratscharte; note the fresh snow

STAGE 2 – FRANZ SENN HUT TO AMBERGER HUT VIA WILDGRATSCHARTE

CAUTIONARY NOTES

The standard time given for the journey is 6hr, but it is rarely achieved. The average time is about 8hr, so you need to be on your way early, by 06:30.

While the crux of the route is the crossing of the Wildgratscharte, the first challenge of the day is to accurately locate the col itself, as from the glacier the route is not obvious and there is a real need to avoid getting trapped following tracks for the Ruderhofspitze. Ensure you continue to bear right once above what remains of the Alpeiner Ferner glacier's ice fall, heading for the rock faces and towers ahead of you, avoiding the easier ground that bears left as the trail levels out and heads into the large glacial amphitheatre that eventually leads to the Ruderhofspitze.

The Wildgratscharte itself is rigged with fixed cables on both sides of the mountain to make the passage easier, and while the ascent is a pretty straightforward climb with plenty of anchor points, it remains very exposed and airy.

On the Schrankogel-side of the mountain, the fixed cables may be used for the descent onto the glacier; however, a 50m single abseil is faster and easier to rig up than making use of the fixed cables, more so if the rocks are snow covered. However, when there is minimal snow, as may be the case later in the season, crossing the Bergschrund below the col can prove to be difficult in itself, and the slopes that follow may be covered in hard ice requiring good axe and crampon skills. As a precaution ask the Hüttenwirt at the Franz Senn Hut whether the col is passable and also check the entries in the hut book.

Cross the river via the footbridge just outside the hut and follow the left bank of the Alpeinerbach south-west for 2½km on **Route 131**, until it starts to rise steeply among old glacial moraines at the foot of the Aperer Turm.

A signpost of sorts, with the words *Neue* (new) and *Alte* (old) painted on a large boulder, indicates the new and old routes to the glacier.

From hereabouts the scenery starts to open up, mostly dominated by the Seespitze and what remains of the ice fall off the Alpeiner Ferner glacier. Continue to follow the red waymarks, bearing left along the new route. The track starts to rise more steeply, following a rocky trail heading south-west through the cliff face to gain access onto the left bank of the **Alpeiner Ferner glacier** at 2700m. **2hr**

After kitting yourself out with rope, axe and crampons, set off across the glacier, heading south-west in a wide arc to avoid the ice fall, to a point due east of the Nördliche Wildgratspitze at about 2900m and a group of crevasses. Now

TREKKING IN AUSTRIA'S STUBAI ALPS

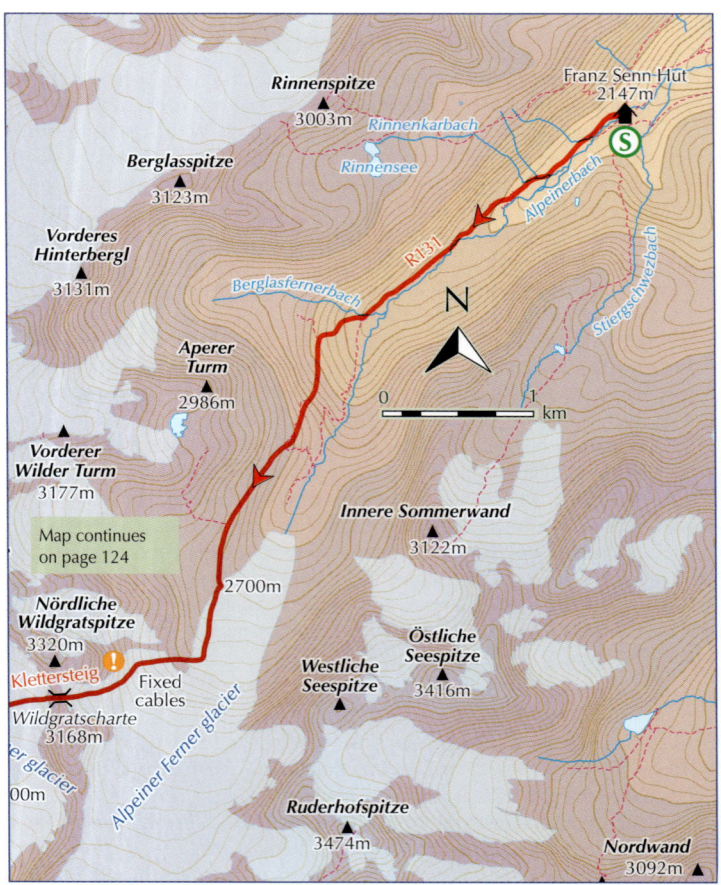

move in a more southerly direction to the foot of the Südliche Wildgratspitze's east ridge. The Wildgratscharte is now placed due west in an obvious gap along the interconnecting ridge marked by a large red-and-white painted circle. **3hr**

Proceed up the steeping snow slopes to the foot of the rocks that guard access to the col. Ensure you have some form of harness deployed, with sling and karabiner, and climb the series of fixed cables, Klettersteig style, up the steep, rocky crag to the **Wildgratscharte** (3168m). **About 1hr** There is a good belay at half height and spectacular views from the col of the Ruderhofspitze and Seespitze group to the east, and of the Schrankogel (3497m) to the west, the Stubai's second-highest mountain with its spectacular north-east face.

From the col, scramble down rocks on the west side of the Wildgratscharte, fixed cables in place but very exposed, and cross the Schwarzenbergferner glacier in a wide arc to a point at approximately **3100m** on the Schrankogel's east flank. Be aware of crevasse danger in the centre of the glacier and on the right bank.

While crossing the glacier, keep an eye open and recce the route to the Hoch Stubai Hut via the Sulztalferner glacier to the south. Those with sharp eyes will be able to locate the hut on its rocky knoll to the south-west.

Negotiating the lower east ridge of the Schrankogel becomes a grotty affair over difficult ground and needs a fair amount of care among ankle-twisting, knee-wrecking boulders, as the route is not always obvious until the path re-establishes itself with the usual daubs of red paint. Look out for cairns and marker posts. **About 1hr**

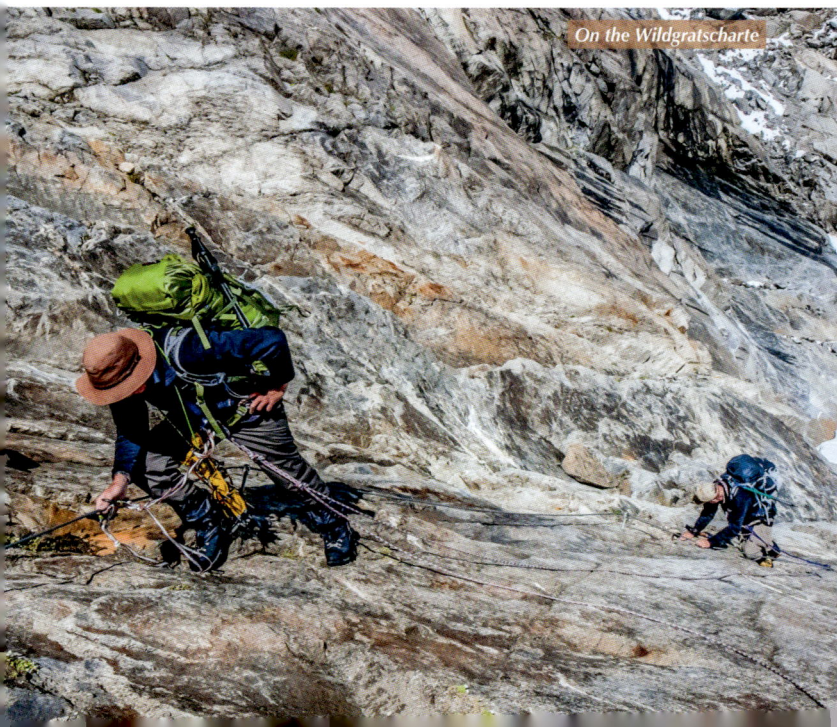

On the Wildgratscharte

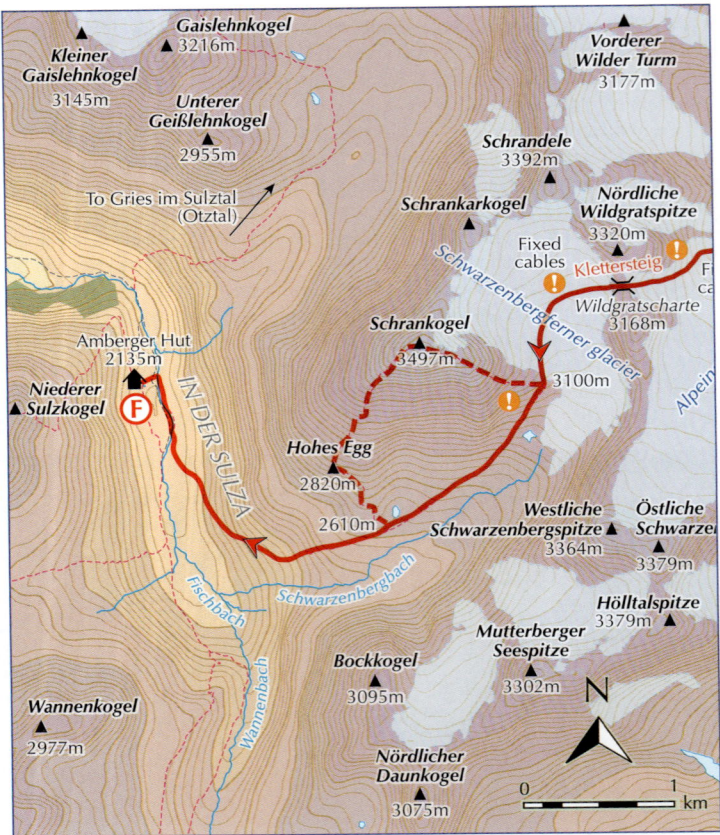

Having regained the path at about 2800m, think in terms of 2hr to get to the hut. Continue to follow the obvious lateral moraines south-west to a **tiny tarn** and junction with the main track and normal route up the Schrankogel, along the Hohes Egg at 2610m (signpost).

The path is now clearly defined, heading west then north-west above the marshy Sulzbach to the **Amberger Hut**. **1hr**

Ascent of Schrankogel (3497m)

Fit climbers may find passing so close to the mountain a temptation they cannot resist, and climbing the east ridge should fulfil that need.

From point **3100m**, at the junction of the east ridge with the right bank of the Schwarzenbergferner glacier, clamber up the steep rocks to gain the ridge proper, then follow it all the way to the summit of **Schrankogel**. **1hr**

It is not unusual to come across a snow crest, which may also be corniced, on the final 100m to the summit; keep a safe distance by staying on the north side of the mountain.

In descent, pick up the trail of the ordinary route via the south-west flank and **Hohes Egg** to rejoin the track at 2610m. **About a 3hr detour**

A POTTED HISTORY OF CLIMBING ON THE SCHRANKOGEL

Not surprisingly, being the second-highest mountain in the Stubai, the Schrankogel attracted attention from early on in the 18th and 19th centuries.

The first ascent by the accepted normal route, by the south-west ridge, remains disputed; it was recorded as climbed in 1824 by botanist JG Hargasser but later confirmed as a pastor called Pfarrer Schöpf in 1840.

In the summer of 1865, the British pair FF Tuckett and FAJ Brown, both of Alpine Club fame, with their Swiss guides F Biner and C Michels, added the east ridge on a rare visit to the Eastern Alps, during the golden age of alpinism.

Interestingly, elsewhere in the Alps, during the same season, a certain Ed Whymper and friends were on the Matterhorn, a climb and ensuing tragedy that entered into mountaineering folklore. While further west, Piz Buin in the Silvretta was climbed by Franz Pöll, Anton Specht and Jakob Pfitscher on 14 July 1865, the same day that Whymper's tragedy unfolded.

Many years would then pass before local alpinists H Hörtnagl and W Löb made short shrift of the north face in 1923. This route also received attention of a different kind when it was skied down in 1935.

STAGE 3
Amberger Hut to Hoch Stubai Hut via Wütenkarsattel

Start	Amberger Hut (2135m)
Standard time	5–6hr
Distance	8.3km
Ascent	1110m
Descent	75m

Stage 3 is another excellent day out full of scenic interest mostly provided by the glaciers: first and midway on the Sulztalferner glacier, when the ice fall is in full view, then later at the Wütenkarsattel, when the Schrankogel and Wilde Leck are seen to advantage and the scale of the Sulztal can be fully appreciated.

The finale of the day is the spectacular location of the Hoch Stubai Hut with its splendid view of the Ötztal mountains.

CAUTIONARY NOTES

Take care crossing the Wütenkarferner glacier, where hidden crevasses in the centre of the glacier and just below the hut can be problematic. These potential dangers will be heightened after fresh snow fall or during bad weather.

From the hut, head south on Route 137 for about 1km, along the flat, open, marshy ground of **In der Sulze**, keeping to the left bank of the many streams generated by the glaciers. At point **2155m** (signpost) the path splits. Route 137 goes west to Sölden via the Atterkarjoch. Continue south, heading in the direction of a large buttress. Climb this in a series of zigzags to a signpost at **2280m** marked 'Hoch Stubai Hut and Dresdner Hut'. **¾hr** Take the right-hand fork, continuing to climb the buttress via a number of ledges until it gives way to the moraines of the left bank (west) of the **Sulztalferner glacier** (2627m). **1½hr** Look out for great views from here of the previous day's route, particularly of the Schrankogel and the ice fall off the Sulztalferner glacier.

After cramponing up, get onto the glacier and proceed more southerly, gradually climbing the snow slopes to the **Wütenkarsattel** (3105m), bypassing the magnificent Wilde Leck halfway. **2hr**

STAGE 3 – AMBERGER HUT TO HOCH STUBAI HUT VIA WÜTENKARSATTEL

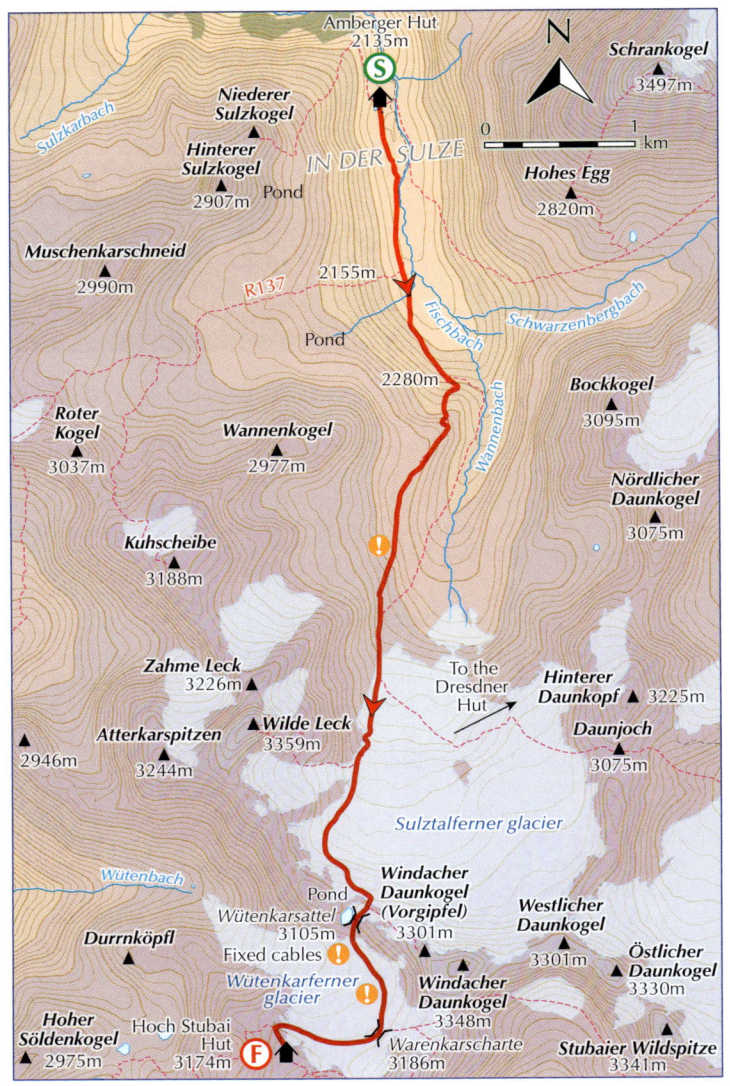

Crossing the Wütenkarsattel, with the Hoch Stubai Hut in the distance

At the pass, the Hoch Stubai Hut is now clearly visible on the far side of the Wütenkarferner glacier.

From the Wütenkarsattel, descend past the glacial pond, then climb down steep rocks and difficult ground to gain access to the **Wütenkarferner glacier**. Cross the glacier in a wide south-easterly arc – crevasses in the centre – before turning west to ascend the final snow slope to a broad col just below the hut, and then onto the **Hoch Stubai Hut**. 1½hr

ESCAPE ROUTE

Should you be caught out by bad weather, there are a couple of descent routes to Sölden in the Ötztal valley. If the weather is foul, however, neither route is pleasant. The best option then would be to stay over and enjoy the ambience of the Hoch Stubai Hut.

From the hut, proceed north for a few metres to the col overlooking the Wütenkarferner glacier, then turn west, descending to the Lauberkarscharte (2760m). Now turn south through the Lauberkar boulder field and on to a signpost indicating the way to Sölden. Continue as before for a short distance to another signpost. Here turn right and follow the forest service roads and track into Sölden. **Allow 5hr**

Alternatively, from the hut, head south-east for 300m to a col at 3114m, then descend very steep, difficult ground overlooking the Seekar alpine pond. Now head south-east along a narrow corridor, then turn south-west again to descend steep, difficult ground of rocks and boulders to the Seekarsee lake (2655m). After 100m you will come to a signpost that indicates the way to Sölden, via the Fiegl Alm, or to the Hildesheimer Hut. **Allow 5hr** on the 2500m contour for around 3km, through the D'Heache, Warenkar and Schussgruben couloirs, then climb out along the ridge of the **Fräulaskofel** (2803m) to a col marked by a large **cairn** on the southern edge of the Windacher Ferner glacier at 3034m. Cross the glacier's snowy remnants towards the ski-tow pylons to the **Eisjoch**. Continue following the route up the snow slope to the Eisjoch restaurant and Schaufeljochbahn cable-car station, following the protective barriers and marker posts down the snow slopes of the Gaisskarferner glacier and rocks to the **Hildesheimer Hut**. About 4–5hr

At the Hildesheimer Hut, looking towards the Pfaffennieder

Stage 4 – Hoch Stubai Hut to Hildesheimer Hut via Bildstöckljoch

Main route
From the Warenkarscharte, descend east over dubious loose rock and steep, difficult ground of snow patches and rubble, with fixed cables in some places, to a large rock buttress with a red circle painted on it, then continue onto a final steep, bouldery snow slope to the **Warenkarferner glacier** proper. **Allow 1hr**

Once on the glacier proper, which is now more snow slope than glacier, traverse it first east, then more south-east below the Östlicher Daunkogel, taking care to keep around the 2950m contour, to a tiny col at the foot of the Stubaier Wildspitze's south-west ridge. From here you should be able to see the ski-tow machinery and other mechanisations located on the Bildstöckljoch.

Continue south-easterly across the Windacher Ferner glacier, following the line of the **ski-tow pylons**. Ascend what remains of the glacier to the **col at 3149m**, complete with restaurant and Schaufeljochbahn cable-car station and the junction of routes joining from the Dresdner Hut. **1hr**

To climb the Schaufelspitze
From the Schaufeljoch, a quick ascent can be made of the Schaufelspitze (3333m) – if you are happy to share the mountain with lots of tourists who are there to ascend to the 'Top of Tyrol' viewing platform. For the Schaufelspitze, walk past the restaurant and head for the Schaufeljochbahn cable-car station. Keep right, south of the col, and scramble up the south-west flank on a path of sorts to **Chapel Schaufeljoch**, then continue over loose rocks to the large cross on the summit of **Schaufelspitze**. **1hr**

Main route
Otherwise, from the broad col (3149m), descend south-east on the **Gaisskarferner glacier**, following the protective barriers and marker posts, where after 30min you will reach the rocks at 3058m. Enjoy the great views across the void to the Pfaffenferner glacier and Zuckerhütl. Continue south-east across the top of the ridge on Route 102, following the red waymarks, along the edge of the glacier overlooking the hut and a small lake. Descend the fixed cables and paved slabs to eventually arrive at the **Hildesheimer Hut**. **1hr**

Poor weather alternative route
Due to the difficult nature of descending from the Warenkarscharte an alternative route to the Hildesheimer Hut is slowly taking shape.

From the Hoch Stubai Hut, descend south, passing the **Seekarsee alpine tarn**, to a junction of paths at point 2493m. Head east, following the track roughly

Trekking in Austria's Stubai Alps

CAUTIONARY NOTES

The signpost at the Hoch Stubai Hut states 4½hr, which is possible; however, extreme care is needed in descending the steep, difficult ground from the Warenkarscharte onto the Warenkarferner glacier. The only real crevasse danger remains on the Hoch Stubai Hut's side of the Warenkarferner glacier, as the crevasses on the ski pistes have been removed by simply filling them in.

This is not a route to undertake in bad weather with poor visibility, when route finding would become difficult and problematic, similarly in rain, when the rocks below the Warenkarscharte turn into streams, making the whole experience unpleasant.

Alternative route to Warenkarscharte

Alternatively, from the hut proceed in the direction of the Warenkarseitenspitze to point **3114m** and descend into the gap, getting onto the Wütenkarferner glacier at the low point in the ridge at approximately 3100m. You will need to recce this route beforehand, but it will shave 45min off the standard time.

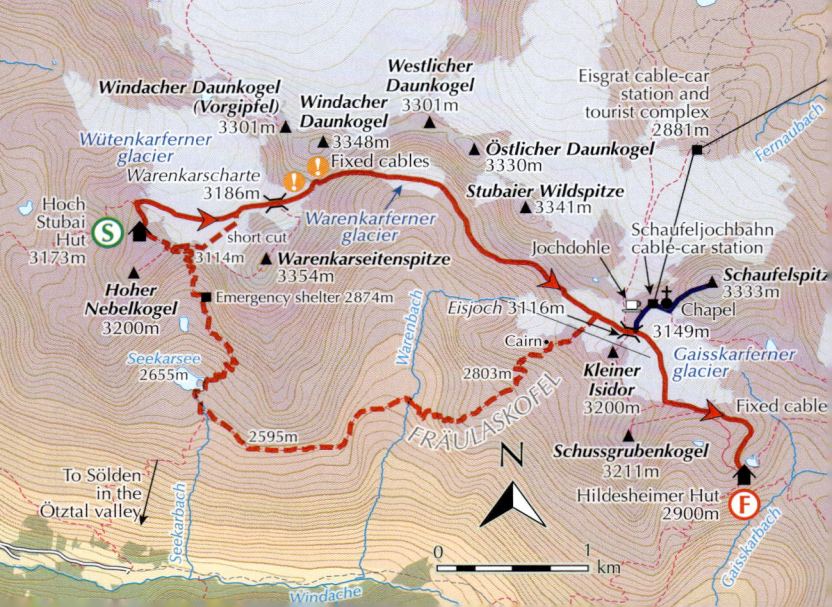

STAGE 4
Hoch Stubai Hut to Hildesheimer Hut via Bildstöckljoch

Start	Hoch Stubai Hut (3174m)
Standard time	5–6hr
Distance	5.9km
Ascent	345m
Descent	615m

This walk is characterised by a long descending traverse; however, before you set out, enquire with the Hüttenwirt if there have been any changes to the route. Although not as spectacular as the previous day's outing, it is still challenging and has some excellent views of the Ötztal mountains.

Presently, it seems that the newish route avoiding the Warenkarscharte is gaining favour, which is a shame as the original route across the Warenkarscharte is infinitely better. The original route needs traffic to remain open, otherwise it will become neglected and be abandoned in favour of the more southern roundabout route (see alternative poor-weather route).

The area around the Bildstöckljoch, Eisjoch and Isidornieder was at one time a splendid alpine glacial plateau. Unfortunately, it is now spoilt by the proliferation of ski-tow machinery installed in the early 1980s and, more recently, the restaurant with viewing platform that boasts of being the highest restaurant in the Tirol – all constructed to satisfy the appetites of skiers and much to the detriment of the mountain and its glaciers. Here you will be able to mix with day trippers from Innsbruck who come to enjoy a 'mountain experience'. The patron, Saint Isidor, whose name graces this once-magical place, would not have been amused. Some consolation is gained by enjoying the particularly fine view of the Wilder Pfaff and Zuckerhütl from the Schaufelspitze.

From the hut, return to the broad col below the hut to regain the **Wütenkarferner glacier**. Cross the glacier's upper snow slope, heading east first to the foot of the prominent buttress off the Warenkarseitenspitze, then turning more north-east, climbing gradually to the broad col of **Warenkarscharte** (3186m). **1½hr**

STAGE 5
Hildesheimer Hut to Müller Hut via Zuckerhütl

Start	Hildesheimer Hut (2900m)
Standard time	5–6hr
Distance	6.1km
Ascent	850m
Descent	600m
Grade	PD

This is the finest alpine promenade of the whole Glacier Tour. Not surprisingly, almost everyone staying at the Hildesheimer Hut will have in mind an ascent of the highest mountain in the Stubai Alps, the Zuckerhütl (3505m). The mountain is best seen from the Grosser Trögler on the Stubai Rucksack Route, where the meaning of its name, 'sugarloaf' in English, becomes apparent. Also apparent from this vantage point is the spectacular view of the Zuckerhütl's glaciers, the Sulzenauferner and Fernerstube.

The route comprises some first-class glacier scenery, particularly at the foot of the Pfaffenferner when passing the ice fall, then later at the Pfaffenjoch as the route opens up to the great expanse of the upper Sulzenauferner glacier, revealing the Zuckerhütl's north face. Unfortunately, due to global warming, the once-famous north face is in decline and is losing its snowy mantel bit by bit, such that it is now only possible to climb the Nordwand in winter.

Obviously, the views from the summit of the Zuckerhütl are spectacular, particularly of its close neighbours, the Sonklarspitze (3467m) with it sculpted east face, and the Triebenkarlasferner, which is superb. Similarly, the Wilder Pfaff, whose own summit reveals its steep, precipitous north face and the reason why it's not called the Wild Priest for nothing! Further afield are the ever-popular Wilder Freiger and Schrankogel, while on the horizon are the mountains of the Ötztal in the west, the Zillertal to the east and the Dolomites to the south.

The route is extremely popular and one to savour. To make the most of this excellent walk, be on your way early, no later than 07:00, before the sun has had a chance to soften up the snow slopes below the Pfaffenjoch and Pfaffensattel.

Zuckerhütl's summit cross

ESCAPE ROUTES

In very poor weather you have a number of options available to you:

1. In extremely bad weather, the correct decision is to descend from the Hildesheimer Hut to Sölden in the Ötztal valley. You will not come to any harm this way. From the hut, follow Route 102 on the (Peter) Aschenbrennerweg, named after the famous Austrian mountaineer, to Gaisstal, at the head of the Windachtal. Continue to follow Route 102, now renamed the Central Alpine Way, all the way down to the valley floor.

2. Alternatively, and provided the cable-car system is operational, you will need to ask the Hüttenwirt at the Hildesheimer Hut to telephone the cable-car station before setting out. Retrace your steps to the Bildstöckljoch and restaurant and take the cable car at the Schaufeljoch down to the Dresdner Hut.

3. Alternatively, when low cloud persists, proceed to the Siegerland Hut by the route described below, via the Gamsplatzl.

At the Pfaffenjoch

STAGE 5A
Hildesheimer Hut to Siegerland Hut (alternative bad-weather route)

Start	Hildesheimer Hut (2900m)
Standard time	3hr
Distance	5.3km
Ascent	345m
Descent	530m

The following two route descriptions – the Hildesheimer Hut to the Müller Hut via the Siegerland Hut (5A) and via Sonklarspitze (5B) – are provided as viable alternatives in bad weather and serve as a means of buying some time. They also provide that much-needed psychological change-of-scene morale booster if you have been confined to the Hildesheimer Hut for more than a day or so. While not on the glacier route proper, the crossing of the Sonklarspitze is a worthy alternative to the Zuckerhütl–Wilder Pfaff traverse.

Unfortunately, this is not an easy undertaking and should equally be avoided in poor weather. Therefore, you must decide whether to sit out the bad weather at the Hildesheimer Hut before attempting the Zuckerhütl or move on to the Siegerland Hut and gamble on the weather improving so you can cross the Sonklarspitze. In very poor weather, the right decision from either hut would be to descend to Sölden in the Ötztal valley.

However, should the weather forecast improve, making the route over the Sonklarspitze possible, you could spend a second night at the Müller Hut and then make a lightweight there-and-back expedition over the Wilder Pfaff to the Zuckerhütl in a single day.

Although a pleasant walk, the route to the Siegerland Hut lacks the excitement of the trek of the previous day. The route, however, has some points of merit, particularly the view of the west face of the Sonklarspitze and the remnants of the steep Triebenkarlasferner glacier, at one time a fine climb in its own right. As you arrive at the Siegerland Hut, you are rewarded with magnificent views across to the Ötztal and Austria's second-highest mountain, the Wildspitze (3770m).

STAGE 5A – HILDESHEIMER HUT TO SIEGERLAND HUT (ALTERNATIVE BAD-WEATHER ROUTE)

> **CAUTIONARY NOTES**
>
> As this route is likely to be undertaken in less than favourable weather, parties should endeavour to stick strictly to the path, to locate the bridge over the Gaiskarbach, and in descending the steep slopes of the Gamsfalle. The Gamsplatzl should also be avoided during storm conditions due to the possibility of lightning strikes.

From the hut, descend the steep, rocky outcrop of the Gaiskar, heading south-east along **Route 140** to the foot of the buttress. Cross the boulder field, crossing the **Gaiskarbach** stream on a rickety footbridge at point 2700m. Continue south up the flank of the Gaiskogel, via a series of zigzags over boulders and large blocks, to the **Gamsplatzl** (3019m), a small col at the foot of the Gaiskogel's north ridge. **1½hr** Across the void there are superb views to the Ötztal and, more closely, the west face of the Sonklarspitze.

Trekking in Austria's Stubai Alps

At the Gamsplatzl, looking towards the Stubaier Wildspitze, with the Hildesheimer Hut to the left of centre

From the col, descend south-east on the steep rock and scree of the Gamsfalle to immediately north of the **Triebenkarsee** at 2656m. The path then continues on easily in a south-east direction to the **Siegerland Hut**. **1½hr**

STAGE 5B
Siegerland Hut to Müller Hut via Sonklarspitze

Start	Siegerland Hut (2710m)
Standard time	5hr
Distance	4.5km
Ascent	775m
Descent	305m
Grade	F+
Note	For map, see Stage 5A

This is an excellent route and equally as challenging as the Zuckerhütl–Wilder Pfaff traverse.

Although the initial start is a disappointing trudge over scrappy glacial debris, once on the south-east ridge, the route gets going and interest abounds. First there is good scrambling, airy and exposed in places, providing excellent opportunities for action photos. The rock ridge then gives way to the Hohes Eis, which, as the name suggests, is often a snow crest, and although it is short, it is quite steep and spectacular.

The Sonklarspitze is more of a flat-top mountain, with a newish large summit cross that acts as a good navigational aid. The views are excellent in all directions, particularly of the Zuckerhütl, the Wilder Freiger and the mountains of South Tirol, especially Botzer. There is also a good opportunity to recce the route across the Übeltalferner glacier to the Müller Hut, and the route up the Wilder Freiger.

Parties who may be tempted to proceed along the north ridge to the Wilder Pfaff should note that the route is graded AD+ with pitches of III, although not sustained. The rock, however, is of Stubai quality and not very good. In descent it is possible to avoid most of the east ridge by getting onto the glacier higher up, around the 3350m contour. Two abseils will then usually get you across the offending Bergschrund.

Thereafter, the crossing of the Übeltalferner glacier, although crevassed, is quite straightforward and full of scenic interest, surrounded by high mountains.

This is a superb day among high mountains. You are advised to be on your way by 07:00 or earlier.

> ## CAUTIONARY NOTES
>
> Although the Sonklarspitze is regularly climbed from the Siegerland Hut, route marking using the customary cairns and rocks daubed with red paint is generally poor. This is first experienced in ascending the broad couloir of the Hohes Eis and then later in descending the east ridge onto the Übeltalferner glacier. Route finding will be further hindered in mist, when trying to locate the east ridge corridor from the Sonklarspitze summit.
>
> While crevasses are not normally a problem, the Bergschrund at the foot of the east ridge onto the Übeltalferner glacier can be difficult to cross in late season, by which time it is usually quite a large gaping hole.
>
> Overall, as previously noted, the Sonklarspitze is as serious an undertaking as the Zuckerhütl, with perhaps more general route-finding difficulties. It should therefore be avoided if the weather is generally poor.

From the back of the hut, ascend rough, broken ground, heading north-north-east, looking for cairns and marker posts as the route is not always obvious, to a **tiny lake** at 2800m.

The route continues north, over glacial debris of blocks and boulders, into a large broad couloir between the Scheiblehnwand and the south-west ridge of the Hohes Eis. Proceed up the couloir to the snowfield, route finding is not always obvious, continuing to gain height to reach the 3000m contour.

Hereabouts, the route turns east over boulders and slabs to the south-west ridge at **3017m**. **1½hr** Continue along the ridge, fixed cables in sections, which is very airy and exposed in places, until it comes to a natural end. Climb the ridge of the **Hohes Eis** (3388m), frequently snow covered in late season, keeping on the south side of the ridge to avoid the steep northern edge of the Triebenkarlasferner glacier. From the Hohes Eis, continue along the upper snow slopes, first east, then north, to point 3432m, past crevasses and onto the large flat-topped summit of **Sonklarspitze** (3467m), complete with large metal cross. **1½hr** Enjoy the excellent panoramic views.

Stage 5B – Siegerland Hut to Müller Hut via Sonklarspitze

From the summit, the Müller Hut and Becherhaus are both clearly visible across the Übeltalferner glacier. Descend the snow slopes south-east to the top of the east ridge; this is an ill-defined area where the north-east and south-east flanks converge. Descend difficult, steep, broken ground, which is grotty and protected in places with in-situ bolts, and continue to scramble down the rocks, keeping on the north side of the ridge where there are cairns in places, until the ridge comes to a natural end. Here proceed cautiously, again some bolts in place, until it is possible to get onto the upper edge of the **Übeltalferner glacier**. **1hr** You will need to negotiate a Bergschrund at the foot of the ridge, and a second one is usually found at 3250m. Thereafter, cross the glacier north-north-east, usually marked with poles, bypassing **crevasses** en route to the **Müller Hut**. **1hr**

Scenic views from the Sonklarspitze, looking across the Übeltalferner glacier to the Wilder Freiger

STAGE 6
Müller Hut to Nürnberger Hut via Wilder Freiger

Start	Müller Hut (3145m)
Standard time	4–5hr
Distance	6.8km
Ascent	330m
Descent	1200m
Grade	F+

CAUTIONARY NOTES

Because of the expanse of glaciers, warm air from the south can quickly condense into thick mist, making route finding particularly difficult on the Übeltalferner glacier and when descending from the summit to the Seescharte

In mist and after fresh snow has fallen, the route may not be so obvious. You should stick strictly to the route over the Signalgipfel and avoid the temptation to cut the corner off the Wilder Freiger's glacier, which suddenly steepens and leads into a labyrinth of crevasses.

The ascent of the south-west ridge is straightforward; however, the rock in places is suspect and needs to be handled with care. Similarly, some of the fixed cables are of dubious quality and best avoided.

For those ascending the mountain via the upper Übeltalferner glacier, the crux of the route will be in crossing the Bergschrund and climbing the steep rock couloir thereafter. This section of the route is subject to seasonal change and can vary dramatically from a straightforward snow slope to one of hard ice requiring good ice axe and cramponing techniques, followed by equally good rock-climbing skills. If in doubt proceed along the normal route via the Signalgipfel from the Becherhaus.

South-west ridge

From the hut, traverse the rocks adjacent to the hut to regain the **Übeltalferner glacier** at 3152m. Proceed east for a short distance, then head north-east, keeping close to the rocks of the south-west ridge to point 3228m. Either gain the south-west ridge here or continue up the glacier to point **3264m** before getting onto the ridge. Climb the ridge, which is rock in its entirety, pitches of II-III with

This superb day out amid fine alpine scenery is full of interest and challenge that is, perhaps, only eclipsed by the ascent of the Zuckerhutl. You have a choice of routes to climb the Wilder Freiger (3418m) from the Müller Hut.

The initial section of the route is mostly influenced by the extent of the Übeltalferner glacier and the immediate scenery into South Tirol, dominated by the multi-buttressed Botzer, a fine mountain in its own right. Parties will also be curious to see what is happening at the Becherhaus, the Müller Hut's close neighbour and previously the highest hut in the Stubai until it was forfeited to Italy after World War 1.

Once you reach the south-west ridge, the scenery opens up dramatically, as does the degree of exposure on both sides of the ridge, reinforcing the need to take care.

All this pales in comparison once you reach the beautiful snow-covered summit of the Wilder Freiger (3418m), for the Freiger is the epitome of the ideal mountain for most climbers, set as it is among the Stubai's largest glaciers, with perhaps the most extensive views in the Stubai.

As the regular route up the mountain from the Nürnberger Hut is straightforward, the Freiger is perhaps the most popular mountain in the Stubai Alps, with views across South Tirol as far south as the Dolomites and the Marmolada, the Queen of the Dolomites. In the west are the Ötztal mountains and other Stubai peaks, including the Zuckerhütl, the Wilde Leck and around to the Ruderhofspitze. To the east are the magnificent Zillertal and Venediger ranges, while on the northern horizon the limestone peaks of the Kalkkögel and Karwendel groups can be easily seen. Those with keen eyesight will be able to locate the Starkenburger Hut above Neustift.

As you descend from the summit, the scenery remains excellent; first, just north of the Gamsspitzl, there is a spectacular view of the Wilder Freiger and its attendant glacier. Somewhat lower, the col of the Seescharte, at the junction of routes from the Sulzenau Hut, provides a similar view of the Freiger but with the peaks of the Feuerstein dominating the scene. But equally important is the profusion of alpine flowers that grow around the col, particularly the vivid blue spring gentian. We are fortunate that spring comes late at this height.

some dubious fixed cables, to the summit of **Wilder Freiger** with its large wooden cross. **2hr**

Trekking in Austria's Stubai Alps

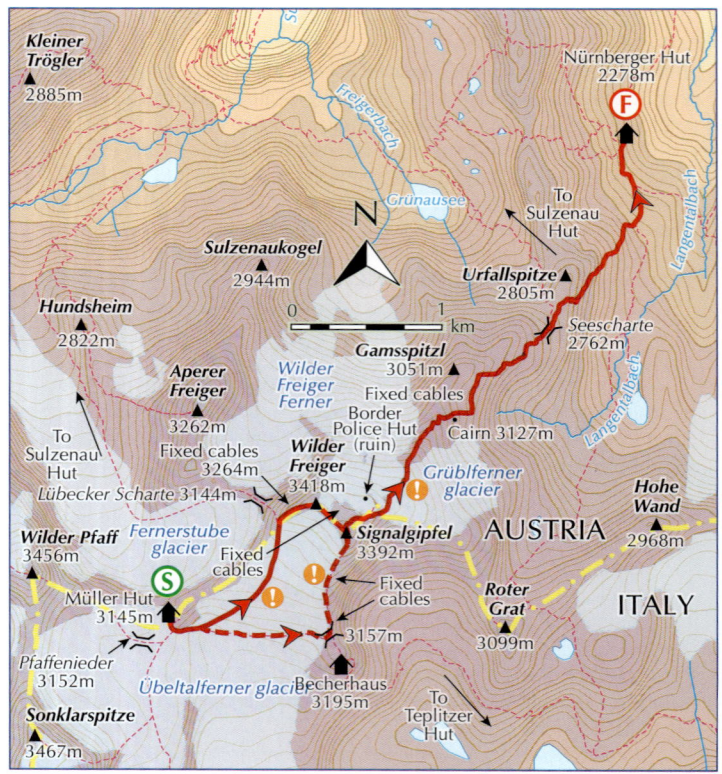

South-west flank

Get onto the Übeltalferner glacier, as previously described, and proceed around the foot of the hut, turning north towards the Freiger's south-west ridge. Continue up the glacier's right bank, heading north-east, keeping parallel to the south-west ridge, passing below point **3264m**. Make a slight detour east away from the south-west ridge until just right of the Wilder Freiger's summit, avoiding a bank of crevasses on the 3300m contour.

Continue up the glacier to the foot of an obvious couloir. Cross the Bergschrund and climb the steepish snow slope to its end, finally climbing up the

Stage 6 – Müller Hut to Nürnberger Hut via Wilder Freiger

ESCAPE ROUTES FROM THE MÜLLER HUT

Because of the remoteness of the hut, there are no easy routes down the mountain, and while both of the following routes are feasible, they do require reasonable visibility to be undertaken safely; otherwise, the safest option is to remain at the hut.

The easiest option is to decend to the Nürnberger Hut. From the Müller Hut, cross directly across the Übeltalferner glacier to the Becherhaus. If the weather remains poor, such as high wind, snow, rain or cloud, stay there; this is a great hut with a lot of history; see 'Hut directory'.

If it is just cloudy, climb the south ridge to the Signalgipfel col. At the Signalgipfel you should take a compass bearing to get you to the large cairn at the Gamsspitzl. Thereafter, the route to the Nürnberger Hut is well marked, even in bad weather (allow 5–6hr).

Alternatively, from the Becherhaus, descend to the Teplitzer or Grohmann huts in South Tirol. Once there you will be safe, although the trek back to Innsbruck and Austria via Sterzing and the Brenner Pass may prove a bit tedious.

Whatever you do, do not attempt to descend to the Sulzenau Hut via the Pffafennieder col and Fernerstube glacier as the col is very difficult, steep ground; it is extremely dangerous and best avoided – even in good weather.

Approaching the Wilder Freiger's summit ridge: note the Becherhaus

Descending easier ground from the summit of the Wilder Freiger, looking towards the peaks of the Feuerstein

Grade II-III rocks to the summit of **Wilder Freiger**. **2hr** Early in the season, this is usually a steep snow slope but come August it is more of a rock climb.

Alternatively, below point **3264m**, roughly on the 3150m contour, traverse the glacier south-east, heading for the Becherhaus. At the small **col** (3157m) below the hut, turn left, heading north, and climb the rocky ridge, fixed cables in place, to the Signalgipfel col on the Austrian–Italian border, and then scramble along the obvious ridge thereafter, fixed cables in place, to the summit of **Wilder Freiger**. **2hr**

Main route

From the summit cross, retrace your steps, descending south-east and keeping on the north side of the ridge to the **Signalgipfel** (3392m) with its unmistakable derelict border police hut. Continue north-east over broken ground, frequently snow covered, to point 3324m and the junction with the Wilder Freiger's east ridge. Get back onto the snow proper and descend north-east along the snow crest to point 3222m. Follow the obvious rock ridge to a large cairn at 3127m, south of the col of the Gamsspitzl (3051m). The views are splendid in all directions, especially of the Feuerstein mountains.

From the cairn, turn right and head east down the steep, rocky ridge, over broken ground, until it is possible to gain a large patch of permanent snow at its base. Get onto the snow and cross it, heading north, then exit onto the rocks via a series of ledges that are not easy to locate in poor weather; look for the usual daubs of red-and-white paint. Regain the rocks, following a good waymarked path, continuing north-east to the **Seescharte** (2762m), at the junction of routes to the Sulzenau Hut. Enjoy fabulous views of the Wilder Freiger Ferner glacier.

From the Seescharte, continue north-east over rocks and easy broken ground, always well marked, to the **Nürnberger Hut**. **2–3hr**

See also Stage 4B of the Stubai Rucksack Route: 'Nürnberger Hut to Sulzenau Hut via Wilder Freiger'.

STAGE 7
Nürnberger Hut to Ranalt

Start	Nürnberger Hut (2278m)
Standard time	2hr
Distance	5.9km
Ascent	Negligible
Descent	910m

After the rigours of the Glacier Tour, the demands of returning to the valley pale into insignificance.

From the hut, follow **Route 134** along an obvious trail, first over rocks, then through the forest, to emerge at the roadside in Ranalt with car park and convenient bus stop. **2hr**

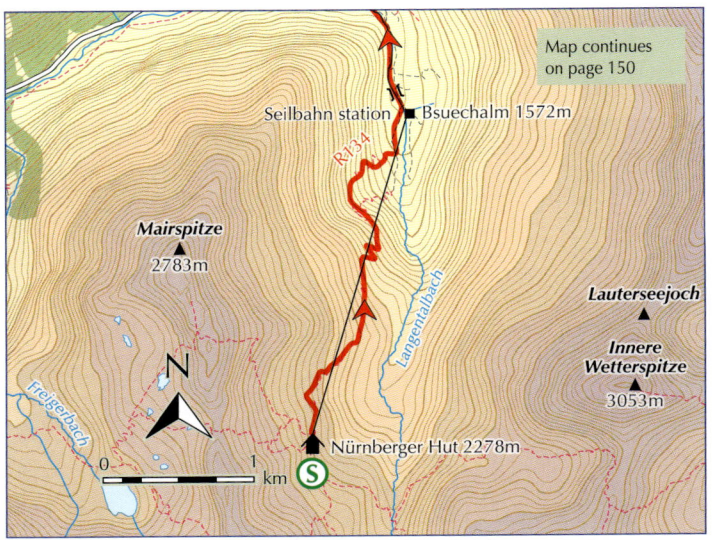

TREKKING IN AUSTRIA'S STUBAI ALPS

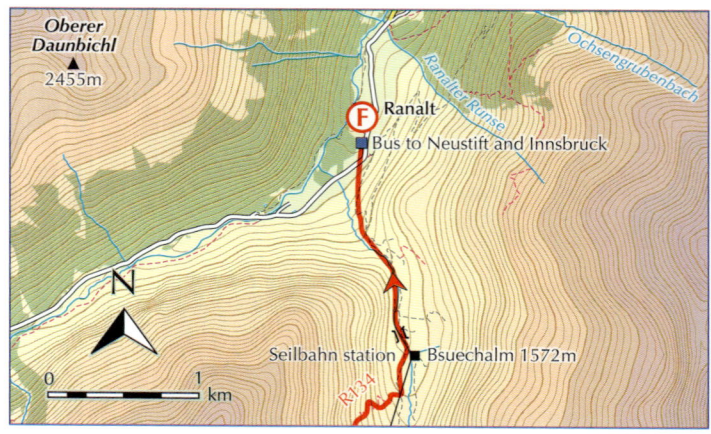

The bus times for Neustift and Innsbruck are as follows; the journey time to Innsbruck is about 1hr. Check at the Nürnberger Hut before departing for any changes to the timetable.

The bus departs from Mutterbergalm on the hour and arrives at the Nürnberger Hut bus stop 8min later, at 09:08 / 10:08 / 11:08.

At the Nürnberger Hut

TREK 2A
Stubai Glacier Tour: South Tirol extension

Start	Mieders (the extension leaves the main route at the Müller Hut)
Finish	Trins, Steinach am Brenner or Obernbergtal valley
Standard time	6 days (South Tirol extension); 11 days in total, including main route
Distance	36.4km/39.5km (South Tirol extension); 83.6km/86.7km in total, including main route
Ascent	2190m/2215m (South Tirol extension); 6735m/6760m in total, including main route
Descent	4120m/3805m (South Tirol extension); 6495m/6180m in total, including main route

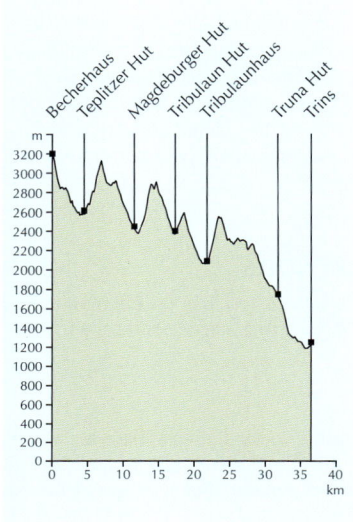

While the original Stubaier Höhenweg, the Glacier Tour, returned to Austria at the Müller Hut, this was at a time, during the 1970s, when the political situation between Austria and Italy in regard to South Tirol was dire. Most if not all of the huts along the border, including the Becherhaus, Teplitzer Hut and Magdeburger Hut, were occupied by the Italian Army's mountain troops, making it impossible to continue the tour through South Tirol, as all the huts were closed to visitors.

Fortunately, such tensions are long gone, but for the visiting mountaineer little has been known in the English-speaking world of the opportunity to extend the Glacier Tour through the mountains of South Tirol as far as the Brenner Pass.

For those of you who have the time to spare, the following extension makes a worthwhile tour, extending the Stubai Glacier Tour to link up with the Gschnitztaler Rundtour at the Magdeburger Hut.

STAGE 6
Becherhaus or Müller Hut to Teplitzer Hut

Start	Becherhaus (3195m); Müller Hut (3145m)
Standard time	4hr; 5hr from Müller Hut
Distance	4.6km; 6km from Müller Hut
Ascent	60m
Descent	630m
Grade	F+

This is a superb day out full of scenic interest, particularly early on in the day, with alpine panoramas across the huge and once-mighty Übeltalferner glacier towards the Sonklarspitze and the multi-faceted pyramid peak of Botzer. As you descend, it is worthwhile remembering that during the latter stages of World War 2, on 8 April 1945, 12 crew were lost when their American Air Force B24 Liberator bomber was shot out of the sky, crash-landing on the glacier. Debris was scattered far and wide, including one of its machine guns, which now resides at the Teplitzer Hut; see 'Hut directory'.

This is a fabulous day out in the mountains with few constraints. It doesn't come much better than this. Enjoy!

CAUTIONARY NOTES
Basically, there are none because this is the safest way off the mountain should the weather be dire. See Stubai Glacier Tour Stage 6 for escape routes from the Becherhaus.

From the Becherhaus, descend south on the rocky staircase path for around 200m, with fabulous views overlooking the Übeltalferner glacier and the fine, multi-faceted peak of Botzer, to the junction of paths at **3008m** indicating the way to the Müller Hut (signpost). **1hr**

Continue to descend the rocky, zigzagging trail, heading more east, to round the foot of the ridge coming down from the Becherhaus. From here on, traverse the wide-open slopes beneath the Freigerscharte in a looping arc, roughly on the

Approaching the Becherhaus

Wilder Freiger Signalgipfel

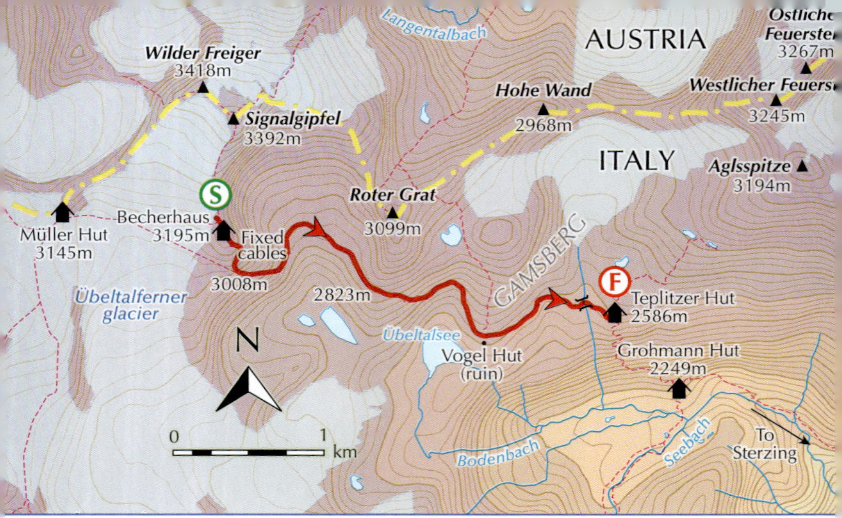

2820m contour, across old snow, rocks and boulders to gain the huge rock buttress of the Roter Grat at point **2823m**. **1hr**

Continue to traverse east across steep, rocky slopes, over difficult broken ground, descending a long rock staircase overlooking the Übeltalsee alpine lake (also known as the Vogelhüttensee) to the bottom of the ridge and the ruins of the old **Vogel Hut** (signpost for the Grohmann Hut). **1hr**

Round the foot of the south ridge of the Gaiswandspitz and start to reascend the broken ground and rocky slopes across the **Gamsberg** to the splendid **Teplitzer Hut**. **1hr**

The scenic Müller Hut from the Becherhaus, with the Zuckerhütl (left) and the Wilder Pfaff (centre)

STAGE 7
Teplitzer Hut to Magdeburger Hut

Start	Teplitzer Hut (2586m)
Standard time	6–7hr
Distance	7.0km
Ascent	615m
Descent	775m

If you want to be alone in the mountains, this is a route to savour as this area is not well frequented, despite providing some superb scenery and a day out full of challenge. While the standard time between the huts is given as 5hr, 6–7hr is more realistic.

The early challenges of the day are in making sure you keep to the trail, as the route up to the Magdeburger Scharte is not always obvious. From the col, the scenery is absolutely stunning, looking across the Übeltalferner glacier towards the Sonklarspitze. Here you can ponder the fate of the young American aircrew blown out of the sky, their lives lost just a few days before the end of the World War 2 in April 1945.

Thereafter, the next challenge is to find the Hoachwand terrace-corridor and the very steep, exposed traverse that leads to the Südliche Stubenscharte. From here, across the void, you can try to locate the Bremer Scharte and the route to the Bremer Hut, as well as the convergence of this route with the Gschnitztaler Rundtour. Whether you follow the Stubenscharte with its tantalising ridge or go down the snow slope, depending on the time of day, they both add-up to a very good mountaineering experience even on the final descent to the Magdeburger Hut.

From the hut, head north over rocky ground where after around 200+m the track of sorts turns right, heading east. If you end up at the alpine tarn, you will have gone too far and will need to retrace your steps to get back on track. Make the turn, climbing steadily over rocky ground to point **2676m**, then turn and head north-east, climbing through a gully to access the ridge of the Hoher Trog, a high, narrow trough. **1hr**

At point **2830m**, overlooking two small lakes, turn right and head south-east around the edge of the pond, climbing a steep, rocky path to the crest of a small

> ## CAUTIONARY NOTES
>
> Sadly, this is a fine-weather route and there is no alternative; the other options in poor-weather conditions are to stay put at the splendid Teplitzer Hut, descend to the Grohmann Hut just 1hr away or abandon the tour altogether, descending to Sterzing then taking the train across the Brenner Pass back into Austria and eventually to Innsbruck.
>
> However, given *Kaiserwetter* (good weather), the main constraint early in the day is one of route finding to the ponds at the Hoher Trog trough. Thereafter, the crossing from point 2991m to the Magdeburger Scharte, traversing old hard-packed snow, is very steep and exposed. Participants who are not totally confident of their snow skills are advised to tackle up and rope up here rather than waiting until they reach the col, as a fall on the snow would be difficult to stop.
>
> The other difficulty is in finding the Hoachwand terrace-corridor. If you miss the exit point off the glacier, easy to do in misty conditions, you will know when you have gone too far, as the glacier starts to descend more steeply and drops away in front of you. In this instance, turn around and return, keeping close to the rocks.
>
> You will know when you have found the exit point, as there is a fairly level platform among the rocks, a good indicator that you are in the right location. (Ignore the obvious steel cables that head north, as these are very old and extremely dangerous!) Turn right and follow the more intact cables to the Stubenscharte and, thereafter, the easier trail down the snow and rocky path to the hut.

ridge at point **2991m** overlooking remnants of the Hangender Ferner glacier. Cross the steep slope ahead, which is frequently snow covered, to the obvious col and gap that is the **Magdeburger Scharte** (3105m). 1½hr The col marks the highest point on the route, as well as providing great panoramas over the Übeltalferner glacier and across the void to the Sonklarspitze.

Tackle up and get onto the **Feuersteinferner glacier**. While what remains of the glacier is usually hard-packed snow and dead-ice, and is generally crevasse-free, it remains best practice and common sense to rope up for the short glacier crossing, as an unroped fall would be difficult to stop.

From the col, head north-east, descending gradually across the glacier towards a fairly level section, in the direction of the Schneespitze. Once below the peak, progress more slowly towards the rocks, looking for a large spot of red paint that indicates the way off the glacier, to access the Hoachwand

STAGE 7 – TEPLITZER HUT TO MAGDEBURGER HUT

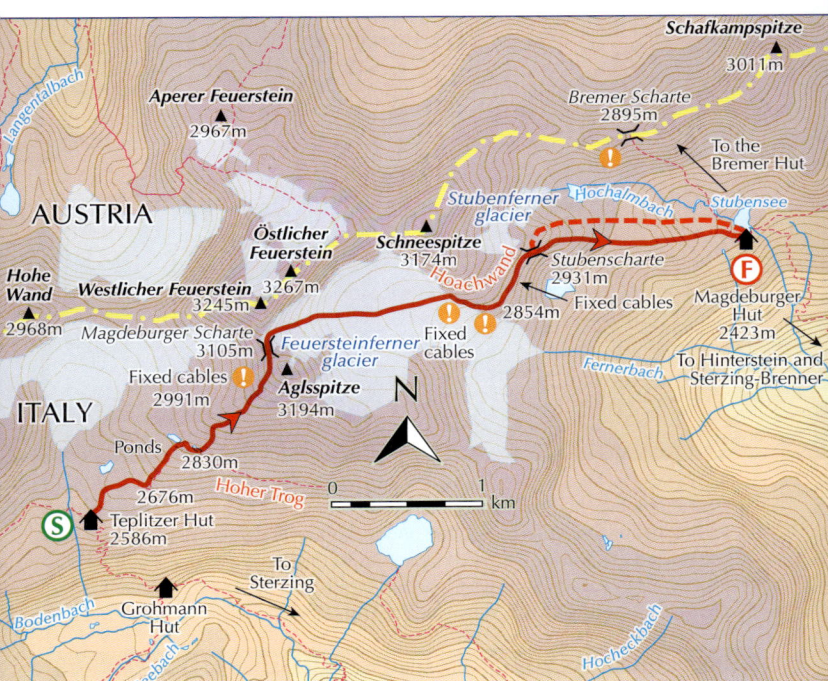

terrace-corridor. Get off the glacier and onto the rocks. Be sure to access the **Hoachwand terrace** here, as there are some tantalising old wire cables that will take you in the wrong direction and onto the old route across the more difficult Alte Stubenscharte. **1½hr**

Once on the terrace, make sure you head eastwards to an obvious rock corner at point **2854m**. From here on, the route is more obvious. Follow a line of fixed cables along a very exposed rocky ledge. This section was hacked out of the rocks when the old route over the Alte Stubenscharte became difficult and dangerous and was abandoned in favour of the established **Südliche Stubenscharte** (2931m). **1hr**

At the col, you have a choice, although this will depend on the time and the weather. If you have time and the weather is good, you can proceed and scramble along the obvious rocky ridge, with fixed cables on the tricky sections, to its base.

Cloud inversion over the Übeltal valley, en route from Becher Haus to the Teplitzer Hut

The alternative, and quicker, option is to get onto the old snow of the shrinking and retreating **Stubenferner glacier** and make a swift parallel descent with the ridge eastward, overlooking the two alpine tarns, one large and one small, to the foot of the ridge at a small gap where both routes converge. **1hr** From here, follow the obvious rocky path to the **Magdeburger Hut**. **½hr**

THE STUBAI GLACIER TOUR AND SOUTH TIROL EXTENSION

From the Magdeburger Hut, the tour continues into the limestone region of the stunning Tribulaun mountains, following the route descriptions for the Gschnitztaler Rundtour. It first heads to either the Italian or Austrian Tribulaun Huts, both highly recommended, then to either the Truna Hut overlooking the Gschnitztal valley or to the picturesque village of Obernberg, both ending at the small town of Steinach am Brenner on the Brenner Pass road, followed by the regional train to Innsbruck.

Incorporating the South Tirol Extension and the Gschnitztaler Rundtour with the Stubai Glacier Tour makes a brilliant and highly recommended mountaineering tour that embraces some of the best scenery there is, taking in some of the least visited mountains and huts of the Stubai Alps.

GSCHNITZTALER RUNDTOUR

A portrait of Serles from above Maria Waldrast (Stage 1A)

TREK 3
Gschnitztaler Rundtour

Start	Trins
Finish	Trins or Steinach am Brenner
Standard time	7 days
Distance	66.7km (69.8km to Steinbach am Brenner)
Ascent	5250m (5275m to Steinbach am Brenner)
Descent	5260m (4945m to Steinbach am Brenner)

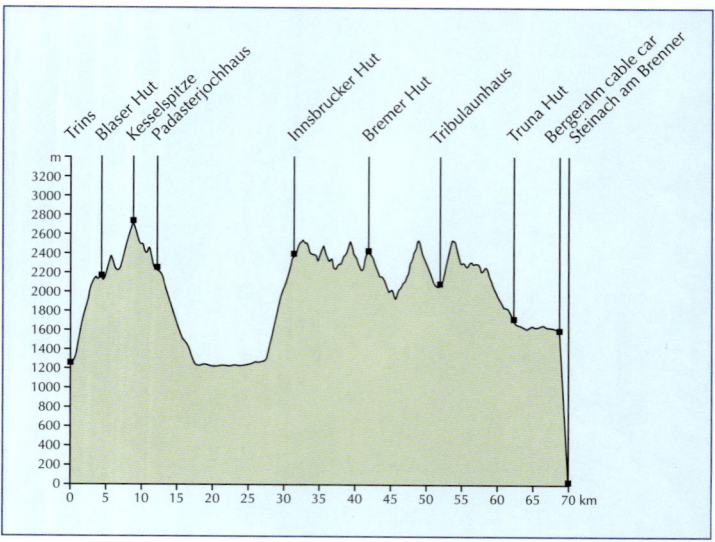

Situated south-west of the old Austrian city of Innsbruck, in the province of Tirol, the Gschnitztal is a lateral valley of the Wipptal valley in the Stubai Alps. The area has no access difficulties and Steinach am Brenner can be easily reached by a regular train service from Innsbruck in less than an hour, as it is located on the old Brenner Pass road and the main route between Austria and Italy.

TREK 3 – GSCHNITZTALER RUNDTOUR

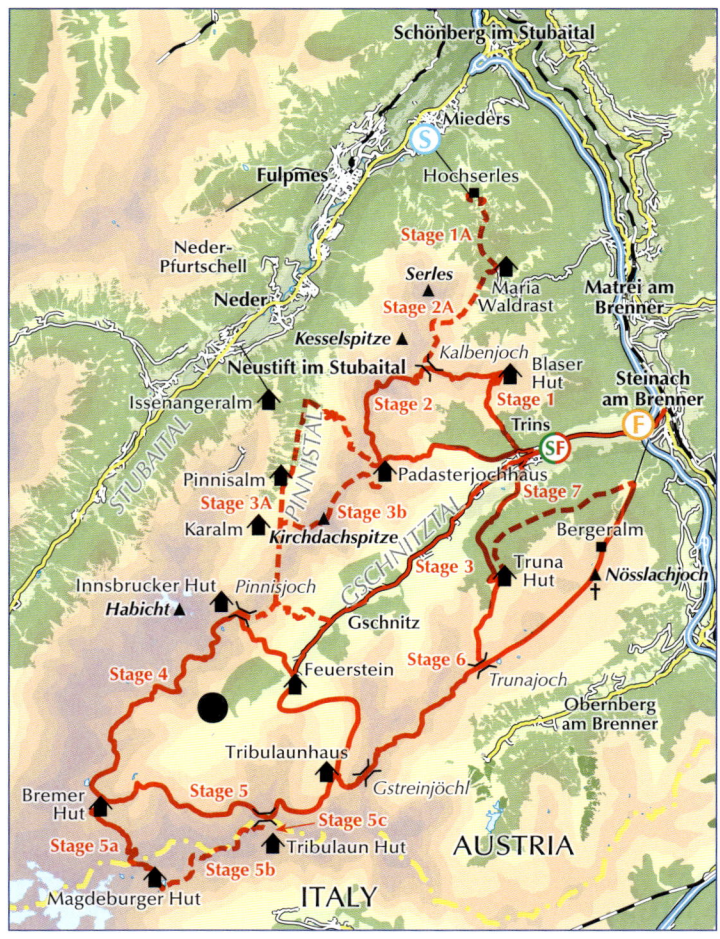

Generally speaking, the Gschnitztaler Rundtour would be more aptly described as an exploration of the peaks of the Serleskamm and the Tribulaun group of mountains. The Serleskamm ridge of mountains – Serles, Kesselspitze and Kirchdachspitze

– runs parallel with the main Stubaital valley and the Tribulaun mountains, following the national border with Italy and the area known as South Tirol, which refers to the Austrian territory that was annexed to Italy after World War 1.

The Gschnitztal valley, with its motto 'Mighty Mountains-Gentle Valleys', has achieved the status of Bergsteigerdörfer (mountaineering villages), which means that unlike the Stubaital with its ongoing tourist development, especially in the mountains adjacent to the Dresdner Hut, the Schaufelspitze and the Daunkogel, the Gschnitztal and villages of Trins, Gschnitz and Feuerstein have protected status. Helga Beermeister from Wipptal's tourist information office explains below:

BERGSTEIGERDÖRF GSCHNITZTAL

The western side valley of the Wipptal, with the villages of Trins and Gschnitz, was able to fulfil the strict criteria of the Alpine Association's Mountaineering Villages and was selected to join the international network in November 2018. The municipalities have thus decided to work together with the Alpine Association towards non-technical, authentic and environmentally friendly mountain tourism.

With its seven 3000m peaks, challenging mountain and ski tours in the Stubai Alps, the Gschnitztal hut tour and several via ferratas, the Gschnitztal valley with its majestic valley head offers the best conditions for mountaineers. The side valley of the Wipptal has managed to preserve its extraordinary biodiversity and unspoilt scenic gems. The municipalities of Trins and Gschnitz view the Mountaineering Villages status as an opportunity to preserve their authentic character and emphasise the valley's alpine potential.

The official admission took place with the accession ceremony on 5 May 2019 in Trins, at which the municipalities committed themselves to the philosophy of the Alpine Association's Mountaineering Villages initiative. Alongside St Jodok with the Schmirn and Vals valleys, which has been a Mountaineering Village since 2012, the Gschnitztal will be the second valley to achieve Mountaineering Villages status in the Wipptal valley tourism region. This confirms that the Wipptal valley will strive for and further develop natural, sustainable mountain tourism in its unspoilt mountain valleys.

For further information, see www.wipptal.at/bergsteigerdoerfer

TREK 3 – GSCHNITZTALER RUNDTOUR

The Gschnitztaler Rundtour came into being around the time of the Millennium and was promoted as a quieter, less frequented alternative to the Stubai Rucksack Route. The tour starts from the village of Trins and heads to the Blaser Hut, followed by the Padasterjoch, Innsbrucker, Bremer, Tribulaun and Truna huts, finishing back at Trins seven days later having embraced along the way some of the best limestone mountain scenery in the Stubai and Eastern Alps.

Technically, the Gschnitztaler Rundtour, like the Stubai Rucksack Route, is a glacier-free tour that does not require participants to carry mountaineering gear, such as ice axe, crampons and rope. However, those undertaking the tour should note that the route is at the top end of seriousness in terms of Alpine walking and involves all sorts of paths; some are very steep and exposed and quite a few are fitted with fixed cables to aid stability and security of passage.

The tour can also be undertaken as a part extension of the Stubai Rucksack Route by visiting the monastery inn of Klostergasthof Maria Waldrast to climb the majestic peak of Serles, known locally as King Serles.

The Gschnitztaler Rundtour is a brilliant tour in a little-known area of the Tirol. If you want a quiet mountain adventure, this is one to savour!

Route summary
- Stage 1 Trins to Blaser Hut
- Stage 2 Blaser Hut to Padasterjochhaus

Alternatively
- Stage 1A Mieders to Maria Waldrast Monastery
- Excursions from Maria Waldrast Monastery
  - Ascent of Serles
  - Ascent of Lämpermahdspitze
- Stage 2A Maria Waldrast Monastery to Padasterjochhaus

Main route continues
- Excursions from Padasterjochhaus
  - Ascent of Kirchdachspitze
- Stage 3 Padasterjochhaus to Innsbrucker Hut via Trins and Gasthof Feuerstein
- Stage 3A Padasterjochhaus to Innsbrucker Hut via Hammerscharte
- Stage 3B Padasterjochhaus to Innsbrucker Hut via Padasterjoch, Silbersattel and Kirchdachspitze
- Stage 4 Innsbrucker to Bremer Hut
- Stage 5 Bremer Hut to Austrian Tribulaunhaus
- Stage 5A Bremer Hut to Magdeburger Hut
- Stage 5B Magdeburger Hut to Italian Tribulaun Hut
- Stage 5C Italian Tribulaun Hut to Austrian Tribulaunhaus via Sandesjöchl

Trekking in Austria's Stubai Alps

- Stage 6 Austrian Tribulaunhaus to Truna Hut via Gstreinjöchl
- Stage 7 Truna Hut to Trins or Steinach am Brenner

Getting to the start

From the main railway station in Innsbruck, get the regional train to Steinach am Brenner. Once in Steinach, simply cross over the platform and exit the railway station for the bus stop, and get the regional 4146 Postbus to Gasthof Feuerstein, getting off the bus in the pretty village of Trins at the *Gemeindeamt* (town council offices). Bus times: 09:10 / 11:40 / 12:42.

Participants who decide to stick with the original route of the Gschnitztaler Rundtour, or who have limited time, should note that they will forfeit the opportunity to climb Serles, which is perhaps the most important peak along the Serleskamm ridge.

Getting to the alternative start

From the main railway station in Innsbruck, get on the Stubaital Mutterbergalm regular bus service 590 from Stand B, getting off the bus in the village of Mieders at the Mieders–Serles cable-car station.

The journey to Mieders takes about 20min and leaves Innsbruck bus station, next to the main railway station, from Stand B at 09:05 / 09:35 / 10:05 / 10:35 / 11:05 / 11:35 / 12:05, similarly timed throughout the afternoon until 17:00.

Approaching the Sandesjöchl, with Habicht in the background

STAGE 1
Trins to Blaser Hut

Start	Trins (1233m)
Standard time	About 2½–3hr
Distance	4.4km
Ascent	1005m
Descent	45m

In the centre of Trins, look out for the signpost pointing to the right, uphill and north, to the Blaser Hut. Walk through the quaint streets for less than 200m to a a signpost pointing the way uphill, north, on **Route 31** for the Blaser Hut. Follow this through scenic woodland and forest until it reaches the end of the forest service road at Zwieselmahder, roughly on the 2000m contour.

From here on, the trail is fairly obvious, passing through more-open countryside and high alpine pasture to the pleasantly located **Blaser Hut**. **About 2½–3hr**

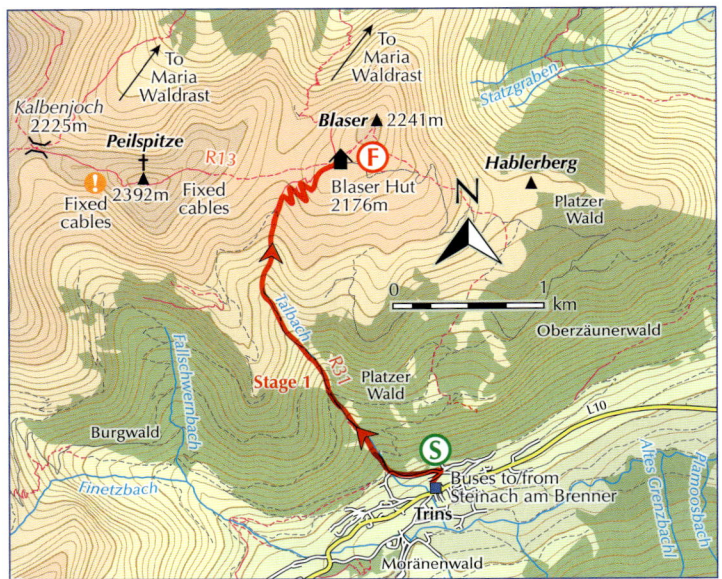

STAGE 2
Blaser Hut to Padasterjochhaus

Start	Blaser Hut (2176m)
Standard time	6hr; 6–7hr via Kesselspitze
Distance	7.8km
Ascent	845m
Descent	790m

Set amid chocolate-box alpine scenery of jagged peaks, lush alpine meadows and ubiquitous pine forest, this lovely walk is topped off with one of the very best huts in the region. Enjoy!

CAUTIONARY NOTES

While the day is one of gentler alpine walking, it does involve quite a lot of uphill and should not be underestimated. Before setting out on the first option, remember to telephone the hut to advise them that you are on your way and, if possible, arrange to be met once you reach the junction with the forest road; this way, for a small fee, your rucksacks can be transported to the hut while you enjoy the forest and the scenery.

At the Blaser Hut

From the hut, head west on **Route 13** across high alpine pasture in the general direction of the Peilspitze (2392m). After half a kilometre the route steepens considerably before making the final traverse over rocks to the summit of **Peilspitze** (2392m) with its large summit cross. **1hr** Brilliant views stretch towards Serles and the Kesselspitze.

From the summit, descend the Peilspitze's west ridge over steep, broken rocky ground, aided by fixed cables and a ladder, until the ground gradually eases before the **Kalbenjoch** (2225m) and the junction with various trails, including our continuation to the Padasterjochhaus (signpost). **1hr**

At the Kalbenjoch you have a choice of routes, which will be mainly dictated by the weather.

The first and easiest option is to descend to the forest service road and follow it to the hut or, second, take the high-level route that heads west over the open rocky ground of the Kugelwand and onto the fine summit of the Kesselspitze (2728m). Thereafter, the route heads south on the obvious rocky path, difficult and exposed in places, over the Roter Kopf (2526m), bypassing the summit of the Wasenwand (2563m), to end the day at the wonderful Padasterjochhaus (2232m).

CAUTIONARY NOTES

The Kesselspitze is definitely not a place to be in poor weather and should definitely be avoided in stormy weather. Being the highest peak around, it becomes a very effective lightning conductor. In wind, rain or cloud, it's best to be cautious and take the low-level forest route from the Kalbenjoch to the Padasterjochhaus.

Forest route

From the **Kalbenjoch**, so named for the many cows that graze there, head south, descending steeply over grassy slopes on Route 53 through the open meadows of the Falschwernalm, turning more south-east until the route joins the forest service road at **Burgwald** (1479). **2hr**

Now turn west and follow the forest service road as it climbs steadily via numerous hairpin bends to eventually reach the splendid **Padasterjochhaus**. **2hr** Take in the brilliant views of the Gschnitztal valley and across the void to the fabulous mountains of the Zillertal Alps, where the Olperer is easily seen. The mountains you are overlooking were much loved by Emperor Maximillian and other gentry when hunting. They were also used as the setting for the film *The Last Valley*, starring Michael Caine and Omar Sharif.

Alternative route via the Kesselspitze (2728m)

This route has been closed in recent years due to a rockfall but is once again open to the mountain wanderer. The route is infinitely more enjoyable and embraces

STAGE 2 – BLASER HUT TO PADASTERJOCHHAUS

some fabulous limestone scenery through very mountainous terrain. Allow 4hr from the Kalbenjoch.

It offers a good day of alpine scenery as you traverse some very interesting, much-neglected peaks, all complemented by colourful high alpine meadows and the ubiquitous pine forest, finally topped off by one of the very best huts in the region.

However, before venturing out, make enquiries at both huts to ensure the route is possible and if the weather is looking dubious, keep to the safer, lower forest route as previously described.

From Kalbenjoch, head south-west over the grassy slopes around the open couloir, heading for the rocks and ridge of the Kugelwand. Ascend steep, rocky scree slopes, zigzagging west to a col with a signpost at 2450m. **1hr** From here the views are excellent across the whole of the Stubaital valley and the snow-covered peaks of the Alpeiner above the Franz Senn Hut.

Continue south-west up the steep, rocky slopes of the north-east ridge of the **Kesselspitze** to eventually reach the large summit cross. **1hr** The scenery from the summit is fabulous.

From the summit, with the track now more obvious, descend south-west along the ridge to point 2450m and the junction with Route 7 on the Kesselmahd coming up from the village of Kampl in the Stubaital valley.

Continue south over easy broken ground and traverse the head of the **Roter Kopf** (2526m). After 1km the trail breaks off left and veers south-east to contour around the rocky flank of the **Wasenwand** (2563m), aided by fixed cables, heading for and crossing a small spur.

With the hut now in sight, descend more steeply, zigzagging over steep, broken ground of scree and boulders until the slope finally relents a few hundred metres from the **Padasterjochhaus**. **2hr**

Panorama from the Peilspitze, looking across the void to the Serleskamm ridge

STAGE 1A
Mieders to Maria Waldrast Monastery

Start	Mieders (952m)
Standard time	1+hr from the Hochserles cable-car station (1605m); 1+hr following the forest trail; 2+hr via Waldraster Jöchl
Distance	3.1km
Ascent	160m
Descent	140m

Any of the routes described are scenically rewarding; they are relaxing and full of interest, with lots of fleeting glimpses of 'King Serles' and later, at Maria Waldrast Monastery, distant views of the Olperer and the peaks of the Zillertal Alps.

CAUTIONARY NOTES

Be mindful of the various route signs, as the area around the Waldraster Jöchl has myriad roads and trails that are heavily used in winter for cross-country skiing.

From Mieders, take the cable car to **Hochserles**. For the shortest route to the monastery, from Hochserles cable-car station, turn right and proceed downhill, following the service road past the **children's adventure park** until you reach a junction of service roads (signpost). ¼hr

Turn right and follow the forest road in an anti-clockwise direction around the hillside of Waldraster Jöchl. After about 20min you will pass the spring of the Golden Well, the Geldenbrunnen, then after a similar distance you will come to a road junction that leads off to the right, downhill to the village of Fulpmes (signpost).

Hereafter, continue to follow the forest service road/track that climbs steadily, passing several small chapels depicting the Stations of the Cross story. When you reach the top of a rise **(1689m)**, you will get a wonderful view of the church and the other fine buildings that make up the monastery. As you approach the **Maria Walrast Monastery**, you will pass the Marienbrunnen well and fountain on the right, famed for its healing powers and medicinal qualities, and a signpost

STAGE 1A – MIEDERS TO MARIA WALDRAST MONASTERY

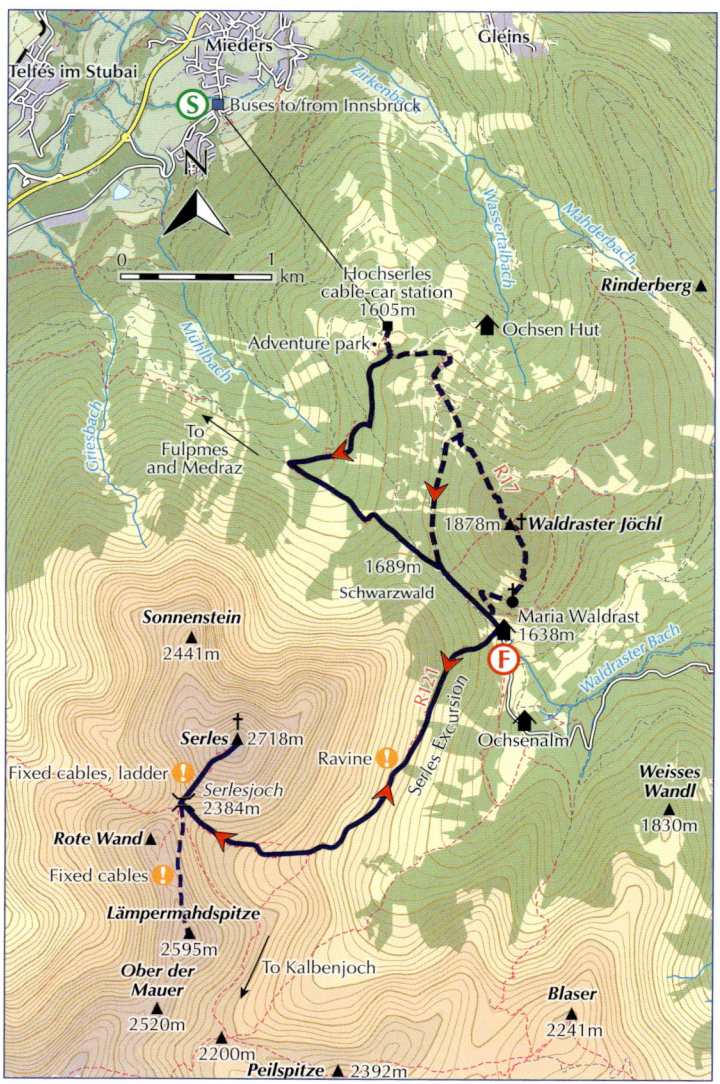

indicating the way to Serles. To the left is the entrance to the chapel and ahead is the entrance to the Klostergasthof, with its sun terrace and magnificent views over the Gschnitztal valley and across the void towards the adjacent peak of Blaser. In the 15th century, this was the favourite hunting ground of Emperor Maximillian I; more recently, it was the location for the filming of *The Last Valley*, which stars Omar Sharif and Michael Caine in the roles of medieval knights. **About 1hr from Hochserles** (depending on how long you spend admiring the scenery along the way.)

Alternative route
Alternatively, from the signboard at Hochserles, turn left and head uphill for a short distance, then follow the waymarked forest trail until it descends to meet the service road. **¼hr**

Alternative main route
At the service road, turn left, following signs for the Ochsen Hut (1582m). Follow this for a short distance until just before the hut where the track heads uphill to the right (signpost).

Follow the zigzag trail through the forest until you reach a clearing (signpost). **½hr**

Here you have a choice of routes: one long and one short. If your intention on arrival at Maria Waldrast is to climb Serles, then the best option would be to turn right and take the shorter route to the monastery to give you more time on this impressive mountain. If your intention is to simply make your way to the monastery for an overnight stay, then the ascent through the forest to the panoramic viewpoint of Waldraster Jöchl (Gleinser Jöchl) (1878m) is recommended. Of course, if it's raining then your route choice is obvious and simple: to get out of the rain by the shortest route.

STAGE 1A – MIEDERS TO MARIA WALDRAST MONASTERY

Alternative short route
For the short route, at the signpost ½**hr**, take the right-hand broad forest path, climbing steadily through the forest until the track descends to meet the forest service road. At the road junction, turn left, uphill, and follow this to its natural conclusion at the magnificent **Maria Waldrast complex**. 1¼**hr**

Alternative longer route
For those who wish to take the longer, more scenic route. At the signpost ½**hr**, head uphill on **Route 17**, signposted for Waldraster Jöchl.

Follow this, climbing steadily along the forest trail, with several zigzags here and there, crossing a number of subsidiary forest service roads until you reach the little summit of **Waldraster Jöchl**, complete with park-bench-type seats, a large wooden crucifix with a logbook and an absolutely stunning view of Serles. This is a brilliant place to stop for a very leisurely break. ½**hr**

Prior to reaching the top, you will have passed a signpost for Maria Waldrast. Reluctantly dragging yourself away from this little summit, return to the signpost and pick up the forest trail once more, now heading south through the forest, passing pretty glades with woodland log cabins. After about 30min you will drop down to the little forest **chapel** (*Kappelle*), where the carving of the Virgin Mary was found in the 13th century. Stay here a while for it's a delightful place: a simple one-room chapel complete with a colourful information flip board outside that tells the story of Maria Waldrast. ½**hr**

Continue as before, descending through the forest which gradually gives you fleeting glimpses of the monastery from high above. Eventually, the forest trail relents to meet the service road just above the monastery from where you can proceed more leisurely to conclude the journey at **Maria Waldrast**. ¾**hr. Allow 2¼ total** (longer if you want to spend time at the chapel)

EXCURSION
Ascent of Serles (2718m)

Start	Maria Waldrast Monastery (1638m)
Standard time	3hr (+2½hr for descent)
Distance	4.0km (+4.0km for descent)
Ascent	1075m
Descent	1075m
Grade	F
Note	For map, see Stage 1A

Also known as Waldrastspitze – due to its proximity to the monastery – King Serles and the Tyrolean Altar, Serles is a particularly fine symmetrical mountain with a conical summit that can clearly be seen from Innsbruck.

Pronounced Ser-less, the mountain was first climbed in the 16th century by a man named Ernstinger, who was probably working on the construction of the monastery at the time. Considering the era, this was a very bold ascent by Erstinger.

This is a fine excursion up a justifiably popular mountain, although it is a little short in duration. Not surprisingly, the views from the summit are superb in all directions, but it will be the Kirchdachspitze and the Habicht that will hold your attention as you gaze across this range of jagged limestone peaks to the snow-capped peaks of the central Stubai Alps. Those with exceptional eyesight should be able to locate the Starkenburger Hut, far away across the void towards the Kalkkögel.

From the monastery, head up the road, past the entrance to the chapel on the right. Almost opposite on the left is the Marienbrunnen well and fountain and a signpost pointing the way to Serles.

Follow the marked track up through the forest, climbing steadily on **Route 121** across the southern flank of the mountain, heading towards the Serlesjoch, which overlooks the fine pastoral valley above Ochsenalm. This area was well frequented by Emperor Maximillian and other gentry when hunting; it was also used as the filming location for *The Last Valley*, which starred Omar Sharif and Michael Caine as medieval knights looking for a place to spend the winter.

Leaving behind dwarf pine trees and alpine rose rhododendron bushes, the route turns west and ascends steeper ground over limestone scree, contouring around a steep, washed-out gully-type **ravine** that demands quite a bit of care to

Pleasant alpine walking approaching the Kalbenjoch, with Serles and Serlesjoch in the background

CAUTIONARY NOTES

First, take care while traversing the washed-out gully-type ravine, as the gravel stone path is very narrow and the adjacent ground quite steep; participants should stay close together for moral support while making good use of those trekking poles.

Second, during the final hour of the ascent, after you have climbed the short ladder, the ground is very exposed and steep, mostly over scree, until you reach the final rock barrier, which is very steep. In ascent this is not so much of a problem, but in descent it is more significant and demands more than a reasonable amount of care, as the ground is always dropping away from you.

Note that the route should be avoided when cloud covered because of the above difficulties, and definitely avoided in the wet and after rain, as the upper scree slopes run with water, and as Serles is the biggest mountain around, it also acts as a very good lightning conductor.

negotiate before giving way to slightly easier ground and a track leading to the **Serlesjoch** (2384m). **2hr**

From the col, scramble up the steep rock and scree slope, heading north-east, where after a short distance you will reach a 5–6m-high ladder with attendant fixed cables. Climb these, then follow the broken, rocky trail over scree and boulders, zigzagging to and fro, to reach Serles' summit mantel. Climb through the rock barrier – very exposed – to the summit of **Serles** (2718m) with its large cross, which overlooks the whole of Innsbruck, the Inn valley and the Brenner Pass. **1hr**

In descent, return by the same route. It's very exposed as the ground is always dropping away from you until you reach the ladder back to the col. Thereafter, the ground becomes easier and eventually leads to **Maria Waldrast**. Allow **2½hr**

EXCURSION
Ascent of Lämpermahdspitze (2595m)

Start	Serlesjoch (2384m)
Standard time	2hr (+1hr for descent)
Distance	1.0km (+1.0km for descent)
Ascent	210m
Descent	210m
Note	For map, see Stage 1A

As mentioned, the ascent of Serles is quite short in duration and adding an ascent of the neighbouring Lämpermahdspitze will help to fill the day.

From Serlesjoch, head south across the scree slope, hugging the rocks and cliff face of the **Rote Wand** on the right, passing a cave with an old signpost for the Kesselspitze. The track thereafter heads steeply over broken, rocky ground to a ridge. Get onto the ridge and follow it – very exposed in places but with excellent scrambling – to the summit of **Lämpermahdspitze** complete with metal summit cross. **2hr** Return to Serlesjoch by the same route. Enjoy the brilliant views over the Stubaital valley and back towards King Serles.

At one time, this was part of a high-level route to the Padasterjochhaus, across the Ober der Mauer (over the wall) to the Kesselspitze. Sadly, it has been much neglected and is now no longer in use. Hopefully, at some future date, this will be corrected, but for the present, and as far as this guidebook is concerned, the route is *Gesprutt, Schweirig und Gefahrlich* (closed, difficult and dangerous).

Good scrambling on the Lämpermahdspitze

STAGE 2A
Maria Waldrast Monastery to Padasterjochhaus

Start	Maria Waldrast Monastery (1638m)
Standard time	6–7hr
Distance	10.2km
Ascent	1245m
Descent	650m

There is a choice of routes for this promenade: one that enjoys picturesque, pastoral scenery of meadows and forest and one that embraces the peaks and passes of the Serleskamm ridge, passing through some very dramatic limestone scenery.

From Maria Waldrast, follow the route description for ascending Serles by taking the forest track, **Route 121**, which starts at the Marienbrunnen well and fountain. Follow this for about **1½hr** to where, a short distance after passing the steep, washed-out gully, a track bears left, heading south-west for the Kalbenjoch. There is no signpost as such and the track is not that obvious. Look out for the usual daubs of red-and-white paint heading south-west. Follow the vague track over high alpine grassy pasture to the **Kalbenjoch** (2225m), joining the route from the Blaser Hut. **2hr**

Alternatively, you can proceed to the Serlesjoch, then head south over a rocky scree-type path to the Kalbenjoch. This option is marginally longer by 30min but it enjoys better scenery **2½ hr** From here there are excellent retrospective views towards King Serles.

From the Kalbenjoch, follow the route description for 'Stage 2: Blaser Hut to Padasterjochhaus', taking either the forest route or the highly recommended route via the Kesselspitze, to finish at the **Padasterjochhaus**. **4hr**

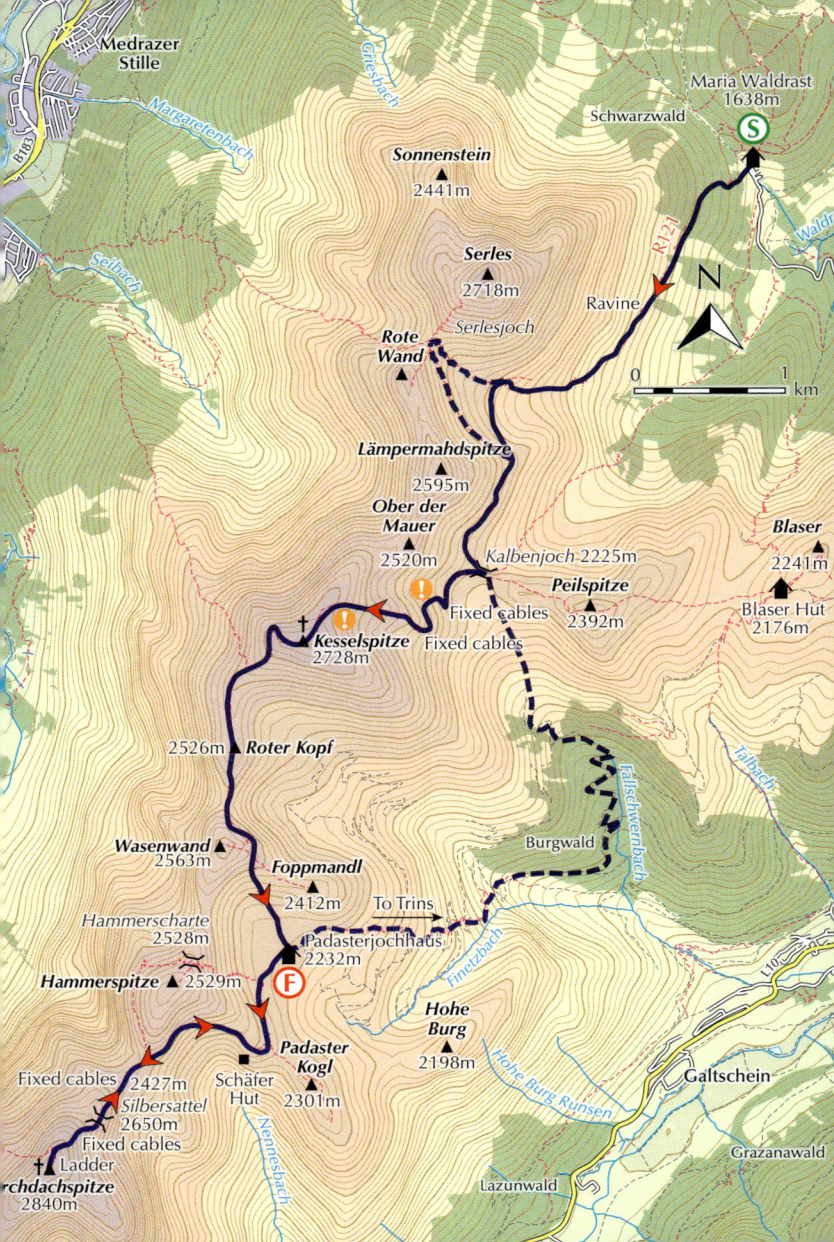

EXCURSION
Ascent of Kirchdachspitze (2840m)

Start	Padasterjochhaus (2232m)
Standard time	2½–3hr (+2hr for descent)
Distance	3km (+3km for descent)
Ascent	610m
Descent	610m
Grade	F
Note	For map, see Stage 2A

As a suggestion, particularly if you have days to spare, consider spending two nights at the Padasterjochhaus which will allow you to enjoy a more relaxing half-day excursion on the Kirchdachspitze before moving on the following day to the Innsbrucker Hut.

This is a challenging, if somewhat short, excursion through some very dramatic and stunning limestone scenery. Not surprisingly, the views from the summit are superb in all directions, but it will be the Feuerstein, the Habicht and the mountains of the Tribulaun that will hold your attention as you gaze across this range of jagged limestone peaks to the snow-capped peaks of the central Stubai Alps.

Those with exceptional eyesight should be able to locate the Starkenburger Hut far away across the void towards the mountains of the Kalkkögel.

From the hut, head south over easy ground where after a short distance a signpost points the way to the Hammerscharte on Route 122. Continue south as the ground rises and cranks up a few degrees, climbing steadily to the Padasterjoch col 2428m. The retrospective views to the hut and the distant peaks of the Zillertal Alps are excellent.

Round the couloir below the Hammerspitze to the very picturesque **Schafer Hut** (shepherd's hut), with the Kirchdachspitze standing tall across the void to the left. Continue traversing west across rocky scree-strewn slopes to a small col and junction with the Rohrauersteig and Jubiläumssteig tracks at point **2427m** (signpost). **1½hr**

Excursion – Ascent of Kirchdachspitze (2840m)

The route turns south-west and climbs steeply over broken, rocky ground to the **Silbersattel** (2650m). **¾hr** Here turn left and scramble along the obvious ridge, following the Klettersteig-type trail over fixed cables and staples, until you are stopped in your tracks just below the summit. Climb the 5m-high ladder to the summit of **Kirchdachspitze** (2840), the mountain with the 'church roof' and 'spire', complete with a large summit cross. **About ¾hr** The views across the entire region are fabulous from the summit.

In descent, return to the hut by the same route, allowing 2hr.

At the Padasterjoch's shepherd's hut, looking towards the Kirchdachspitze: the mountain with the 'church roof' and 'spire'

STAGE 3
Padasterjochhaus to Innsbrucker Hut via Trins and Gasthof Feuerstein

Start	Padasterjochhaus (2232m)
Standard time	6hr without transport
Distance	19.2km via Trins
Ascent	1160m via Trins
Descent	1035m via Trins

From the Padasterjochhaus you have a choice of three routes to the Innsbrucker Hut; one entails gentle alpine walking while the other two will test your alpine walking skills to the limit. The least demanding is more suitable when the clouds are gathering and for those participants who are not at peak fitness.

The preferred route taking in the Kirchdachspitze, via the Silbersattel to Karalm, demands fine, settled weather and a good level of personal fitness, coupled with agility on all types of ground, some of which is exceedingly steep. The route via the Hammerscharte is less so, but it is still demanding, making an alternative descent into Issenangeralm in the Pinnistal valley.

This promenade is the least demanding and is in complete contrast to the other two more difficult routes, and although much less demanding, it remains enjoyable without burning needless energy.

CAUTIONARY NOTES

It's not a caution as such, but you do need to be organised and think about transport arrangements, otherwise, frustratingly, you could find yourself hanging around in Trins.

A regular bus service operates up and down the Gschnitztal valley, between Steinach and Gasthof Feuerstein. Check the times at the Padasterjochhaus before leaving or see www.postbus.at for details. For Wipptal Taxi, tel 0043 664 12 23 055.

From the hut, proceed east on **Route 122**, through upper alpine meadows and scrub woodland, descending a well-marked path that criss-crosses the forest

service road. After 4km of downhill walking through sweet-smelling pine forest, you will reach the delightful village of **Trins**. **2hr**

If you made arrangements with the Hüttenwirt your rucksacks will have been transported ahead of you and a taxi will be waiting at the forest parking area to take you up the **Gschnitztal valley** to **Gasthof Feuerstein**, a good place for lunch.

If you have not done so, you will have to wait in Trins for the local bus service that operates between Steinach and Feuerstein or walk! **1hr**

From Gasthof Feuerstein, proceed up the road for a short distance, turning right at a large signpost for the Innsbrucker Hut and the hut's Seilbahn station.

Proceed north-west, zigzagging up through the forest on a good trail that generally follows the line of the Seilbahn cables. After an hour or so the forest gives way to a large open rocky couloir of the Alfairalm, then ramps up to climb more steeply below the Kalkwand to the Pinnisjoch (2370m) and the **Innsbrucker Hut**. There are great views towards the three mountains that form the Tribulaun group, then later of the fabulous Habicht. **3hr**

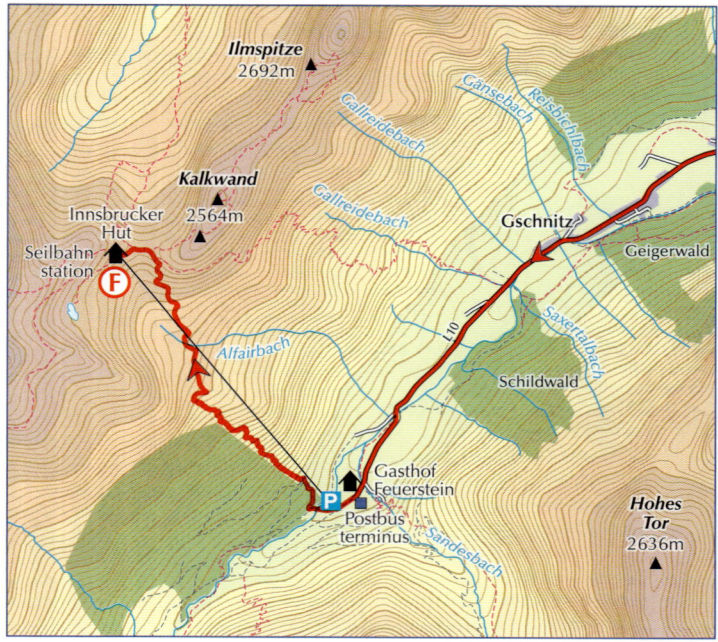

STAGE 3A
Padasterjochhaus to Innsbrucker Hut via Hammerscharte

Start	Padasterjochhaus (2232m)
Standard time	7–8hr
Distance	13km
Ascent	1290m
Descent	1160m

Despite the difficulties, this is a brilliant trek through some stunning limestone scenery, particularly early on in the day when the three towering peaks of the Tribulaun reveal their various facets, challenged by the equally dominant bulk of the Kirchdachspitze, which along with Serles ranks as one of the two most important mountains in the Serleskamm group. However, once the Habicht comes into view, it dominates the whole of the Pinnistal valley, reminding us why it is named Hawk Mountain as it towers high above all of its close neighbours.

CAUTIONARY NOTES

The two main issues with this and the similar Jubiläumssteig option are the weather and the amount of up and down. The weather needs to be fine and settled, as descending over difficult ground is not a place to be caught in rain or thick cloud. You also need to be fit enough to descend and reascend 1000m in one day and be sufficiently recovered the following day to climb the Habicht or to continue the tour to the Bremer Hut.

Also, the middle section of the route was severely damaged during the violent storm of 2022, which took all the fixed cables with it, and a Gesprutt sign now warns that the route ahead is difficult and dangerous. The route now continues via a semi-new route, which is actually an old hunters' trail. The ground is very steep as it descends into the Pinnistal valley, and it demands a lot of care and good mountain skills as the rock is quite loose in places and of dubious quality.

From the hut, head south over easy ground where after a short distance a signpost points the way to the Hammerscharte on **Route 122**.

Make the turn and head west, zigzagging over relatively easy ground to the rocky slopes of the **Hammerscharte** (2528m). **1hr** The views over the Pinnistal valley and towards the Habicht are excellent. Look out for ibex at the col as there is a sizeable herd residing in the area.

From the col, descend the rocky path for a short distance to the junction of paths with the Jubiläumssteig and the Rohrauersteig (signpost).

The left-hand trail goes off in the direction of the Silbersattel and Kirchdachspitze. Take the right-hand trail heading north on the Rohrauersteig. From here you have a 1000m descent into the valley, so take some time to work out the route line, as the trail is not that obvious.

From the signpost, the route starts off gradually, first descending open ground of dwarf pine trees, then cranking up and descending more steeply, zigzagging below the Wasenwand. After levelling out a bit, the trail, vague in places, starts to descend once again, this time more steeply in a series of zigzags, until eventually giving way to some easier ground. The way ahead now involves crossing some difficult ground, letting you know it's time to sort out your improvised harness.

The difficult, steep ground of the Rohrauersteig below the Wasenwand

Stage 3A – Padasterjochhaus to Innsbrucker Hut via Hammerscharte

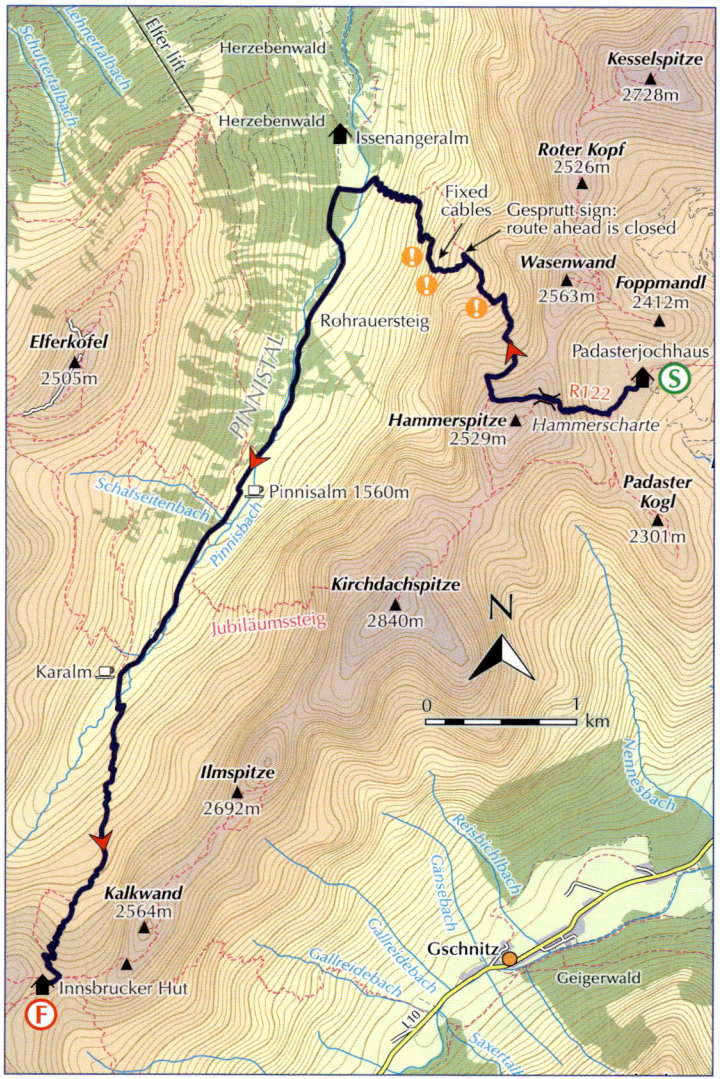

TREKKING IN AUSTRIA'S STUBAI ALPS

Ahead is a washed-out gully and an obvious ridge. Make for this, crossing the rocky gully to the scree slope ahead and to the ridge. Here a **Gesprutt sign** notifies you that the route ahead is closed due to a fierce storm in 2022. **1½hr** At the sign turn left, east, and start to descend to the ridge through dwarf alpine scrub bushes. After around 20min the ground steepens and starts to drop away from you. At the bottom of the ridge, you will be forced into the gully watercourse system that you crossed earlier higher up. Proceed slowly and traverse across a difficult limestone rock buttress, fitted with cables and staples, until it eventually meets an old hunters' track. **1hr**

From here on, you are now on easier ground. Follow the gravelly track north, through the usual scrub vegetation, until your reach the head of a zigzag staircase. Descend the very steep slope, with zigzags in close succession, until you reach the **Pinnistal valley** floor (signpost). **1hr**

Here you can either turn right for Issenangeralm or left to Pinnisalm; both are good places for lunch, but you have to remember that you still have a long way to go. If you choose to go to Issenageralm, which is only a short distance away, albeit in the wrong direction, ask the Hüttenwirt to call Neustifter Funktaxi (tel 0043 664 2877 000) to take you to the Karalm, thus avoiding a 2hr trudge up the Pinnistal valley.

Otherwise, at the signpost turn left for the short 2km walk to the superb **Pinnisalm ½hr**, then onwards to the **Karalm** and eventually the **Innsbrucker Hut**. **2hr**

Innsbrucker Hut

STAGE 3B
*Padasterjochhaus to Innsbrucker Hut via Padasterjoch,
Silbersattel and Kirchdachspitze*

Start	Padasterjochhaus (2232m)
Standard time	7–8hr
Distance	10.7km
Ascent	1355m (plus an extra 200m for Kirchdachspitze)
Descent	1220m

CAUTIONARY NOTES

As mentioned in the notes for Stage 3A, the main issues with this route are the weather and the amount of up and down over difficult ground. The weather needs to be fine and settled, as it is not a place to be caught in rain or thick cloud. You also need to be fit enough to descend and reascend 1000m in one day and be sufficiently recovered the following day to climb the Habicht or to continue the tour to the Bremer Hut.

Note that the middle section of the route involves a very steep descent into the Pinnistal valley, which will demand a lot of care and good mountain skills as the rock is quite loose in places and of dubious quality.

This is a highly recommended, challenging promenade through some very dramatic and stunning limestone scenery. See also 'Excursion: Ascent of Kirchdachspitze (2840m)'.

As with the previous tour, this alternative route is in the top drawer of Alpine trekking, and despite covering some very challenging ground, this is a brilliant day in the mountains, with chocolate-box Alpine scenery on the approach to the Kirchdachspitze.

However, on crossing the Silbersattel, the scenery changes dramatically to an expansive panorama over the whole of the Pinnistal valley. At its head, it is dominated by the great bulk of Habicht, the Hawk Mountain, which towers high above all of its close neighbours.

Trekking in Austria's Stubai Alps

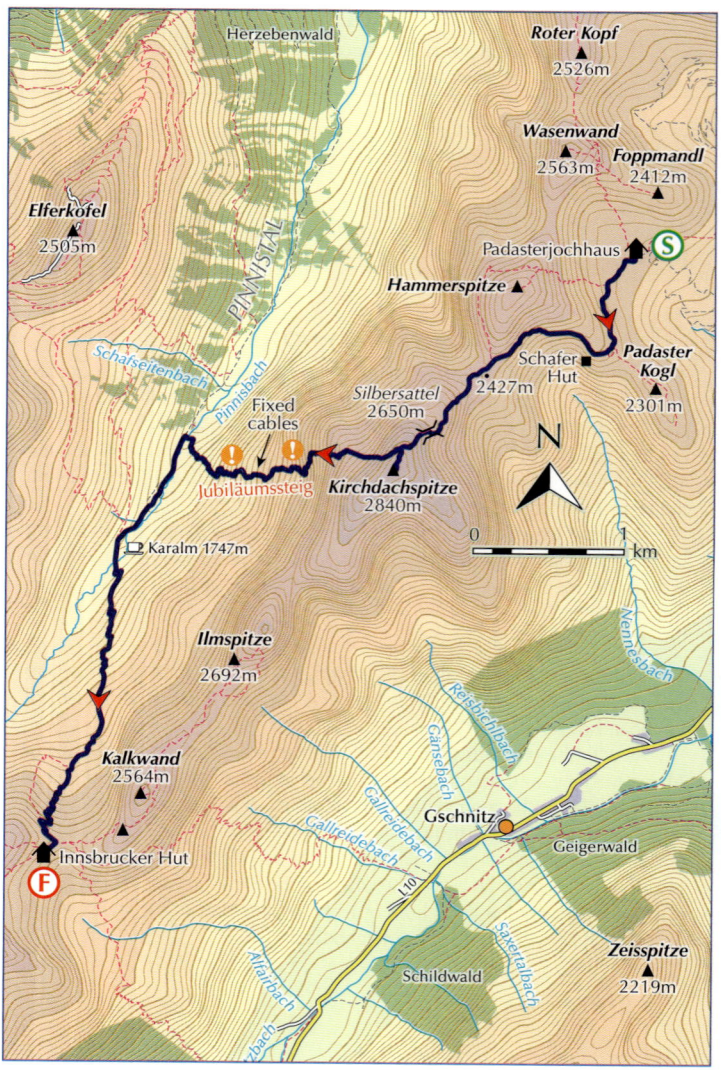

STAGE 3B – PADASTERJOCHHAUS TO INNSBRUCKER HUT

From the hut, head south over easy ground where after a short distance a signpost points the way to the Hammerscharte on Route 122. Continue south as the ground rises and cranks up a few degrees, climbing steadily to the Padasterjoch (2428m).

Round the couloir below the Hammerspitze to the **Schafer Hut** (shepherd's hut), traversing west across rocky scree-strewn slopes to a small col and junction with the Rohrauersteig and Jubiläumssteig tracks at point **2427m** (signpost). **1½hr**

The route turns south-west and climbs steeply over broken, rocky ground to the **Silbersattel** (2650m). **1hr** Those with sufficient energy can now follow the Klettersteig-type trail of fixed cables to the large summit cross of the **Kirchdachspitze** (2840m) – highly recommended.

From the Silbersattel, Route 7 turns west and drops 1000m in 2km, descending the 60–45-degree slope over rocks, scree and other steep, difficult, broken ground, fitted here and there with fixed cables and staples (make good use of your improvised harness), until it finally relents several hours later on the Pinnistal valley floor, midway between Pinnisalm and Karalm. **2–3hr** The Habicht dominates the stunning views of the Pinnistal valley.

With knees and ankles aching, pick up the obvious trail on Route 123 on Stage 1 of the Stubai Rucksack Route approach, heading south to **Karalm** (1747m). Thereafter, follow the rocky trail south, climbing steadily over the boulder slopes of the Alfairgrube to the Pinnisjoch and the very splendid **Innsbrucker Hut**. **2hr**

Ascent of the Kirchdach Spitze

STAGE 4
Innsbrucker Hut to Bremer Hut

Start	Innsbrucker Hut (2369m)
Standard time	7–8hr
Distance	10.4km
Ascent	890m
Descent	850m

This part of the Gschnitztaler Rundtour is shared with the popular Stubai Rucksack Route, which is fully described in Stage 2 of Trek 1. Briefly, and to avoid duplication, the route is characterised by lots of up and down, plenty of challenge and super mountain scenery.

From the hut, the trail follows **Route 124** throughout, contouring south-west across the hillside over various ridges and spurs of the Pfannalm and **Pramarnspitze**, high above the Gschnitztal valley, to the Simmingalm basin around the 2400–2600m contours, reaching its conclusion above the Lauterersee at the magnificently sited **Bremer Hut**. **7–8hr**

At the Bremer Hut

STAGE 4 – INNSBRUCKER HUT TO BREMER HUT

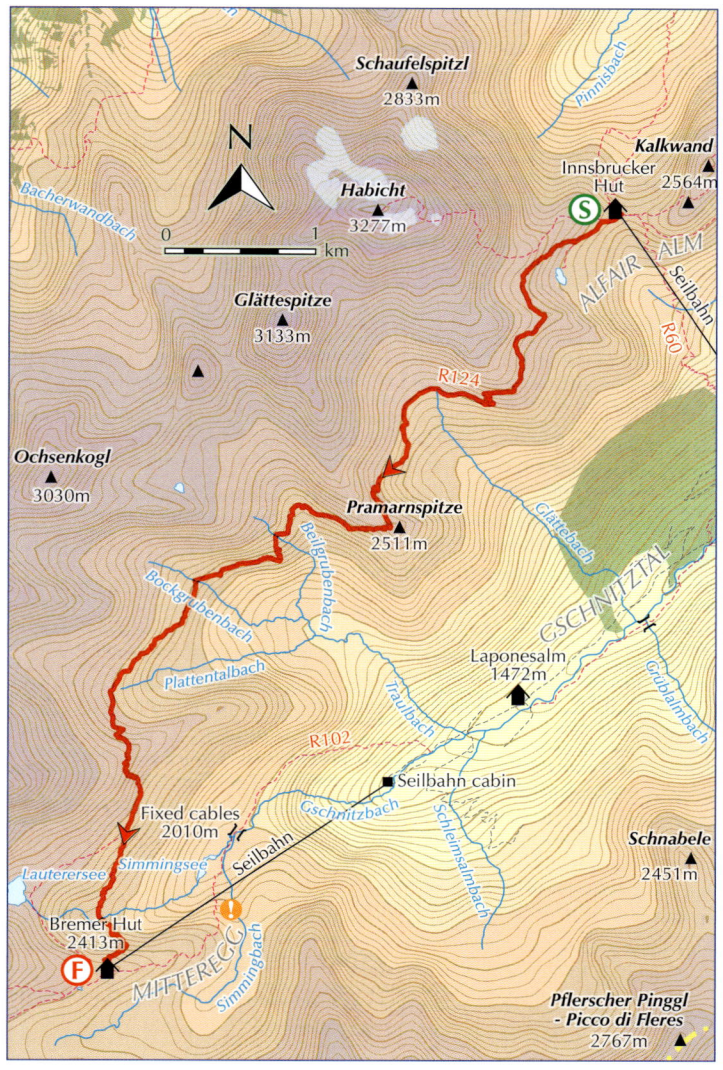

STAGE 5
Bremer Hut to Austrian Tribulaunhaus

Start	Bremer Hut (2413m)
Standard time	7–8hr
Distance	10.1km
Ascent	680m
Descent	1030m

As mentioned above, there is a choice of routes for the next section of the Gschnitztaler Rundtour, which is best described as an exploration of the peaks and passes of the Serleskamm and Tribulaun Mountains, as this section of the tour enters the very heart of the mountains. Whichever route you take, you will not be disappointed.

The Austrian Tribulaunhaus is the next official destination on the Gschnitztaler Rundtour, located on the northern side of the three peaks of the Tribulaun mountains and not to be confused with the Tribulaun Hut, which is located in South Tirol on the south side of the mountains.

However, the preferred and highly recommended route, which extends the tour by two days, is the one from the Bremer Hut that crosses the Bremer Scharte into the Italian South Tirol, ending with a night at the Magdeburger Hut. From there you can make your way to the Austrian Tribulaunhaus by way of the Italian Tribulaun Hut on the more dramatic south side of the Tribulaun peaks.

This route is very similar to the previous day's outing, being quite long with lots of up and down; however, this trek follows the remote Jubiläumssteig, which is an adventurous route that will tick all the boxes for the experienced alpine walker: duration, remoteness, challenge and varied scenic interest.

Early in the day the fine panoramas over the Gschnitztal valley are dominated by the great bulk of the Habicht. Thereafter, crossing the footbridge over the raging torrents of the Simmingbach river, the Jubiläumssteig throws up quite a number of challenges; route finding is not always obvious and a bit of trail bashing may be needed to navigate some of the paths dominated by overgrown shrubs.

STAGE 5 – BREMER HUT TO AUSTRIAN TRIBULAUNHAUS

Once clear of the Schwarze Wand, the route opens up again with some fabulous Dolomitic limestone mountain scenery. The real show stopper is on reaching the Sandesjöchl (Pflerscher Scharte), which reveals stunning wall-to-wall mountain scenery that reveals both aspects of the Tribulaun mountains. All in all, this is a fabulous day in the mountains.

CAUTIONARY NOTES

The Jubiläumssteig is quite long and not a route to be undertaken in iffy weather as there are few escape routes. The middle section of the route, from the footbridge to the Pflerscher Scharte (Sandesjöchl), is the main difficulty. In poor weather the correct decision is to descend to Feuerstein and take the service road track to the hut.

The Jubiläumssteig is also quite a remote route, and you are very unlikely to meet many folk on the trail – if any. Both these constraints make the route quite a serious undertaking and not one suitable for small groups of two, and even less so for solo walkers.

From the hut, retrace your steps, heading east on **Route 124**, as if you are going to the Innsbrucker Hut or returning to the valley at Feuerstein, until you reach a familiar signpost with the word 'Jubiläumssteig' inscribed upon it. Enjoy exceptional views towards the Habicht. Here continue to follow the main track down the top of the Mitteregg ridge to reach a signpost indicating the route to the Tribulaunhaus and a continuation of the Jubiläumssteig. Turn right, south-east, and follow the zigzag track, descending to an obvious **footbridge** at 2228m over the Simmingbach stream-cum-river. A short 1hr

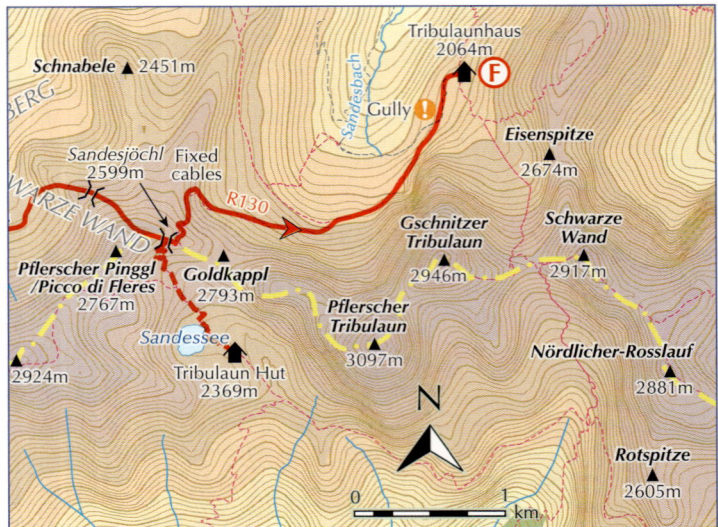

Continue as before, first on rocks then descending more steeply via a series of zigzags, passing a couple of marshy alpine ponds. Round the foot of a buttress, the Am Stöller, on a vegetated trail fitted with some fixed cables, before entering the more-open landscape of the **Kühberg** on the 2000m contour, below the peaks of Weisswandspitze and Pflerscher Pinggl.

The route now starts to climb steadily in a south-westerly direction, over varied ground of scrub vegetation and open rocky slopes. At the foot of the Schwarze Wand, it turns to climb more steeply into an open couloir with the ridge of the Schnabele to the left, east. Here a small col becomes obvious. Ascend the rocky trail, making use of the fixed cables to reach the **col**. Descend the far side, over steep, rocky, broken ground (fixed cables in place) to its base, then turn south to head up to the obvious col of the **Sandesjöchl** (Pflerscher Scharte) (2599m), which overlooks the fabulous peaks of the Tribulaun (signpost). **4–5hr**

Here you have a choice of progressing to either the Austrian Tribulaunhaus or the Italian Tribulaun Hut. Both huts are very good but the Italian Tribualaun Hut holds a special attraction for the mountain wanderer for its location alone – the choice is yours.

Crossing the Kühberg boulder field

However, for the sake of these notes, and route correctness, from the Pflerscher Scharte, with the Austrian Tribulaunhaus in clear sight, descend the steep, rocky limestone slope, zigzagging track to and fro, east, until it levels out at a junction of paths and a signpost with Routes 61 and 63. Turn right, south, for a short distance to another signpost and junction with Route 60. Route 60 follows a high-level trail beneath the peak of the Gschnitzter Tribulaun, over a rugged scree-strewn slope, while Route 61 descends more easily, following a more distinct rocky path. Both routes eventually meet up not far from the **Tribulaunhaus**. **1hr**

Alternative to the Italian Tribulaun Hut
For the Italian Tribulaun Hut, from the Pflerscher Scharte and the white border marker posts with Italy, simply descend and follow the well-marked rocky path to the shores of the Sandessee alpine tarn to the magnificent **Tribulaun Hut** overlooking the massive rock face of the Pflerscher Tribulaun. **1hr**

STAGE 5A
Bremer Hut to Magdeburger Hut

Start	Bremer Hut (2413m)
Standard time	5hr
Distance	5km
Ascent	565m
Descent	565m

While strictly not on the Gschnitztaler Rundtour, this route is an opportunity too good to miss. Walking this particular promenade in favour of the traditional route provides the experienced alpine walker with a really challenging day out in a big mountain environment offering some exceptional scenery. This route is described as *Nur fur Geubte* (only for the experienced), and indeed it is only suitable for those who are confident on all types of terrain. If you are unsure of your fitness and mountain skills, stick with the easier of the two routes.

Global warming has resulted in few advantages in the mountains and has led to the recession of the Stubai's much-loved glaciers. A few years ago, a crossing of the Bremer Scharte would only have been possible for the mountaineer equipped with ropes, ice axes and crampons. With most of the glacier gone, apart from what remains of the winter snow, this route to the rarely visited Magdeburger Hut is now possible for the experienced alpine walker.

This fabulous day out in the high mountains is full of challenge and scenic reward. The highlight of the day is the crossing of the Bremer Scharte, where the scenery is simply stunning, particularly towards the Pflerscher Hochjoch and the Seespitze, then back across the void to the Habicht.

CAUTIONARY NOTES

Note that this is a mountaineering route without the need for mountaineering equipment. It is only suitable for experienced walkers who are confident on all types of ground, who are surefooted and who are vertigo-free. Needless to say, this route should only be undertaken in good weather.

STAGE 5A – BREMER HUT TO MAGDEBURGER HUT

From the hut, head west on the popular Stubaier Höhenweg and Route 102 of the Central Alpine Way, heading for the Simmingjochl pass. After a short distance you will reach a signpost indicating the way to the Innere Wetterspitze. Continue for a similar distance to where a vague track heads south-east in the direction of the Bremer Scharte (signpost). **¼hr**

Turn left, descend a little and make your way towards the great wall of mountains ahead, with the Pflerscher Hochjoch and Schneespitze dominating the scene. Cross over the rocky slopes and streams of the Am Hintersimming, then start to make the gradual climb through the rocky slopes of the Fernerschröfen, which many years ago created the Simmingferner glacier ice fall.

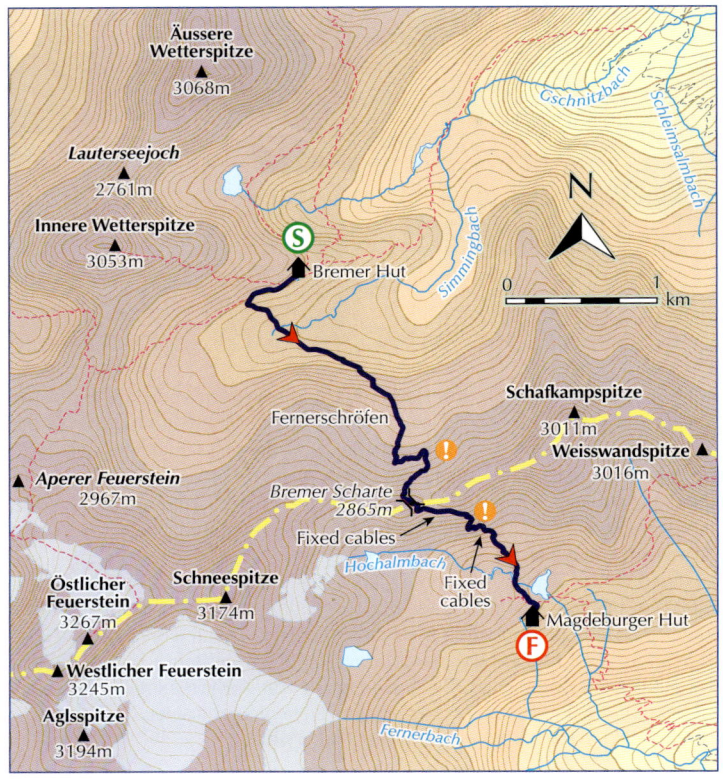

The Bremer Hut

Continue to negotiate the steep, gnarly, broken ground until the route emerges on remnants of the glacier roughly on the 2600m contour. Cross the small patch of snow, be careful as it can be icy, to the rocks on the far side. Here the route turns right, to the south, climbing a steep, rocky couloir to the tiny col that is the **Bremer Scharte** (2865m), marking the border with South Tirol. The 360-degree scenery is magical, with both the Bremer and Magdeburger huts in clear view. **About 2hr**

From the col, which is no more than a gap in the ridge, make your descent into Italy, heading east and gradually descending a rocky corridor until you come to an abrupt stop when the route steepens considerably. Make use of your improvised harness to scramble over and downclimb a series of steep mountaineering-type zigzags. The ground finally eases near the small alpine tarns left behind as reminders of the once-mighty Stubenferner glacier. Continue over easier ground to the superb **Magdeburger Hut**. **2½hr**

STAGE 5B
Magdeburger Hut to Italian Tribulaun Hut

Start	Magdeburger Hut (2423m)
Standard time	4hr
Distance	5.7km
Ascent	610m
Descent	655m

Welcome to Italy, to the Südtirol, also known as the Alto Adige in Italian. With good scenic variety and quite a bit of challenge, this is a great day out.

Participants will notice that after passing through the boulder-strewn slopes of the Schafflecke and on past the Hoher Zahn, the so-called 'high tooth', the geology suddenly changes to limestone, which is more evident on reaching the Sandesjöchl, where there are brilliant views across the 600m-high cliff face of the Gschnitztaler Tribulaun – just fabulous.

CAUTIONARY NOTES

This route is difficult in poor weather. Route finding through the rocky slopes and boulders of the Schafflecke is particularly problematic as the route is not obvious. Care also needs to be exercised when crossing the exposed slopes and terrace around the Hoher Zahn, especially if snow covered.

From the hut, progress east past the edge of the Stubensee alpine lake on a good path. After a short distance you will reach the junction with the path from the valley (signpost). **About ¼hr**

Continue as before. After a kilometre or so the path becomes less obvious and turns north into the wide-open amphitheatre of the **Schafflecke**. Follow this, climbing steadily over gnarly, broken ground of loose rocks and boulders for 500m. The route then turns to the right and almost back on itself to enter a barrier of cliffs, climbing to a small knoll and col. Be careful hereabouts as the route is not that obvious. Once at the little col, the route turns north-east on the Tiroler Höhenweg, meandering over broken, rocky ground to a small col between the Weisswandspitze and Hoher Zahn, roughly on the 3000m contour. Enjoy the excellent scenery around the various rocky teeth of the Hoher Zahn. **1½hr**

TREKKING IN AUSTRIA'S STUBAI ALPS

The peaks of the Pflerscher Tribulaun viewed from the Sandesjöchl

STAGE 5B – MAGDEBURGER HUT TO ITALIAN TRIBULAUN HUT

The route continues east over broken, rocky ground on a slightly better path, rounding the **Hoher Zahn** to the south to re-emerge on a broad col overlooking the peaks of the Tribulaun, the Sandessee alpine lake and the superb Italian Tribulaun Hut. **1+hr** Continue as before but now in more-open countryside, descending the rocky gravel scree slopes to a junction with the path to the Sandesjöchl (2599m) and the Tribulaun Hut. **¾hr**

Here it's decision time. The highly recommended option is to descend to and overnight at the splendid Italian **Tribulaun Hut**. The only downside is that this extends the tour by another day, but if you have the time this is well worth the effort.

Alternatively, if you don't have those extra days at your disposal, at the path junction simply turn left and follow the obvious path, returning to Austria and the Alte Nord Tirol to the Sandesjöchl (2599m), complete with border post signs. Descend the far side, down the rocky scree slopes under the great rock face of the Gschnitzer Tribulaun to the **Tribulaunhaus**.

Trekking in Austria's Stubai Alps

STAGE 5C
Italian Tribulaun Hut to Austrian Tribulaunhaus via Sandesjöchl

Start	Italian Tribulaun Hut (2369m)
Standard time	2½hr
Distance	4.5km
Ascent	235m
Descent	550m

From the hut, retrace your steps and head towards the **Sandesjöchl** (2599m) and the border with Austria. Thereafter, follow the route as described above and in Stages 5 and 5B to the **Tribulaunhaus**. About 2½hr

At the Tribulaunhaus you have to decide whether you stay over and enjoy the ambience of the hut; it's a great place to stay. If you have time constraints, there is the easy walk down to Feuerstein for the Postbus to Steinach am Brenner and then the train to Innsbruck. Alternatively, you can continue and follow Stage 6 to the Truna Hut and opt for the shorter promenade to Obernberg. Should you choose to climb the Gschnitzer Tribulaun (2946m) via the Schneetalscharte, note that the route is very steep at the top – a Grade B Klettersteig climb – and without the appropriate gear it is beyond the scope of these notes.

Looking towards the Gschnitzer Tribulaun. View from the Tribulaun Haus

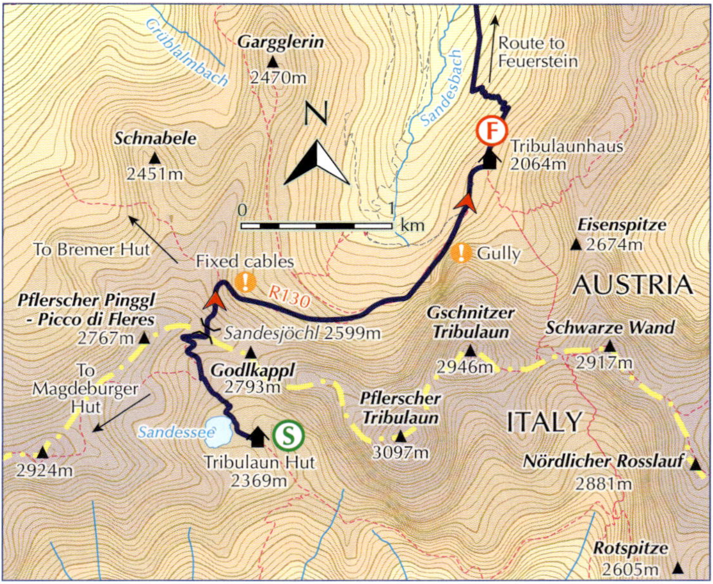

STAGE 5C – ITALIAN TRIBULAUN HUT TO AUSTRIAN TRIBULAUNHAUS VIA SANDESJÖCHL

At the Italian Tribulaun Hut

STAGE 6
Austrian Tribulaunhaus to Truna Hut via Gstreinjöchl

Start	Austrian Tribulaunhaus (2064m)
Standard time	6hr
Distance	10.3km
Ascent	635m
Descent	980m

As mentioned, there is a choice of routes for this promenade; however, it is important to mention that for participants with limited time, the easy option is to follow the service road for the Tribulaunhaus and Route 127 down the valley to Gasthof Feuerstein and then take the bus to Steinach am Brenner, followed by the train back to Innsbruck.

This is a truly magnificent day out in the mountains on a route that passes through some very impressive Dolomite-like limestone mountain scenery.

CAUTIONARY NOTES

This route is quite weather-dependent and not one to undertake on a falling barometer. In very poor conditions, the correct decision is to descend to Gasthof Feuerstein.

From just behind the hut, pick up the trail for the climb to the Gschnitzer Tribulaun, heading south on **Route 127** where after a short distance a branch track heads east to an obvious col that is the Gstreinjöchl (signpost).

Make the turn, and continue on Route 127, climbing the steep rock and gravel path, huffing and puffing on the zigzag trail to its conclusion at the **Gstreinjöchl**. **About 2hr** The views overlooking the Obernberger Tribulaun are fabulous.

From the col, continue to climb, following the rocky path north along an open ridge on Route127. After a short kilometre you will come to a point where the path diverges at the Innere Wildgrube. The higher path is for those who are more surefooted, as the track is a quite narrow and stony. The other track descends quite steeply at first then eases out at point **2299m**, where it meets the

At the Gstreinjöchl

track coming from Obernberg (signpost) before continuing to converge with the higher track at a small pond.

This is the first opportunity for those wishing to descend to the Obernbergtal valley.

Continue as before, but now heading more east to another small col 300m distant. Here again the paths split. The higher path, noted as Route 38, crosses an open rocky couloir to a crucifix cross and wayside shrine below the Muttenjoch col. The alternative route makes a descent of around 100m to round the base of the Muttenkopf's south-east ridge before turning north to traverse the open slopes of the Kastnerberg where after a short distance it rejoins Route 126 from Obernberg. This marks the point and second option for those wishing to descend to Obernberg. **1hr**

Whichever path you choose, continue heading north-east until both paths converge at a col to the east of the Am Hohen Kreuz.

Continue as before, now on the more obvious track of Route 94, on the broad ridge of open ground to the **Trunajoch** (2152m), just over 1km away,

STAGE 6 – AUSTRIAN TRIBULAUNHAUS TO TRUNA HUT VIA GSTREINJÖCHL

with its massive cross (signpost). The scenery across both the Gschnitztal and Obernbergtal valleys is superb. **1hr**

For those descending to Obernberg, this is your last opportunity to do so via the Lichtsee alpine lake.

From Trunajoch, simply make the turn north and follow **Route 125**, descending the obvious path through the beautiful open countryside of Schöne Grube, past the hay barns at the Trunaalm and on to the forested enclave at the farm-complex cabin that is the **Truna Hut**. **2hr**

Completing the Tour via the Obernbergtal valley

Your first option, and the quickest way, is to descend from point **2299m** at Innere Wildgrube, aptly named the wild ditch, parts of which are gully-like, from where a short 2hr walk will take you to the head of the valley at Waldesruh (car park) and the bus stop for Steinach am Brenner.

The second option heads off from where the paths converge with Route 126 on the upper slopes of the Kastnerberg, then continues via the Kastnerbergalm to Obernberg.

Then last, from the Trunajoch, you can descend via the charming lake at Lichtsee on Route 99, or take the alternative, slightly shorter but steeper Route 125.

The routes via Obernberg offer the shortest way out of the mountains other than descending from the Austrian Tribulaunhaus direct to Feuerstein, followed by the bus to Steinach am Brenner and train to Innsbruck.

> Bus 4146 from Feuerstein to Steinach am Brenner: 09:16 / 09:46 / 12:16 / 13:16 / 14:16

Gasthof Feuerstein

STAGE 7
Truna Hut to Trins or Steinach am Brenner

Start	Truna Hut (1750m)
Standard time	4hr
Distance	4.5km to Trins; 7.6km to Steinach am Brenner
Ascent	35m to Trins; 60m to Steinach am Brenner
Descent	530m to Trins; 215m to Steinach am Brenner
Note	For map, see Stage 6

From the Truna Hut you have a choice of routes to bring the Gschnitztaler Rundtour to an end. You can descend to Trins, or take a longer route round to the Bergeralm cable car, and down to Steinach am Brenner.

From the alm, simply follow the forest service road on Route 43, or short-cut the footpaths of Route 125, through the Trunawald forest to the village of Trins and the bus for **Steinach am Brenner** or walk the last four kilometres to Steinach. **2hr to Trins plus 2hr to Steinach.**

Alternatively, from the hut follow the service road on Route 43 as far as the junction at **Fallzambach** (1608m), then continue to round the hillside on Route 527 to Gerichtsheralm and on to the Bergeralm cable-car ride, followed by a short walk into **Steinach am Brenner** and the regional train to Innsbruck. **Allow 3hr**

At the Trunajoch

DAY WALKS AND EXCURSIONS

As mentioned several times throughout the guidebook, most of the huts in the main Stubai connect directly with the Stubaital valley, which means there are lots of opportunities for short day walks, particularly if you have young children with you or if things don't go to plan or if the weather is not so good. Here are some options to consider:

Innsbrucker Hut
See Stubai Rucksack Route Stage 1. Follow the route as described from either Neustift or Neder, but it's best to use the minibus taxi service to the Karalm, then make the 2hr walk to the hut. Return by the same route, not forgetting to reserve your return seat in the shuttle-service minibus.

Pinnisalm
See Stubai Rucksack Route Stage 1. This excellent day out amid beautiful alpine scenery is highly recommended. From Neustift, via the Elfer cable car, you have the option of a 40min walk to the Elfer Hut for refreshments. From the cable-car station, follow the broad path (signposted) past the Globe tourist attraction and scenic viewpoint, gradually descending through the forest to the open pastureland at the Pinnisalm; this is a great place for refreshments. Return to Neustift, making use of the minibus shuttle service.

Dresdner Hut
See 'Hut directory'. This route is highly recommended if you have young children.
  Take the bus service from Innsbruck to the Stubai Gletscher Mutterbergalm terminus, followed by cable car to the Dresdner Hut or onwards to the Eisgrat cable-car station. Both the Dresdner Hut and Eisgrat have children's play areas.

Sulzenau Hut
See Stubai Rucksack Route Stage 5A. For this excellent day out, take the bus service from Innsbruck to Stubai Gletscher Mutterbergalm terminus, followed by cable car to the Dresdner Hut, then reverse the route via the Peiljoch to the Sulzenau Hut, returning to the valley via the Sulztal valley and bus back to Neustift. Allow 3hr to the hut and 2hr for the walk out.

Day walks and excursions

Franz Senn Hut
See Stubai Glacier Tour Stage 1. Take the bus to Neustift, followed by the minibus shuttle service to the Oberissalm. Thereafter, you have a 3hr walk to the hut. Remember to reserve your return journey.

Starkenburger Hut
Take the bus service to Fulpmes Bergbahn cable-car station and then on to the Kreuzjoch (children's play area). Follow the botanical trail via Sennjoch, through the avalanche barriers, to the hut. The return by the same route will take 2hr. The scenery is excellent throughout, particularly of the mini-Dolomite range, the Kalkkögel and Schlicker Seespitze. Highly recommended.

Hotel Klostergasthof Maria Waldrast
See Gschnitztaler Runde Tour Stage 1. From Innsbruck, follow the itinerary as described, taking the shortest route to the monastery inn. This route is highly recommended and not to be missed.

At the Globe viewpoint en route to Pinnisalm

Trekking in Austria's Stubai Alps

Gschnitztal: the Alte Mühlenmuseum and Laponesalm
Take the bus service from Steinach am Brenner to the bus terminus at Gasthof Feuerstein. Cross the road and follow the farm-type track until you reach the interesting Alte Mühlen (old grist mill) museum. It's interesting to see the methods used not so long ago to grind cereals into flour. Thereafter, take the shortcuts and then follow the service road to the popular Laponesalm for refreshments.

Wipptal: Nösslachjoch
Take the bus service to Steinach am Brenner, then walk through the town to the Bergeralmbahn cable-car station. Take the lift to the top station, followed by a 20min ascent to the summit of the Nösslachjoch, with its excellent views over the Wipptal, Brenner and Zillertal. Return by the same route or walk down to the middle station and the children's play area.

Nosslachjoch summit

HUT DIRECTORY

The Bremer Hut

HUT DESCRIPTIONS AND LOCATIONS

The hut descriptions are derived from the Alpenverein Hut Directory Volume 1 Ostalpen (previously known as the 'Green Book'), published by Rother of Munich, together with information available from various tourist offices and that published by the ÖAV, DAV, AVS and the huts themselves.

Other comments and observations are entirely those of the author.

More and more of the huts in the Stubai Alps are developing websites and adding email addresses, which means readers can now make reservations online and check for up-to-date information on the huts by visiting the following sites:

www.alpenverein.at/britannia
www.alpenverein.at
www.bergsteigen.at/de/huttendetail.aspx

Abbreviations		
B	Beds	As in bedrooms
M	*Matratzenlager*	As in dormitory-style accommodation
N	*Notlager*	As in the winter room or other available space but more commonly known as 'sleeping with the furniture'

AMBERGER HUT (2135M)

Owner	DAV Sektion Amberg
Location	Located on a rocky platform east of the Sulzkogel, above the marshy alpine pasture of In der Sulze
Open	Early June to early October
Facilities	3B (1x2, 1x6, 1x14)/14N. The hut has recently been totally refurbished, making it very pleasant and comfortable. Excellent restaurant and toilet facilities, complete with showers and hot water
Connections	To Gries in Sulztal, then Postbus to Längenfeld; Franz Senn Hut 6–7hr. Hoch Stubai 4–5hr
Address	Lydia and Serafin Gstrein, Amberger Hütte, Seestrasse 10, A-6450 Sölden, Ötztal, Austria
Telephone	Hut (0043) 676 952 3426
Email	info@ambergerhuette.at
Website	www.ambergerhuette.at

This old hut was established in 1888, fully refurbished in 1938 and again in 1978, with renovation to the dining areas and bedrooms in 2010 making it very comfortable indeed. It stands just above the raging river of the Fischbach, at the foot of the Niederer Sulzkogel where the valley of In der Sulze opens up.

Its location and height mean that the hut is quite hemmed in and as such does not enjoy panoramic views of any of the local peaks. However, the hut is pleasant and comfortable, and it does have popular additions to the menu which are not available at other huts, namely, ice cream and *pommes frites* (french fries).

It is also one of the few huts where hot water is available throughout the day.

BECHERHAUS (3195M)

Owner	CAI Verona Sektion
Other names	Rifugio Gino Biasi al Bicchiere
Location	Located at the foot of the Wilder Freiger's south ridge
Open	Mid July to mid September
Facilities	40B/65M/6N. Good restaurant facilities but, because of its height and location, not as comprehensive as other huts. Toilet facilities are very basic due to the limited water supply; take your wet wipes with you
Connections	No easy valley connections due to the proximity of the glaciers. If you have to make an escape, the route into Italy and Sterzing is the safest option. Müller Hut 1hr. Sulzenau Hut 4–5hr. Hildesheimer Hut 5hr. Nürnberger Hut 4hr
Address	Becherhaus, Familie Lantschner, Lukas and Edeltraud, Via Valais 14, I-39050 San Genesio, Bolzno, Italy
Telephone	Hut (0039) 329 234 6943
Email	info@becherhaus.it
Website	www.becherhaus.it

The history of the Becherhaus is very similar to that of the Müller Hut in as much as it was forfeited to Italy after World War 1.

First established by D and J Pfurtscheller and Professor Langbein in 1886 and opened on the Kaiser's birthday on 18 August 1894, this three-storey hut was then extended in 1900 and 1920. Due to a combination of general neglect, deterioration as a result of the weather and occupation by the Italian alpine troops, the Alpini, who plundered the hut, the Becherhaus fell into a ruinous state of dilapidation. This was rectified when the hut was extensively refurbished in 1988 after the army had vacated it. The hut is currently enjoying a renaissance having been extensively modernised to mark the hut's 125th anniversary.

Prior to World War 1, the hut was the highest in the Stubai, being 22m higher than the Hoch Stubai Hut (3174m), and the third-highest in Austria.

However, the main intrigue relating to the hut is its correct name, Kaiserin Elisabeth Haus. Also known as Sisi the reluctant Empress, Kaiserin Elisabeth was the wife of Kaiser Franz Joseph. She was murdered in Geneva on 10 September 1898 when a 25-year-old Italian anarchist Luigi Lucheni, who hated aristocrats, stabbed her through the heart. Her husband, Franz Josef, would outlive her by 17

HUT DIRECTORY

The Becherhaus

years, dying on 21 November 1916 as a consequence of old age and the ravages of World War 1.

The Kaiser's brother Archduke Franz Ferdinand, third heir to the throne after Prince Rudolf, who committed suicide at the Vienna hunting lodge at Mayerling on 31 January 1889, was assassinated along with his wife, Countess Sophie of Bavaria, in Sarajevo on 28 June 1914. Their murder by a Bosnian Serb Nationalist Gavrilo Princip was an act that led directly to the outbreak of World War 1.

Those of you fortunate to wander the lofty heights around the Wilder Freiger may ponder the logistics of arranging a visit to the hut for HRH Elisabeth and her entourage, which was planned shortly before her unfortunate death.

Before accepting the name Becherhaus, named after the lump of rock on which the hut sits, the Becherspitze, for a short time after World War 1, the Italians renamed the hut Rifugio Regina Elena after Queen Elena.

Whatever its name, set amid a great sea of peaks and glaciers, the hut is a splendid place to be and certainly lives up to its more modern name of the 'Castle in the Clouds'.

BLASER HUT (2176M)

Owner	Private, Family Nocker
Location	Superbly located on the rounded plateau overlooking Serles, with a full 360-degree panoramic view of mountains near and far
Open	June to mid October
Facilities	6B/20M. Good restaurant and toilet facilities but cold water only! Taxi-jeep service from Trins available with prior arrangement
Connections	Trins 2hr, Maria Waldrast 2½hr, Padasterjochhaus 6hr,
Address	Familie Nocker, Blaser Hütte, Trins 162, A- 6152, Trins-Gschnitztal, Austria
Telephone	(0043) 664 100 3778; mobile (0049) 173 530 8556
Email	n.georg67@gmail.com
Website	www.blaserhuette.at

This super little hut, which has maintained the Gemütlichkeit tradition over many years, is enjoying increased popularity and something of a renaissance due to its inclusion in the Gschnitztaler Rundtour.

Built in 1928 by the Nocker family from Trins, this two-storey, shingle-clad hut enjoys a relaxed atmosphere as it is not on any of the main hut-to-hut routes. The hut enjoys stunning 360-degree panoramic views due to its location on a ring contour, but if you have time on your hands take in the summit of Blaserspitze (2241m), just 15min walk from the hut, where a panoramic signboard points out all of the mountains near and far. The near horizon is dominated by the peaks of the Serleskamm ridge, particularly Serles, the peak clearly visible from Innsbruck railway station, and the Kirchdachspitze, the peak with the 'church roof' and 'spire'. Further afield the limestone giants of the Tribulaun, the snow-capped peaks of the Stubai Alps and the more distant peaks of the Dolomites can be seen.

The hut is popular with day visitors who are prepared to make the 3hr trek from Trins; however, for participants heading out on the Gschnitztaler Rundtour, you will more than likely have the hut to yourselves once the sun has gone down, when you will be able to enjoy the hut's rustic charm, not forgetting perfect views of the night sky.

BREMER HUT (2413M)

Owner	DAV Sektion Bremen
Location	The Mitteregg plateau, above the Gschnitztal valley
Open	Mid June to early October
Facilities	23B/64M/12N. Good restaurant facilities but limited toilet facilities that can be cramped when the hut is full
Connections	Postbus to and from Steinach am Brenner to Feuerstein at the head of the Gschnitztal valley 3hr. A taxi service runs from the Feuerstein car park as far as the lovely Laponesalm (tel 0043 664 163 4190), which will save you around 1½hr. For a few euros your rucksack can be transported to the hut via the Seilbahn station, located just beyond the Laponesalm. Innsbrucker Hut 6–7hr. Nürnberger Hut 3–4hr. Tribulaunhaus 6–7hr
Address	Bremer Hut, Gschnitz 40, A6150 Austria; Patscher Famile, Stefanie and Christian Höllrigl, Bremer Hütte, Unterrain 268, A 6481, Austria
Telephone	Hut (0043) 720 270 660; Patscher 0043 664 304 7360
Email	office@bremerhuette.at
Website	www.bremerhuette.at

Dating back to 1897, the Bremer is an old, cosy, friendly hut in a true mountain situation close to the Simmingferner glacier and the north faces of the Schneespitze and Pflerscher Hochjoch.

Clad in timber shingles, the roof is lashed down at each corner, reminding us that the original roof was lost in a fierce storm in the early 1960s. The creaking timbers and warmth of the dining room add to the mountain environment at its best.

Recently extended in 2005, this hut is very popular due to the growing popularity of the Stubai Rucksack Route and the Gschnitztaler Rundtour, plus the new route just across the border to the Magdeburger Hut. Make sure to reserve beds.

DRESDNER HUT (2308M)

Owner	DAV Sektion Dresden
Location	At the head of the main Stubai valley, below the Schaufelspitze
Open	Early July to end September
Facilities	154B in two multi-functional bedrooms/14B in the recently modernised Zollhütte. Good all-round facilities that would be expected at the largest and most commercial hut in the Stubai, including toilet facilities, hot water and showers for a nominal fee. Excellent self-service restaurant with those little extras not found at other huts, such as pommes frites, ice cream, fruit salad. Internet facility. Rucksack transportation available to the Neue Regensburger Hut for a modest fee
Connections	Postbus to/from Mutterbergalm, then Stubai Gletcherbahn cable car 1hr. Neue Regensburger Hut 6–8 hr. Sulzenau Hut 3–4hr. Hildesheimer Hut 4hr. Müller Hut 6–8hr.
Address	E & H Hofer, Dresdner Hütte, Scheibe 64, A-6167 Neustift im Stubaital, Austria
Telephone	Hut (0043) 5226 8112
Email	info@dresdnerhuette.at
Website	www.dresdnerhuette.at

Opening in 1875, this was the very first *Schutzhuette* (shelter hut) to be established in the Stubai; it was subsequently enlarged in 1926 and 1968. In 2000, major expansion took place, turning the hut into the very modern, substantial four-storey structure seen today. More recently, the interior of the hut has been refurbished, including the modernisation of all bedrooms and the Matratzenlager.

The hut is managed by the local Hofer family, who have been the custodians since the turn of the 19th century. Photographs on the wall of the old dining room bear witness to the early development of the hut, proudly displaying members of the Dresden Section of the German Alpine Club. The old dining room retains much of its original timber panelling together with plaques and other mementoes of a bygone age, all in stark contrast to the newer parts of the dining room.

HUT DIRECTORY

The Dresdner Hut

Sadly, with the construction of the cable car and ski-tow facilities across the Daunkogel and Schaufelferner glaciers, purely for the benefit of skiers, much of the Dresdner Hut's immediate surroundings below the hut has been spoilt, which means genuine walkers now mingle with the many day trippers drawn in from Innsbruck and other tourist resorts.

Fortunately, once the sun has gone down and the clatter of machinery has been silenced, the hut reverts to its true role: to provide mountaineers and other mountain lovers with simple accommodation. It continues to do this very well, but it can never recapture the charisma it enjoyed many years ago.

This is a popular hut with a good view of the Schaufelspitze, made even more spectacular when seen from the Klettersteig rock-climbing garden by those with excess energy and a good head for heights.

ELFER HUT (2080M)

Owner	Private
Location	Large box-like, four-storey structure located on a level platform just below the Elferspitze, overlooking the Stubaital valley
Open	June to early October
Facilities	52B. Good restaurant and toilet facilities, hot water and showers. Internet facility
Connections	Postbus to/from Neustift via Elfer cable car. Pinnisalm 1hr. Innsbrucker Hut 4–5hr
Excursions	Elferspitze Klettersteig route for those folk who brought their gear; otherwise, there is a circular walking tour around the mountain with some excellent limestone scenery
Address	Familie Fritz Hass, Elfer Hut, A-6167 Stubaital, Austria
Telephone	(0043) 5226 2818
Email	hass@elferhuette.at

Perhaps one of the least visited huts in the Stubai Alps as it's not on any of the popular trails. Having said that, the hut is a favourite spot for the many parapenting pilots who use the nearby slopes for take-off.

FRANZ SENN HUT (2147M)

Owner	ÖAV Sektion Alpenverein Innsbruck
Location	Situated on a plateau at the head of the Obernbergtal valley, below the Ruderhofspitze and peaks of the Alpeiner
Open	June to early October
Facilities	70B/70M/12N. Good restaurant and toilet facilities, hot water and showers. Internet facility
Connections	Postbus to/from Neustift via the Oberiss Hut. Taxi service available to/from the Oberiss Hut: tel Neustifter Funktaxi (05226 2877 or 0664 287 7000) or Danler Taxi (05226 3333). Note that the road is currently closed between Seduck and Oberiss due to damage caused by a severe storm in 2022. It may be some years before sufficient funds are raised to get the road and bridges reinstated. The walk now takes 3hrs from Seduck. Starkenburger Hut 6–7hr, Neue Regensburger Hut 4hr, Amberger Hut 6–7hr
Excursions	Rinnnen See 2–3hr. Sommerwand 2hr. Lisenser Fernerkogel 5–6hr. Ruderhofspitze 6–8hr
Address	Herr Thomas Fankhauser, Franz Senn Hütte, Schulweg 18, A-6127 Neustift im Stubaital A6176, Austria
Telephone	Hut (0043) 05226 2218
Email	office@franzsennhuette.at
Website	www.franzsennhuette.at

This is perhaps the premier of all the Stubai huts because of its close links with the history of the Austrian Alpine Club and its founding member, after whom it is named. A portrait of Franz Senn can be found in the dining room.

The hut is also synonymous with Alpenverein Britannia, which is held in high esteem due to its close links with Walter Ingram and Henry Crowther who founded Sektion Britannia in 1948. The hut has been used many times for various Alpenverein Britannia training meets and was a beneficiary of funding for its seminar training room. Elsewhere, there is a portrait of Tony Freake, affectionately known as 'Papa Tony', president of Alpenverein Britannia from 1995 until his death in 2010, who is rightly honoured for the work he undertook for the Alpenverein as a whole.

Trekking in Austria's Stubai Alps

The Franz Senn Hut

This very substantial four-storey, stone-built hut started life in 1885 with accommodation for 37 people, with four reserved places for ladies. Thereafter, it was enlarged in 1891, 1907, 1932 and again in 1960 to its present four-storey status. The hut is strategically placed for climbing the peaks of the Alpeiner area high above the Obernbergtal valley; the Ruderhofspitze, Schrankogel and Lisenser Fernerkogel are all regularly climbed from the hut.

The hut is equally popular with day trippers because of fairly easy access by jeep service from Milders to the Oberiss Hut. Similarly, the hut is popular for ÖAV/DAV climbing courses and aspiring alpinists. Because of the hut's popularity, it is sometimes a little crowded, but it's a big hut and everyone seems to fit in and enjoy their stay.

There is much history surrounding the hut, but most of its original internal architecture, other than the dining room, seems to have been lost at some time during refurbishment. The hut will be celebrating its 140th anniversary on 2 October 2025.

This is a fine hut with excellent views towards the Kalkkögel and the peaks of the Alpeiner.

HILDESHEIMER HUT (2900M)

Owner	DAV Sektion Hildesheim
Location	Located on a rocky platform above the junction of the Gaisskarferner and Pfaffenferner glaciers south of the Schaufelspitze
Open	Late June to end September
Facilities	24B/46M/12N. Good restaurant and toilet facilities
Connections	To Gaisstal then to Sölden in the Ötztal valley. Postbus to Oetz. Hoch Stubai 5hr. Dresdner 3hr. Siegerland 3–4hr. Müller 6hr
Address	Anna Kuisle, Hildesheimer Hütte, Oberwindau Strasse 43, A-6450 Sölden, Austria
Telephone	Hut (0043) 5254 2300
Email	info@gustl-Sölden.com
Website	www.hildesheimerhuette.at

One of the highest huts in the region at 2900m, this solid, three-storey, buttressed stone building was built in 1896 and is ideally placed for the adjacent peaks, particularly the Stubai's highest peak, the Zuckerhütl (3505m).

Not surprisingly, most people staying at this fine hut will have in mind an ascent of the mountain or its neighbouring peaks, the Pfaffenschneide and Wilder Pfaff. This means that the hut is always busy and at weekends may be full.

The dining room is particularly pleasant and retains much of the original timber panelling from the 1937 refurbishment. The general creaking of timbers is reflected on the first floor, where bedrooms are named after the various districts of Hildesheim, such as Bockenem, Giesen, Lamspringe, Duigen and Elze. The hut, as expected, is very well run with a lot of effort being put into maintaining its Gemütlichkeit tradition.

Looking out from the hut's front door, visitors are quickly reminded of the height of the hut by the spectacular view of the ice fall off the Pfaffenschneide's Pfaffenferner glacier.

The Hildesheimer Hut

HOCH STUBAI HUT (3174M)

Owner	DAV Sektion Dresden
Location	Located on the Wildkarspitze, overlooking the Wütenkarferner glacier
Open	Early July to mid September
Facilities	8B/32M/6N. Good restaurant facilities but owing to its height, not as comprehensive as other huts. Toilet facilities are modest, and washing facilities are limited due to scarce water resources
Connections	To Sölden in the Ötztal valley 5hr. Postbus to Oetz. Hildesheimer Hut 4–6hr. Dresdner 4hr. Amberger 4hr
Address	Thomas Grollmus, Hoch Stubai Hütte, Hütten Sölden 204, A 6450 Sölden, Austria
Telephone	Hut (0043) 676 924 3343; mobile (0043) 720 920 305
Email	grollmustom@tmo.at
Website	www.hochstubaihuette.at

This is a brilliant hut in the Gemütlichkeit tradition. It is the highest in the Stubai and the third-highest hut in Austria after the Erzherzog Johann Hut (Adlersruhe) on the Grossglockner and the Brandenburger Hut in the Ötztal. The hut was built in the early 1930s to allow climbers to explore the mountains of the Daunkogel and to provide a base midway between the Amberger and Hildesheimer huts.

During World War 2, the hut was used as a base to train the elite German alpine troops of the Wehrmacht, the Gebirgsjäger. Thereafter, plundered and abandoned, the hut reopened in 1951 albeit in a semi-ruinous state. Struggling to make ends meet, the Hoch Stubai Hut saw various Hüttenwirts through the 1950s and 1960s until the Fiegl family took over in 1972, managing the hut until recently.

Today the hut is managed by the charismatic Thomas Grollmus, and long may it continue. This is a large hut for its location, superbly situated on a rocky knoll overlooking the Ötztal and the adjacent peaks of the Daunkogel with their attendant glaciers.

Not surprisingly, the views from the hut are magnificent.

The Hoch Stubai Hut

KLOSTERGASTHOF MARIA WALDRAST (1638M)

Owner	Private
Location	Situated in a forest clearing on the Gleinser Jöchl, on the eastern slopes of Serles
Open	From mid June to end September
Facilities	45B. Excellent restaurant and toilet facilities, similar to that of a modest hotel. Internet facility
Connections	To Mieders at the head of the Stubai valley. To Matrei in the Wipptal valley. Padasterjochhaus 6hr via the Kalbenjoch (2215m). Taxi service available from Christopher Mader tel (0043) 664 788 0540; Michael Eller www.busreisen-eller.at (only available with prior reservation)
Excursions	Serles (2717m) 3hr
Address	Klostergasthof Maria Waldrast, Mützens 27, A-6143 Mützens, Tirol, Austria
Telephone	Hut (0043)05273 6219
Email	info@mariawaldrast.at
Website	www.mariawaldrast.at

This is not so much a hut or a hotel but a fine group of monastic buildings, including a church, which has been a centre of pilgrimage for several hundred years. The monastery provides visitors with overnight accommodation and simple but excellent food. Now renamed Waldrast Nature Resort, the monastery specialises in all sorts of wellness, from religious to yoga retreats. It is a fabulous place and a visit is highly recommended.

For those who are interested, the resident priests are more than happy to provide guided tours.

STORY OF MARIA WALDRAST

The actual chapel is located in the forest above the monastery, midway between the monastery and the little peak of Waldraster Jöchl (1878m).

In the 13th century two young shepherd boys discovered an image of the Virgin Mary in a tree trunk. On returning home, the boys described what they had seen and all the villagers went to see for themselves. Impressed with what they saw, they took it back to their village and then to the parish church in Matrei, at that time a considerable distance away.

Jakob Lusch, a young man from Matrei, is said to have heard a voice telling him to build a church at the place where the boys had found the image of the Virgin Mary. He hesitated at first, but when out in the forest one day he fell asleep under a tree. Waking to the sound of church bells, he saw a young woman with a child in her arms.

And so, in 1407, Jakob began to build the church of Maria Waldrast, which was consecrated 20 years later in 1429. It has remained an important place of pilgrimage ever since. The original church was demolished in 1724, with rebuilding taking place from 1724–38, to its present size.

Nearby, adjacent to the signpost for the climb to Serles, is a holy well, the Marienbrunnen, where, according to folklore, two blind pilgrims had their eyesight restored by drinking its holy waters.

It is fine water indeed and well worth replenishing your water bottle with, to refresh aching limbs with youthful vigour.

Maria Waldrast, with the Zillertal Alps on the horizon to the left

INNSBRUCKER HUT (2369M)

Owner	ÖAV Sektion Tourist Club, Innsbruck
Location	Situated on the Pinnisjoch, at the foot of the Habicht east ridge
Open	From late June to end September
Facilities	30B/70M/12N. Excellent restaurant and toilet facilities, with hot water on tap most of the day. Token-operated showers. Internet facility. Rucksack-delivery service to the Bremer Hut available for a modest fee
Connections	To Neustift in the Stubai valley and Gschnitz. Postbus from Neustift to Innsbruck or Feuerstein to Steinach. Jeep service available from Neder to the Pinnisalm and Karalm: departs at 09:00. Taxi service available from Neustifter Funktaxi tel 0664 287 7000 or 05226 2877. Feuerstein 2hr. Bremer Hut 7–8hr
Address	Franz and Marlene Egger, Innsbrucker Hütte, Schulweg 12, A-6167 Neustift im Stubaital, Austria
Telephone	Hut (0043) 5276 295
Email	office@innsbrucker-huette.at
Website	www.innsbrucker-huette.at

This superbly sited hut, first established in 1884 then extended in 1982 and modernised in 2000, has excellent facilities.

Of interest to Alpenverein Britannia members is the Britannia Stube, dedicated to member Harry Parkes who was generous in bequeathing the funds for the refurbishment of the dining room. Harry was an active member for many years, having a great affection for the Tirol and the Stubai in particular.

Because of the hut's proximity to the Habicht (3277m) and its relatively easy access from Innsbruck via the Pinnistal, the hut is very popular as a weekend venue, when it is often packed to capacity. This pressure on bed space has been somewhat exacerbated with the creation of the Gschnitztaler Rundweg.

It is a charming hut with an unrivalled view of the Tribulaun mountains and the pinnacles of the Serleskamm. For those with sharp eyes, the Austrian Tribulaunhaus is clearly visible across the great void of the Gschnitztal valley. Sadly, the original Tribulaunhaus hut was blown to smithereens in 1975 when it was hit by a huge avalanche off the Eisenspitze.

The Innsbrucker Hut

MAGDEBURGER HUT (2423M)

Owner	CAI Vipiteno, Sterzing, South Tirol
Other names	Alte Magdeburger Hut 2423m; Rifugio Cremona alla Stua
Location	Also known as the Schneespitze Hut, the hut is situated near the Stubensee glacial pond, overlooking the Innerpflersch-St Anton valley
Open	Late June to end September
Facilities	35B/20M. Good restaurant and toilet facilities. Token-operated showers
Connections	Innerpflersch-St Anton 4hr. Bremer Hut 7hr. Teplitzer Hut 5hr. Austrian Tribulaunhaus 5hr. Italian Tribulaun Hut 3–4hr
Address	Anna Kumpf, Erica Sorte, Mauro Scattolini, Magdeburger Hütte, I-39040 Val di Fleres, Italy
Tel	Hut: (0039) 0472 632472; mobile: (0039) 338 2428278
Email	rifugiocremon@gmail.com
Website	www.rifugiocremona.com

The Magdeburger Hut

HUT DIRECTORY

This substantial two-storey shingle-clad hut was built in 1886, extended in 1970 and fully renovated in 1980. Since then the hut has remained largely unchanged apart from a few cosmetic improvements. As it is not situated on any of the main hut-to-hut routes, it enjoys a relaxed atmosphere.

The hut was originally owned by the DuÖAV Sektion Magdeburg, named after the medieval city of Magdeburg in the province of Saxony-Anhalt in Northern Germany, previously in the East German Democratic Republic before German reunification in October 1990.

In 1919 at the end of World War 1, the Magdeburger was one of 72 huts forfeited to Italy during the Treaty of St Germain. The new Neue Magdeburger Hut, built to replace it, is located in the Karwendel Mountains near Innsbruck. Thereafter, the hut has a chequered history, similar to other huts along the Austrian–Italian border, particularly the Teplitzer Hut, when it was closed to visitors as it was used as a border control point by the Italian military.

After World War 2, the hut remained closed, mostly due to the political shenanigans of the 1960s resulting from the South Tirol Question, when the hut was once again occupied by the Italian military. During those difficult years, all of the hut's provisions had to be delivered on foot or transported by horses.

This is a good hut for all the right reasons: location, food, beds and friendliness.

MÜLLER HUT (3145M)

Owner	CAI Sektion Bolzano
Other names	Rifugio Cima Libera 3145m, also known as the Pfaffennieder Hut
Location	Located at the foot of the Wilder Freiger's south-west ridge, a little above the Pfaffennieder col
Open	From mid June to mid September
Facilities	23B/65M/6N. Good restaurant facilities, but because of its height and location, not as comprehensive as other huts. Toilet facilities are very basic due to the limited water supply; take your wet wipes with you!
Connections	No valley connections. There are no easy ways off the mountain from this hut as all involve glacier crossings. The safest route is to retreat to Italy and Sterzing. Becherhaus 1hr. Sulzenau Hut 4hr. Nürnberger Hut 4–5hr
Address	Heidi Wettstein, Müller Hütte, Mühlenweg 35, A-6167 Neustift, Austria
Telephone	Hut (0043) 699 186 78965
Email	info@muellerhuette.eu
Website	www.muellerhuette.eu

Karl von Müller first established a hut here in 1907, naming it Erzherzog Franz Josef in honour of the emperor. The hut soon fell apart and was abandoned. A second hut was built on the present site; this also was sadly neglected for many years, being one of the huts forfeited to Italy after World War 1.

Since the hut sits on the Austrian–Italian border, it was more or less closed to alpinists between 1926 and 1973 as a result of the political tit for tat going on between the two countries. During the years of instability, the Italian border police and military frequently used the hut as a base from which they could patrol the border.

Not surprisingly, over this long period the hut was misused and bit by bit fell into a ruinous state. In the early 1970s the CAI made efforts to patch up the old hut using materials scavenged from its interior or from its close neighbour, the Becherhaus, which had fallen into a similar derelict state. Fortunately, both

HUT DIRECTORY

The Müller Hut

huts have since been rebuilt and reopened. In the case of the Müller Hut, rebuilt means patched up using old doors and timbers. Consequently, the hut is very much a ramshackle building full of creaking and groaning timbers, but it has a character not found in other huts.

At best the hut is functional and perhaps a poignant reminder of what all huts would have been like not so many years ago, before the advent of electricity, showers and flush toilets.

But more importantly, from the alpinist's point of view, the hut is located in a prominent position, set as it is among the Stubai's highest mountains and its biggest glaciers. Therefore, for mountaineering purposes, the hut is ideally placed for excursions along the Frontier Ridge. While the hut is a bit basic, the views from the terrace are some of the best there are. Perhaps there is a certain amount of Gemütlichkeit in the old building after all.

NEUE REGENSBURGER HUT (2286M)

Owner	DAV Sektion Regensburg
Location	Located on the marshy plateau of the Falbesoner valley, below the Ruderhofspitze.
Open	From mid June to end September
Facilities	26B/57M/5N. Excellent restaurant facilities but a bit limited on toilet provision for the size of the hut. Token-operated showers. Internet facility
Connections	To Falbesoner in the main Stubai valley 2½hr. Postbus to Neustift and Innsbruck. Dresdner Hut 6–8hr. Franz Senn Hut 4–5hr
Address	Familie Tomaselli, Neue Regensburger Hütte, A-6150 Gschnitz 50, Austria
Telephone	Hut (0043) 664 202 95 or (0043) 664 202 5070
Email	info@regensburgerhuette.at also office@n-r-h.at
Website	www.regensburgerhuette.at

Built in 1931, this fairly modern hut was subsequently enlarged in 1967–68. It was built to replace the original hut, which was forfeited to Italy after World War 1. The original hut is sited in the Geisler region of the Dolomites, to the north of the Langkofel Group (Sassopiatto).

Reputed to be the cleanest of all the huts in the Stubai, it is a very pleasant hut with an excellent view of the Habicht.

NÜRNBERGER HUT (2278M)

Owner	DAV Sektion Nürnberg
Location	Situated at the head of the Langtal valley
Open	From mid June to October
Facilities	45B/75M/10N. Excellent restaurant and toilet facilities, including showers on tap most of the day
Connections	To Ranalt in the main Stubai valley 2hr. Postbus to Neustift and on to Innsbruck: 09:08 / 10:08 / 11:08. Bremer Hut 4hr. Sulzenau Hut via the Niederl 3hr, via the Mairspitze 4hr. Müller Hut or Becherhaus via Wilder Freiger 5hr
Address	Herr Leonhard Siller, Nürnberger Hütte, Dorf Schulweg Nr 28, A-6167 Neustift im Stubaital, Austria
Telephone	Hut (0043) 664 165 74611
Email	info@nuernberghuette.at
Website	www.nuernbergerhuette.at

This magnificent old hut, four stories high, is more akin to a hotel for tourists than a hut for mountain climbers, but its size does not detract from its obvious popularity and charm. Built in 1886 and then extended in 1898 and 1908 to its present size, the hut underwent general refurbishment in 1962.

The Nürnberger Hut

The hut has a lot of history and like a number of other huts owned by the DAV, it reflects the great wealth of the German Alpine Club prior to World War 1. Many of the bedrooms are fitted with wash basins with hot and cold water, and a number of water fountains are placed along its corridors, with an absolutely magnificent fountain in the main dining room.

The main dining room is very pleasant in the Gemütlichkeit tradition, with some fine carpentry details embracing the panelled walls. Not surprisingly, the hut is very popular due to its close proximity to the Wilder Freiger and the summits of the Feuerstein, with what remain of the Feuerstein's hanging glaciers in clear view from the hut's front door.

Its popularity has also been greatly enhanced by the excellent service rendered by the Siller family for the best part of 100 years.

PADASTERJOCHHAUS (2232M)

Owner	Naturfreunde Innsbruck
Location	Situated in the large open combe below the peaks of the Wasenwand and Hammerspitze
Open	June to late September
Facilities	Good restaurant facilities, but limited toilet facilities that can be cramped when the hut is full
Connections	Trins 2½hr. Innsbrucker Hut via Trins 6hr. Blaser Hut 5hr. Innsbrucker Hut via Kirchdachspitze and Silbersattel 8hr, described as a full-on Bergtour. To Innsbrucker Hut via Issenangeralm and Hammerscharte 6–7hr. Note the route has partly changed following the violent storm of 2022
Address	Paul Pranger, Padasterjochhaus, Naturfreunde, Plöven 60, A-6165 Telfes, Austria
Tel	(0043) 699 111 753 52
Email	info@padasterjochhaus.at
Website	www.padasterjochhaus.at

The hut is managed by Paul and Agi Pranger, who have provided visitors with top-drawer service in the Gemütlichkeit tradition over many years.

Built in 1907, the hut enjoys a relaxed atmosphere since it is not on any of the main hut-to-hut routes. It has stunning views of the Tribulaun and the more distant peaks of the Zillertal. That said, the main excursion from the hut is an ascent of the

Kirchdachspitze (2840m), the mountain with the 'church roof' and 'spire', which along with Serles makes up the two most important peaks in the range.

When travelling from Maria Waldrast, phone the hut to arrange to be met at the forest track where rucksacks can be transported to the hut for a modest fee.

For those visitors arriving from the Kesselspitze, as you approach the hut, don't be surprised to see Paul's one-hole golf course. Golf balls really do zing at that altitude.

SEDUCKER HOCHALM (2256M)

Owner	Private, Marcus Illmer
Location	Situated just below the Wildkopfscharte, which leads to the Potsdamer Hut, and approximately halfway between the Franz Senn Hut and the Starkenburger Hut, overlooking the Obernbergtal valley
Open	End June to mid September
Facilities	8M. Good but limited restaurant facilities due to its location. Toilet facilities are very modest but adequate for its size
Connections	Franz Senn Hut 3hr. Starkenburger Hut 4hr
Address	No address as such
Telephone	(0043) 0650 968 229 or 0664 7390 7959
Email	seduckerhochalm@gmail.com

Situated on the Franz Senn–Starkenburger trail, this superb little hut was at one time a sheperd's hut with the motto 'my kingdom is a flock of white sheep and my little hut is my castle'. The hut was also used by hunters searching for the *Gams* goat-antelope. Being where it is, the hut is frequently used by visitors escaping poor weather. That aside, if you are a small group why not split your journey and stay over at the hut to experience what huts would have been like over a hundred years ago.

It's a magical place!

SIEGERLAND HUT (2710M)

Owner	DAV Sektion Siegerland
Location	Located at the foot of the south-west spur of the Sonklarspitze, on a rocky platform overlooking the Windach valley
Open	From early July to end September
Facilities	26B/21M/6N. Good restaurant and toilet facilities
Connections	To Gaisstal then to Sölden in the Ötztal valley. Hildesheimer Hut 3hr. Müller Hut 5hr
Address	Herr Raimund Gritsch, Siegerland Hütte, Hütten Sölden 203, A6450 Sölden, Ötztal, Austria
Telephone	Hut (0043) 664 241 4040
Email	office@sigerlandhuette.com
Website	www.siegerlandhuette.com

This is a fine stone building with a large circular buttress and a commanding view of the Ötztal.

The hut was built in 1930 and has remained virtually unchanged since then. Its dining room is particularly warm and pleasant in the Gemütlichkeit tradition. Most visitors will relish sitting in its bay windows, enjoying a meal and a superb view across the Ötztal.

It is one of the most charming huts in the Stubai.

The Siegerland Hut

STARKENBURGER HUT (2237M)

Owner	DAV Sektion Darmstadt-Starkenburg
Location	On the hillside above Neustift, at the foot of the Hoher Burgstall
Open	From June to October
Facilities	30B/24M/6N. Excellent restaurant and toilet facilities
Connections	To Neustift or Fulpmes in the main Stubai valley 3hr. Franz Senn Hut 6–7hr. Adoplf Pichler Hut 2–3hr
Address	Karin and Martin Tanzer, Starkenburger Hütte, Ausserain 573, A-6167 Falbeson im Stubaital, Austria
Telephone	Hut (0043) 664 503 5420
Email	office@starkenburgerhuette.at or km.tanzer@gmx.at
Website	www.alpenverein-darmstadt.de/huetten

A tiny hut was first built here in 1900 as a base for exploration of the limestone peaks of the Kalkkögel. Thereafter, the hut has been regularly enlarged, in 1905, 1914, 1965, 1975 and 1981, with internal renovation taking place in 2000, when the porch was added.

The hut is extremely popular with day visitors from Neustift, who are prepared to sweat up 1300m to reach it. This means that the hut is likely to be packed on arrival, but it is not unusual to have the run of the place once the sun has gone down. If you are lucky with the weather, the sunset and night sky from the hut are truly memorable.

The Starkenburger is a friendly hut whose guardians, the Tanzer family, will often be seen fussing over their UK visitors to ensure they have as pleasant a stay as possible. That is Gemütlichkeit by example.

The Starkenburger Hut, with Habicht in the distance

Trekking in Austria's Stubai Alps

SULZENAU HUT (2191M)

Owner	DAV Sektion Sulzenau
Location	Situated below the snout of the Sulzenauferner glacier, above Grawa Alm in the Stubaital
Open	From mid June to end September
Facilities	40B/100M/12N. Excellent restaurant and toilet facilities, with hot water on tap throughout the day. Coin-operated showers. And if you are ill, the hut has a resident doctor to take care of you
Connections	To Grawa Alm then Neustift in the main Stubai valley 2+hr. Nürnberger Hut 3–4hr. Dresdner Hut via the Peiljoch 3–4hr, via the Grosser Trögler 4hr
Address	Familie Gleirscher, Sulzenau Hütte, Schmieden 10, A-6167 Neustift im Stubaital, Austria
Telephone	Hut (0043) 5226 24320
Email	info@sulzenauhuette.at
Website	www.sulzenau.com

The Sulzenau Hut

This entirely new hut was built in 1976–78 to replace the original hut, which was completely demolished by an avalanche off the Sulzenaukogel in 1975. Splendid pictures in the dining room lay testimony to the awesome powers of nature that were unleashed on that fateful day. While the hut shows off its new sign, the old sign is still proudly displayed on the wall in the hallway.

The hut is managed by the Schöpf family from Neustift, who have provided a sterling service in the Gemütlichkeit tradition for many generations, spanning almost 100 years.

The Sulzenau is a popular hut, due to its close proximity to the Zuckerhütl (3505m) and Wilder Freiger (3418m), and because of this it is frequently used for climbing courses organised by the DAV-ÖAV, whose practice crags are evident en route to the Peiljoch.

This is a justifiably popular hut with a fine view across the Stubai towards the Kalkkögel and the Starkenburger Hut.

TEPLITZER HUT (2586M)

Owner	CAI, Landeshütter, Provincial Administration of South Tirol; Bolzano
Other names	Rifugio Vedretta Pendente
Location	A fine location overlooking remnants of some of the area's biggest glaciers, including the fast-shrinking Übeltalferner
Open	Late June to end September
Facilities	30B/27M. Good restaurant facilities, including a small bar. Hot water on tap all day
Connections	Ridnaun-Maiern 3½hr. Grohman Hut 1hr. Becherhaus 3–4hr. Magdeburger Hut via Magdeburger Scharte 6–7hr
Address	Familie Haller Davis, Teplitzer Hütte, Ridnaun-Reid 13, I-39040 Ratschings, Bolzano, Italy
Tel	(0039) 0338 135 8371; (0043) 699 103 21999
Email	info@teplitzerhuette.com
Website	www.teplitzerhuette.com

This hut is in the top drawer of all huts, having maintained the Gemütlichkeit tradition over many years, and enjoys stunning views towards the Übeltalferner glacier and the more distant peaks of the Dolomites.

It was built in 1880 and extended in 1898, when the second floor was constructed, with the new dining room being added many years later in 1992. The two-storey, shingle-clad hut enjoys a relaxed atmosphere since it is not on any of the main hut-to-hut routes.

The hut was originally owned by the DuÖAV Sektion Teplitz-Schönau and is named after the old Bohemian town of Teplitz (Teplice) on the northern Czech border with East Prussia, south of Dresden. In 1919, at the end of World War 1, it was one of the 72 DuÖAV huts forfeited to Italy during the Treaty of St Germain. Thereafter, the hut suffered a chequered history, but mostly it was closed to visitors as it was occupied by the Italian military and used as a border control point, similar to the other newly acquired huts along the Austrian–South Tirol border. The difference is that it took 60 years for the army to leave.

During World War 2, the hut came under attack more than once from the American Air Force as the Allied Armies advanced through Italy. During a raid on Sterzing, an American Liberator bomber crashed onto the Übeltalferner glacier, scattering wreckage far and wide, including a 50-calibre machine gun. The rusting relic is now displayed at the hut.

After the war, the hut was closed, and then with smuggling and political shenanigans of the 1960s because of the South Tirol Question, the hut was once again occupied by the Italian military, who trashed it. The hut was eventually reopened in 1979 by Karl Markart with the help of the local mountain rescue team, who helped to clean the place up.

Since that time the hut has been associated with the Haller family, first by Grandfather Karl Markart and then by Grandmother Margareth, who managed the hut more or less single-handedly for 30 years. During those difficult early years, all of the provisions had to be physically carried to the hut, including the 100kg stove necessary for cooking meals. During this period, there was some problem with licensing the hut, so the position of Hüttenwirt was transferred to Margareth Markart. Fast forward to the present day and the hut is now managed by the fourth generation, Davis Haller and his wife Mary. Today the hut is provisioned by helicopter, ferrying anything between 20 and 25 loads during the short 12-week season.

This is a brilliant hut for all the right reasons: location, food, beds and friendliness. In fact, Alpenverein Britannia members on the Stubai Sud Tirol Bergtour were unanimous in voting the Teplitzer the 'Best Hut' of the tour.

TRIBULAUNHAUS (AUSTRIAN) (2064M)

Owner	Naturfreunde, Ortsgruppe, Innsbruck
Location	Located in a fine situation at the foot of the Gschnitzer Tribulaun, overlooking the head of the Gschnitztal valley towards the Serleskamm ridge dominated by the peaks of Serles, the Kirchdachspitze, the Habicht and, for those with eagle eyes, the Innsbrucker Hut
Open	June to end September
Facilities	2B/45M/12N. Good restaurant facilities, including a small bar. Hot water on tap all day. The hut specialises in yoga retreat weekends
Connections	Gasthof Feuerstein 2hr. Italian Tribulaun Hut 2½hr. Bremer Hut via Jubiläumssteig 6–7hr. Magdeburger Hut 5hr. Gschnitzer Tribulaun (2946m) 3hr. Gargglerin (2470m) 2½hr. Truna Hut 6–7hr. Obernberg 6–7hr
Address	Verena Salchner, Tribulaun Hütte
Tel	(0043) 664 4050 951
Email	info@tribulaunhuette.at
Website	www.tribulaunhuette.at

The modern, two-storey, shingle-clad hut that you see today enjoys a relaxed atmosphere and hides quite well some of the tragedies it has had to endure.

The Tribulaunhaus started life in 1922 as a typical two-storey mountain hut with a pitched roof and accommodation for around 20 people. It was used as a base for climbing on the peaks of the Tribulaun when access to the south side of the mountains was barred because of the annexation of South Tirol to Italy at the end of World War 1. A major extension of the hut took place in 1927 and then again in 1934 when, during the rise of National Socialism, ownership of the hut was acquiesced to the state. This didn't matter much, as the hut was totally destroyed by an avalanche in 1935.

A new hut was built more or less on the same site in 1936, with beds for 24 and Matratzenlager for 64. In 1938 the hut was renamed the 'Reichsverband fuer Deutsche Jugendherbergen', the Hitler Youth, and given to DAV Sektion Bamberg to manage between 1940 and 1945.

Immediately after the end of World War 2, the Naturfreunde nature group from Innsbruck regained control of the (their) hut in May 1945 and reinstated its original name, the Tribulaunhaus.

The Tribulaunhaus

Peace and quiet returned to the hut until March 1975 when the hut was totally destroyed by an avalanche that lifted the hut entirely off its base and dumped it unceremoniously down the mountainside, scattering debris far and wide. Only the foundations survived; these can still be seen adjacent to the winter room.

In 1979 a new hut was opened, one that stood in complete contrast with the traditional architecture of the previous hut. The new hut was functional in style: a low-cost, prefabricated, two-storey, shingle-clad shoebox with a large dining room and beds for 24 and Matrazenlager for 36. This arrangement served well until 2014 when the hut was completely refurbished with a new kitchen, bathrooms and bedrooms and the exterior was reclad in the larch shingles that you see today.

As you sit peacefully on the terrace, imagine the roar of the avalanche as it swept down from the mountains of the Tribulaun.

The hut is delightful and would be worthy of a 'Best Hut' award if there were one. Just watching Verena and her family team of four generations, from great-grandma to great-granddaughter, pitching in to help out makes this a fabulous hut in every sense of the word.

TRIBULAUN HUT (ITALIAN) (2369M)

This hut is in the top drawer of all huts, having maintained the Gemütlichkeit tradition over many years.

Owner	CAI Sektion Sterzing (Vipiteno)
Other names	Rifugio Cesare Calciati al Tribulaun

Location	A fine location in a glacial bowl adjacent to the Sandesee lake and wholly dominated by the 500m-high limestone cliffs of the Pflerscher Tribulaun Sud Wand (3097m)
Open	Late June to end September
Facilities	19B/18M/10N. The menu is a bit limited because of the hut's size, but the food provided is excellent and home-cooked. Since the hut is quite small (part of its charm), reservations are advised, particularly at weekends
Connections	Pflersch 3hr. Obernberg 6hr. Tribulaun Hut via Sandesjöchl 3hr, via Schneetalscharte 6–7hr. Magdeburger Hut via Weissenwandspitze 5hr. Bremer Hut 7hr
Address	Daniela Eisendle and Fabrizio Ballerini, CAI Tribulaun Hütte, Pflersch, I-39040 Gossenass, Bolzano (Bozen), Italy
Telephone	(0039) 0472 632470; (0043) 0699 103 21999
Email	info@tribulaunhuette.com
Website	www.tribulaunhuette.com

The DuÖAV Sektion Magdeburg first proposed a hut in the area as early as 1873, but for whatever reason another 20 years would pass before the small single-storey hut was built and opened in 1892 with bed spaces for 18 people.

Thereafter, a major refurbishment of the hut took place in 1907 when the hut doubled in size with the addition of a two-storey extension with several bedrooms. During this period the route was established to the Magdeburger Hut, across the Hoher Zahn and Weissandwand and across the Schneetalscharte (2657m), on what is now the border with Austria, to Gschnitztal and the now Austrian, TVN (Touristenverein Naturfreunde) Tribulaunhaus, established in 1935.

All was fine up to World War 1, during which time the Haus was mostly closed. At the end of the war the hut was transferred to Italy along with 72 other DuÖAV huts as part of Austria's war reparations. Little is recorded about the period between the war years, but during World War 2 the hut was attacked and strafed by the American Air Force as the Allied Armies advanced through Italy, not surprising bearing in mind how close the hut is to the Brenner Pass.

At the end of World War 2 the hut was more or less a ruined shell, without a roof or windows. In 1949 ownership of the hut passed from CAI Cremona to CAI Sterzing, with construction of the new hut starting in 1953. The biggest problem at the time was getting material to the hut, and mule trains a hundred strong were used. Again, many years would pass before the newly rebuilt hut finally opened

The Tribulaun Hut

in 1960. But difficulties continued for the hut because of the Austrian-Italian tension on the border resulting from the long-standing problem of the South Tirol Question. The Italian military occupied the hut from 1963 to 1972 when, fortunately for CAI Sterzing, the hut reopened with Paul Eisendle taking on the role of Hüttenwirt for almost 30 years, retiring in 2000 when his daughter Daniela and Fabrizio Ballerini took over the management of the hut.

The scenery around the hut is simply stunning, being wholly dominated by the sheer rock faces of the Gschnitzer Tribulaun (2946m) and the Pflerscher Tribulaun (3097m), which provide aspiring rock climbers with many challenging routes.

This is a brilliant hut for all the right reasons: location, scenery, food, beds and friendliness. In fact, Alpenverein Britannia members on the Exploring the Peaks and Passes of the Serleskamm and Tribulaun Bergtour were unanimous in voting the CAI Tribulaun the 'Best Hut' of the tour.

TRUNA HUT (1750M)

Owner	Private
Location	Located on the upper Trunawald forest zone where the forest meets the upper pastures overlooking the Gschnitztal valley
Open	June to mid September

Hut directory

Facilities	2B(1x3 and 1x4)/10M. Good restaurant and toilet facilities, with a spacious bar. Popular as a day venue from Trins or the cable-car station at Bergeralm. Taxi service also available with prior arrangement
Connections	Trins 2hr. Tribulaun Hut 6–7hr. Bergeralm cable-car station 3hr.
Address	Familie Schlögl, Truna Hütte, Trins 195, A- 6152, Trins-Gschnitztal, Austria
Tel	(0043) 676 413 4880; mobile (0043) 6764134880
Email	schloegl@graf-ferdinand.at
Website	www.trunahuette.at

This semi-two-storey converted *Alm* (old farmhouse) is a super little hut that has maintained the Gemütlichkeit tradition over many years. Built in 1928, the hut enjoys a relaxed atmosphere with its pleasant location in the forest. Sadly, the hut is a little too low down to enjoy views of the high peaks.

Just outside the hut an information board tells the story of an unfortunate American Airforce bomber crew that was shot out of the sky just before the end of World War 2. The debris was scattered far and wide, and you will recall that one of the plane's machine guns now rests peacefully at the Teplitzer Hut.

Visitors on the Gschnitztaler Rundtour should note the importance of making a reservation. By not doing so, and if there are no other guests, the lady of the house, Ingrid, will have simply locked up and gone home.

The Truna Hut

APPENDIX A
Useful contacts

Websites and tourist information
Some of these are currently in German, but they will inevitably be translated into English at some stage.

Visit Austria
www.Austria.info

Stubai
www.stubai.at

Neustift tourist information
www.stubai.at

Austrian National Tourist Office
tel 020 7440 3830
london@austria.info
www.austria.com
www.austriatourism.com

Stubai Rucksack Route
www.stubai.at/stubaier-hoehenweg

Wipptal Tourist Office
tourismus@wipptal.at
http://www.wipptal.at

Transport
Austrian State Railways
www.oebb.at

Bus service
www.postbus.at

Four Seasons Travel
A-6020 Innsbruck
tel 0043 512 58 41 57
office@airport-transfer.com
www.tirol-taxi.at

Stubaital taxi services
Taxi Pranger
tel 0043 664 16 34 190

Wipptal Taxi
tel 0043 664 12 23 055

Bus Reisen
Eller, Brennerstrasse 29, A-6150
Steinach am Brenner, Tirol, Austria
http://www.busreisen-eller.at
0043 5272 210 7012

Alp Transfer Trins and Wipptal
info@alptransfer.tirol
http://www.alptransfer.tirol
tel 0043 664 230 9392

Austrian Alpine Club
Austrian Alpine Club (UK) Alpenverein Britannia
Austrian Alpine Club (UK)
28 South Street
Wareham
Dorset
BH20 4LU
tel 0044 1929 556870
aac.office@aacuk.org.uk
www.alpenverein.at/britannia

Austrian Alpine Club Head Office in Austria
Österreichischer Alpenverein
Olympiastrasse
A-6020 Innsbruck
tel 0043 512 59547
office@alpenverein.at
www.alpenverein.at

Appendix A – Useful contacts

Professional mountain guides (Bergführer)

Should you require the services of a professional mountain guide, these can be hired in Neustift.

Bergfuehrerburo Stubai Alpin
A-6167 Neustift im Stubaital
Austria
tel 0043 5226 3461, 2322 or 2983
alpin@stubai.org
www.stubai-alpin.com

Also, the British Association of International Mountain Leaders, to which the author belongs.

British Association of International Mountain Leaders
www.baiml.org

Accommodation

For mountain huts, see
www.alpenverein.at/huetten
www.alpsonline.org
www.alpenverein.at/britannia
www.bergsteigen.at/de/huttendetail.aspx

In **Steinach am Brenner** and starting point for the Gschnitztal Rune Tour:

Zur Rose Hotel
Located within ten minutes walk from the village railway station. Good, inexpensive hotel accommodation. You can leave surplus bags there to pick up on your return.
tel 0043 (0) 5252 6221
info@hotelrose.at

Should you have to stay in **Innsbruck**, the following hotels are recommended.

Hotel Mondschein
Located just across the Innbrücke bridge on the north side of the River Inn, less than a 5min walk to the old part of the city, the Alte Stadt.
tel 0043 512 22784
office@mondschein.at
www.mondschein.at

Basic Hotel
There is nothing basic about this hotel, other than it caters for short-stay clients. Located close to the River Inn and a 5min walk to the old part of the city, the Alte Stadt.
tel 0043 512 586385
info@basic-hotel.at
www.basic-hotel.at

Alternatively, there are a handful of hostels:

Nepomuk's Backpackers' Hostel
Located just off the main square, in the old part of the Alte Stadt, above the Konditorei cake shop. Highly recommended.
tel 0043 664 7879197 or 0043 512 584118
mail@nepomuks.at
www.nepomuks.at

Jungendherberge Fritz-Prior-Schwedenhaus
Rennweg 17b
A-6020 Innsbruck
Located in the district of Saggen by the River Inn.
tel 0043 512585 814–27
info@hostel-innsbruck.com
hostel-innsbruck.com

Volkshaus Hostel Innsbruck
Redetzky Strasse 47
A-6020 Innsbruck
Located in the district of Reichenau.
tel 0043 664 266 7004
info@hostel-innsbruck.at
www.hostel-innsbruck.at

Jungendherberge Innsbruck and Studentenheim
Reichenau Strasse 147
A-6020 Innsbruck
Located to the north-east of the city, in the district of Reichenau by the River Inn.
tel 0043 512 346179/346180
info@youth-hostel-innsbruck.at
youth-hostel-innsbruck.at

If you have to stay overnight in **Neustift**, the Hotel Berghof (info@berghof-tirol.com www.berghof-tirol.com), located adjacent to the Elfer cable-car station, is a very good place to stay.

If you have to stay overnight in **Salzburg**, the family-run Das Grüne Hotel zur Post (tel 0043 662 8323390 info@hotelzurpost.info) is recommended, located 5min from the airport and a 15min walk from the centre of this fine old city.

Weather

For weather forecasts on the go, visit:

Tyrol.com, then choose an area

AccuWeather.com, then choose an area

Weather25.com, then choose the country and area

Emergencies

- Mountain rescue (*Bergrettung Austria*) 140
- Mountain rescue (*Bergrettung Italy*) 118
- Red Cross (*Rotes Kreutz*) 144
- European emergency phone number 112

APPENDIX B
German–English glossary

German	English
Getting around	
Flughafen	airport
Hauptbahnhof	railway station
Bushaltestelle	bus stop
Ausgang/Eingang	exit/entrance
Ankunft/Abflug/Abfahrt	arrivals/departures
Auskunft	information office
Platz – Reservierung	booking office
Fahrkarten schalter	ticket office
Gleis/Bahnsteig	platform
Einfach	one way/single
Ruckfahrkarte/Hin und Zuruck	round-trip/return
Ich möchte	I would like …
Wo ist …	Where is …?
Ich suche …	I'm looking for …
At the table	
Frühstück	breakfast
Mittag	lunch
Abendessen	dinner
Speisekarte	menu
Tasse	cup
Teller	plate
Schussel	bowl
Messer	knife
Gabel	fork
Loffel	spoon
Selected menu	
Apfelstrudel	apple pie
Bergsteigeressen	mountaineers' meal: low cost and potluck
Brot/Brotchen	bread/bread rolls
Compote	fresh or tinned fruit
Gemischter salat	mixed salad
Gemuse	vegetables
Gruner salat	green salad
Gulash	cubes of beef in a rich sauce
Jager Schnitzel	veal/pork fillets with mushroom topping
Kaiserschmarren	sweet pancakes
Kartoffel mit Spiegeleier	pan-fried potatoes with fried egg
Kartoffel-gaertreide-bratlinge	pan-fried potatoes
Kartoffeln	potato

German	English
Käsebrot	cheese and bread
Kasspatzle	cheese with noodles
Knodelsuppe	soup with dumplings
Mit Salatgarnitur	with salad garnish
Pfeffer	pepper
Reis	rice
Salt	salt
Schinken Brot	ham and bread
Senf	mustard
Spiegeleier und Schinken	fried eggs and bacon
Tagesuppe	soup of the day
Tyroler Grotzl	fried potato and eggs
Vegetarische	vegetarian
Wiener Schnitzel	breaded veal/pork fillets
Wurst Brot	sausage and bread
Wurstsuppe	soup with sausages
Zweibelrostbraten	broiled or fried beef with onions

Drinks

German	English
Bier	beer
Gross/Klein	large/small
Heiss/Kalt	hot/cold
Schnapps	clear, strong alcoholic spirit, aka rocket fuel!
Tee/Café/Milch	tea/coffee/milk
Viertel/Halb	quarter/half
Weiss/Rot Wein	white/red wine
Zitronen	lemonade

Ordering and paying

German	English
Wie bitte	Excuse me
Sprechen Sie Englisch?	Do you speak English?
Kann ich haben …?	Can I have …?
Haben sie …?	Have you …?
Haben sie vegetarische Gerichte Essen …?	Do you have vegetarian meals?
Wieviel?/Mein zahlen, bitte	How much?/My bill, please
Die Rechnung, bitte	The bill, please

Mountain terminology

German	English
Alm	alpine hut/pastures
Alpenvereins	Alpine Association
Bach/Wasserfal	river/stream/waterfall
Band/Grat/Kamm	ledge/ridge
Berg	mountain
Bergführer	mountain guide
Bergrettung	mountain rescue
Eis	ice
Gefahrlich	dangerous
Gesprutt	route is closed/barred

Appendix B – German–English glossary

German	English
Gipfel/Spitze	summit
Gletscher/Kees	glacier
Hinter/Mittler/Vorder	further/middle/nearer
Inner/Ausser	inner/outer
Kabel/Pickle	rope/ice axe
Kessel/Grube/Kar	couloir/basin/combe
Links/Rechts/Geradeaus	left/right/straight ahead
Nadel	needle/pinnacle
Nord/Sud/Ost/West	north/south/east/west
Nur fur Geubte	only for the experienced
Randkluft/Spalten Bergschrund	crevasses
Schweirig/Leicht	difficult/easy
See/Lac	tarn/lake
Steinslag	stone fall
Tal	valley
Törl/Scharte/Sattel/Nieder	col/saddle/pass
Uber/Unter	over/under
Wald/Baum	forest/tree
Wanderkarte	map
Weg	way/footpath
Wilde/Aperer	snow peak/rock peak

APPENDIX C
Further reading

Die Alpenvereinshütten: Band 1: Ostalpen (previously the Green book), (Bergverlag Rother, 2005)

Dieter Siebert, *Eastern Alps: The Classic Routes on the Highest Peaks* (Diadem Books, 1992)

Frank Smythe, *Over Tyrolese Hills* (Hodder and Stoughton, 1936)

Kev Reynolds, *Trekking in the Alps* (Cicerone Press Ltd, 2011)

Sir William Martin Conway, *The Alps from end to End* (Nelson Books, 1894)

Wolfgang Heitzmann, *Stubaier Alpen: 50 Selected Walks* (Kompass Wanderführer, 1999)

Street scene in the Tirolean city of Innsbruck at the Triumphal Arch looking towards Maria Theresian Strasse and the mountains of Nordkette

DOWNLOAD THE ROUTES IN GPX FORMAT

All the routes in this guide are available for download from:

www.cicerone.co.uk/1065/GPX

as standard format GPX files. You should be able to load them into most online GPX systems and mobile devices, whether GPS or smartphone. You may need to convert the file into your preferred format using a conversion programme such as gpsvisualizer.com or one of the many other such websites and programmes.

When you follow this link, you will be asked for your email address and where you purchased the guidebook, and have the option to subscribe to the Cicerone e-newsletter.

www.cicerone.co.uk

LISTING OF CICERONE GUIDES

BRITISH ISLES CHALLENGES, COLLECTIONS AND ACTIVITIES
Great Walks on the England Coast Path
Map and Compass
The Big Rounds
The Book of the Bivvy
The Book of the Bothy
The Mountains of England and Wales:
 Vol 1 Wales
 Vol 2 England
The National Trails
Walking the End to End Trail

SHORT WALKS SERIES
Short Walks Hadrian's Wall
Short Walks Lake District — Keswick, Borrowdale and Buttermere
Short Walks Lake District — Windermere Ambleside and Grasmere
Short Walks Lake District — Coniston and Langdale
Short Walks in Arnside and Silverdale
Short Walks in Nidderdale
Short Walks in Northumberland: Wooler, Rothbury, Alnwick and the coast
Short Walks on the Malvern Hills
Short Walks in Cornwall: Falmouth and the Lizard
Short Walks in Cornwall: Land's End and Penzance
Short Walks in the South Downs: Brighton, Eastbourne and Arundel
Short Walks in the Surrey Hills
Short Walks on Dartmoor — South: Ivybridge and Princetown
Short Walks on Exmoor
Short Walks Winchester
Short Walks in Pembrokeshire: Tenby and the south
Short Walks in Dumfries and Galloway
Short Walks on the Isle of Mull
Short Walks on the Orkney Islands
Short Walks on the Shetland Islands

SCOTLAND
Ben Nevis and Glen Coe
Cycling in the Hebrides
Cycling the North Coast 500
Great Mountain Days in Scotland
Mountain Biking in Southern and Central Scotland
Mountain Biking in West and North West Scotland
Not the West Highland Way
Scotland
Scotland's Best Small Mountains
Scotland's Mountain Ridges
Scottish Wild Country Backpacking
Skye's Cuillin Ridge Traverse
The Borders Abbeys Way
The Great Glen Way
The Great Glen Way Map Booklet
The Hebridean Way
The Hebrides
The Isle of Mull
The Isle of Skye
The Skye Trail
The Southern Upland Way
The West Highland Way
Walking Ben Lawers, Rannoch and Atholl
Walking in the Cairngorms
Walking in the Pentland Hills
Walking in the Scottish Borders
Walking in the Southern Uplands
Walking in Torridon, Fisherfield, Fannichs and An Teallach
Walking Loch Lomond and the Trossachs
Walking on Arran
Walking on Harris and Lewis
Walking on Jura, Islay and Colonsay
Walking on Rum and the Small Isles
Walking on the Orkney and Shetland Isles
Walking on Uist and Barra
Walking the Cape Wrath Trail
Walking the Corbetts Vol 1 South of the Great Glen
Walking the Corbetts Vol 2 North of the Great Glen
Walking the Fife Pilgrim Way
Walking the Galloway Hills
Walking the John o' Groats Trail
Walking the Munros
 Vol 1 — Southern, Central and Western Highlands
 Vol 2 — Northern Highlands and the Cairngorms
Walking the West Highland Way
West Highland Way Map Booklet
Winter Climbs in the Cairngorms
Winter Climbs: Ben Nevis and Glen Coe

NORTHERN ENGLAND ROUTES
Cycling the Reivers Route
Cycling the Way of the Roses
Hadrian's Cycleway
Hadrian's Wall Path
Hadrian's Wall Path Map Booklet
The Coast to Coast Cycle Route
The Coast to Coast Map Booklet
The Coast to Coast Walk
The Pennine Way
Pennine Way Map Booklet
Walking the Dales Way
The Dales Way Map Booklet

LAKE DISTRICT
Bikepacking in the Lake District
Cycling in the Lake District
Great Mountain Days in the Lake District
Joss Naylor's Lakes, Meres and Waters of the Lake District
Lake District Winter Climbs
Lake District: High Level and Fell Walks
Lake District: Low Level and Lake Walks
Mountain Biking in the Lake District
Outdoor Adventures with Children — Lake District
Scrambles in the Lake District —
 North
 South
Trail and Fell Running in the Lake District
Walking The Cumbria Way
Walking the Lake District Fells —
 Borrowdale
 Buttermere
 Coniston
 Keswick
 Langdale
 Mardale and the Far East
 Patterdale
 Wasdale
Walking the Tour of the Lake District

NORTH-WEST ENGLAND AND THE ISLE OF MAN
Cycling the Pennine Bridleway
Isle of Man Coastal Path
The Lancashire Cycleway
The Lune Valley and Howgills
Walking in Cumbria's Eden Valley
Walking in Lancashire
Walking in the Forest of Bowland and Pendle
Walking on the Isle of Man
Walking on the West Pennine Moors
Walking the Ribble Way
Walks in Silverdale and Arnside

NORTH-EAST ENGLAND, YORKSHIRE DALES AND PENNINES
Cycling in the Yorkshire Dales
Great Mountain Days in the Pennines
Mountain Biking in the Yorkshire Dales
The Cleveland Way and the Yorkshire Wolds Way
The Cleveland Way Map Booklet
The North York Moors
Trail and Fell Running in the Yorkshire Dales
Walking in County Durham

Walking in Northumberland
Walking in the North Pennines
Walking in the Yorkshire Dales:
  North and East
  South and West
Walking St Cuthbert's Way
Walking St Oswald's Way and
  Northumberland Coast Path

DERBYSHIRE, PEAK DISTRICT AND MIDLANDS
Cycling in the Peak District
Dark Peak Walks
Scrambles in the Dark Peak
Walking in Derbyshire
Walking in the Peak District —
  White Peak East
  White Peak West

WALES AND WELSH BORDERS
Cycle Touring in Wales
Cycling Lon Las Cymru
Great Mountain Days in Snowdonia
Hillwalking in Shropshire
Mountain Walking in Snowdonia
Offa's Dyke Path
Offa's Dyke Map Booklet
The Pembrokeshire Coast Path
Pembrokeshire Coast Path Map Booklet
Scrambles in Snowdonia
Snowdonia: 30 Low-level and Easy Walks — North, South
The Cambrian Way
The Snowdonia Way
The Wye Valley Walk
Walking Glyndwr's Way
Walking in Carmarthenshire
Walking in Pembrokeshire
Walking in the Brecon Beacons
Walking in the Wye Valley
Walking on Gower
Walking the Severn Way
Walking the Shropshire Way
Walking the Wales Coast Path

SOUTHERN ENGLAND
20 Classic Sportive Rides in South East England
20 Classic Sportive Rides in South West England
Cycling in the Cotswolds
Mountain Biking on the North Downs
Mountain Biking on the South Downs
The North Downs Way
North Downs Way Map Booklet
Walking the South West Coast Path
South West Coast Path Map Booklet
  — Vol 1: Minehead to St Ives
  — Vol 2: St Ives to Plymouth
  — Vol 3: Plymouth to Poole
Suffolk Coast and Heath Walks
The Cotswold Way
The Cotswold Way Map Booklet
The Kennet and Avon Canal
The Lea Valley Walk

The Peddars Way and Norfolk Coast Path
The Pilgrims' Way
The Ridgeway National Trail
The Ridgeway Map Booklet
The South Downs Way
The South Downs Way Map Booklet
The Thames Path
The Thames Path Map Booklet
The Two Moors Way
Two Moors Way Map Booklet
Walking Hampshire's Test Way
Walking in Cornwall
Walking in Essex
Walking in Kent
Walking in London
Walking in Norfolk
Walking in the Chilterns
Walking in the Cotswolds
Walking in the Isles of Scilly
Walking in the New Forest
Walking in the North Wessex Downs
Walking on Dartmoor
Walking on Guernsey
Walking on Jersey
Walking on the Isle of Wight
Walking the Dartmoor Way
Walking the Jurassic Coast
Walking the Sarsen Way
Walks in the South Downs National Park
Cycling Land's End to John o' Groats

ALPS CROSS-BORDER ROUTES
100 Hut Walks in the Alps
Alpine Ski Mountaineering Vol 1 — Western Alps
The Karnischer Hohenweg
The Tour of the Bernina
Trekking the Tour du Mont Blanc
Tour du Mont Blanc Map Booklet
Trail Running — Chamonix and the Mont Blanc region
Trekking Chamonix to Zermatt
Trekking in the Alps
Trekking in the Silvretta and Ratikon Alps
Trekking Munich to Venice
Walking in the Alps

FRANCE, BELGIUM, AND LUXEMBOURG
Camino de Santiago — Via Podiensis
Chamonix Mountain Adventures
Cycling London to Paris
Cycling the Canal de la Garonne
Cycling the Canal du Midi
Mont Blanc Walks
Mountain Adventures in the Maurienne
Short Treks on Corsica
The Grand Traverse of the Massif Central
The Moselle Cycle Route
Trekking in the Vanoise
Trekking the Cathar Way

Trekking the GR10
Trekking the GR20 Corsica
Trekking the Robert Louis Stevenson Trail
The GR5 Trail
The GR5 Trail —
  Vosges and Jura
  Benelux and Lorraine
Via Ferratas of the French Alps
Walking in Provence — East
Walking in Provence — West
Walking in the Auvergne
Walking in the Brianconnais
Walking in the Dordogne
Walking in the Haute Savoie: North
Walking in the Haute Savoie: South
Walking on Corsica
Walking the Brittany Coast Path
Walking in the Ardennes

PYRENEES AND FRANCE/SPAIN CROSS-BORDER ROUTES
Shorter Treks in the Pyrenees
The Pyrenean Haute Route
The Pyrenees
Trekking the Cami dels Bons Homes
Trekking the GR11 Trail
Walks and Climbs in the Pyrenees

SPAIN AND PORTUGAL
Camino de Santiago: Camino Frances
Costa Blanca Mountain Adventures
Cycling the Camino de Santiago
Mountain Walking in Mallorca
Mountain Walking in Southern Catalunya
Spain's Sendero Historico: The GR1
The Andalucian Coast to Coast Walk
The Camino del Norte and Camino Primitivo
The Camino Ingles and Ruta do Mar
The Mountains Around Nerja
The Mountains of Ronda and Grazalema
The Sierras of Extremadura
Trekking in Mallorca
Trekking in the Canary Islands
Trekking the GR7 in Andalucia
Walking and Trekking in the Sierra Nevada
Walking in Andalucia
Walking in Catalunya —
  Barcelona
  Girona Pyrenees
Walking in the Picos de Europa
Walking La Via de la Plata and Camino Sanabres
Walking on Gran Canaria
Walking on La Gomera and El Hierro
Walking on La Palma
Walking on Lanzarote and Fuerteventura
Walking on Tenerife
Walking on the Costa Blanca
Walking the Camino dos Faros
Portugal's Rota Vicentina